Python Standard Library

Python Standard Library

Fredrik Lundh

O'REILLY®

Beijing · Cambridge · Farnham · Köln · Paris · Sebastopol · Taipei · Tokyo

Python Standard Library

by Fredrik Lundh

Published by O'Reilly & Associates, Inc., 101 Morris Street, Sebastopol, CA 95472.

Editor: Frank Willison

Production Editor: Catherine Morris

Cover Designer: Hanna Dyer

Printing History:

      May 2001:   First Edition.

ISBN: 0-596-00096-0

[M]

Table of Contents

Preface

*"We'd like to pretend that 'Fredrik' is a role, but
even hundreds of volunteers couldn't possibly keep up. No,
'Fredrik' is the result of crossing an http server with a
spam filter with an emacs whatsit and some other stuff besides."*
—Gordon McMillan, June 1998

The Python 2.0 distribution comes with an extensive standard library, comprised of over 200 modules. This book briefly describes each module and provides one or more sample scripts showing how to use it. All in all, this book contains 360 sample scripts.

About This Book

*"Those people who have nothing better to do than post on
the Internet all day long are rarely the ones
who have the most insights."*
—Jakob Nielsen, December 1998

Since I first stumbled upon Python some five years ago, I've spent hundreds of hours answering questions on the `comp.lang.python` newsgroup. Maybe someone found a module that might be exactly what he wanted, but he couldn't really figure out how to use it. Maybe someone had picked the wrong module for the task. Or maybe someone tried to reinvent the wheel. Often, a short sample script could be much more helpful than a pointer to the reference documentation.

After posting a couple of scripts each week, for a number of years, you end up with a rather large collection of potentially useful scripts. What you'll find in this book are the best parts from over 3,000 newsgroup messages. You'll also find hundreds of new scripts added to make sure every little nook and cranny of standard library has been fully covered.

I've worked hard to make the scripts both understandable and adaptable. I've intentionally kept the annotations as short as possible. If you want more background, there's plenty of reference material shipped with most Python distributions. In this book, the emphasis is on the code.

Comments, suggestions, and bug reports are welcome. Send them to *fredrik@pythonware.com*. I read all mail as soon as it arrives, but it might take a while until I get around to answering.

For updates, addenda, and other information related to this book, point your web browser to *http://www.pythonware.com/people/fredrik/librarybook.htm*

What About Tkinter?

This book covers the entire standard library, except the (optional) Tkinter user-interface library. There are several reasons for this, mostly related to time, space, and the fact that I'm working on several other Tkinter documentation projects.

For current status on these projects, see *http://www.pythonware.com/people/fredrik/tkinterbook.htm*.

Production Details

This book was written in DocBook SGML. I used a variety of tools, including Secret Labs' PythonWorks, Excosoft Documentor, James Clark's Jade DSSSL processor, Norm Walsh's DocBook stylesheets, and a bunch of Python scripts, of course.

Thanks to my referees: Tim Peters, Guido van Rossum, David Ascher, Mark Lutz, and Rael Dornfest, and the PythonWare crew: Matthew Ellis, Håkan Karlsson, and Rune Uhlin.

Thanks to Lenny Muellner, who turned my SGML files into the book you see before you, and to Christien Shangraw, who pulled all the different text and code files together for the book and the CD-ROM.

Conventions Used in This Book

The following typographic conventions appear in this book:

Italic
> Is used for filenames and command names. It is also used to define terms the first time they appear.

`Constant Width`
> Is used in examples and in regular text to show methods, modules, operators, functions, statements, and attributes.

About the Examples

Unless otherwise noted, all examples run under Python 1.5.2 and Python 2.0. I've tried not to depend on internal details, and I expect most scripts to work with upcoming 2.x versions as well.

The examples have been tested on Windows, Solaris, and Linux. Except for a few scripts that depend on platform-specific modules, the examples should work right out of the box on most other platforms as well. (If you find something that doesn't work as expected, let me know!)

All code is copyrighted. Of course, you're free to use one or more modules in your own programs, just don't forget where you got them.

Most script files are named after the module they're using, followed by the string "-example-" and a unique "serial number." Note that the scripts sometimes appear out of order; it's done this way on purpose, to match the filenames used in an earlier version of this book, *(the eff-bot guide to) The Standard Python Library*.

You'll find copies of all scripts on the CD provided with this book. For updates and more informaiton, see *http://www.pythonware.com/people/fredrik/library-book.htm*. That page also explains what you need to know to decrypt and unpack the archive.

How to Contact Us

You can write to:

O'Reilly & Associates, Inc.
101 Morris Street
Sebastopol, CA 95472
1-800-998-9938 (in the U. S. or Canada)
1-707-829-0515 (international/local)
1-707-829-0104 (FAX)

You can also send us messages electronically. To be put on the mailing list or request a catalog, send email to:

info@oreilly.com

To ask technical questions or comment on the book, send email to:

bookquestions@oreilly.com

We have a web site for the book, where we'll list examples, errata, and any plans for future editions. You can access this page at:

http://www.oreilly.com/catalog/pythonsl/

For more information about this book and others, see the O'Reilly web site:

http://www.oreilly.com

1

Core Modules

*"Since the functions in the C runtime library are not part of
the Win32 API, we believe the number of applications that will be
affected by this bug to be very limited."*
—Microsoft, January 1999

Introduction

Python's standard library covers a wide range of modules. It includes everything from modules that are as much a part of the Python language as the types and statements defined by the language specification, to obscure modules that are probably useful only to a small number of programs.

This chapter describes a number of fundamental standard library modules. Any larger Python program is likely to use most of these modules, either directly or indirectly.

Built-in Functions and Exceptions

The following two modules are even more basic than all other modules combined: the _ _builtin_ _ module, which defines built-in functions (like len, int, and range), and the exceptions module, which defines all built-in exceptions.

Python imports both modules when it starts up, and makes their content available for all programs.

Operating System Interface Modules

There are a number of modules modeled after the POSIX standard API and the standard C library that provide platform-independent interfaces to the underlying operating system.

The modules in this group include os, which provides file and process operations, os.path, which offers a platform-independent way to pull apart and put together filenames, and time, which provides functions to work with dates and times.

To some extent, networking and thread support modules could also belong in this group, but they are not supported by all Python implementations.

Type Support Modules

Several built-in types have support modules in the standard library. The string module implements commonly used string operations, the math module provides math operations and constants, and the cmath module does the same for complex numbers.

Regular Expressions

The re module provides regular expressions support for Python. Regular expressions are string patterns written in a special syntax, which can be used to match strings and extract substrings.

Language Support Modules

sys gives you access to various interpreter variables, such as the module search path, and the interpreter version. operator provides functional equivalents to many built-in operators. copy allows you to copy objects. And finally, gc gives you more control over the garbage collector facilities in Python 2.0.

The __builtin__ Module

This module contains built-in functions that are automatically available in all Python modules. You usually don't have to import this module; Python does that for you when necessary.

Calling a Function with Arguments from a Tuple or Dictionary

Python allows you to build function argument lists on the fly. Just put all the arguments in a tuple, and call the built-in apply function, as illustrated in Example 1-1.

Example 1-1. Using the apply Function

```
File: builtin-apply-example-1.py

def function(a, b):
    print a, b
```

Example 1-1. Using the apply Function (continued)

```
apply(function, ("whither", "canada?"))
apply(function, (1, 2 + 3))
```

whither canada?
1 5

To pass keyword arguments to a function, you can use a dictionary as the third argument to apply, as shown in Example 1-2.

Example 1-2. Using the apply Function to Pass Keyword Arguments

```
File: builtin-apply-example-2.py

def function(a, b):
    print a, b

apply(function, ("crunchy", "frog"))
apply(function, ("crunchy",), {"b": "frog"})
apply(function, (), {"a": "crunchy", "b": "frog"})
```

crunchy frog
crunchy frog
crunchy frog

One common use for apply is to pass constructor arguments from a subclass on to the base class, especially if the constructor takes a lot of arguments. See Example 1-3.

Example 1-3. Using the apply Function to Call Base Class Constructors

```
File: builtin-apply-example-3.py

class Rectangle:
    def __init__(self, color="white", width=10, height=10):
        print "create a", color, self, "sized", width, "x", height

class RoundedRectangle(Rectangle):
    def __init__(self, **kw):
        apply(Rectangle.__init__, (self,), kw)

rect = Rectangle(color="green", height=100, width=100)
rect = RoundedRectangle(color="blue", height=20)
```

create a green <Rectangle instance at 8c8260> sized 100 x 100
create a blue <RoundedRectangle instance at 8c84c0> sized 10 x 20

Python 2.0 provides an alternate syntax. Instead of apply, you can use an ordinary function call, and use * to mark the tuple, and ** to mark the dictionary.

The following two statements are equivalent:

```
result = function(*args, **kwargs)
result = apply(function, args, kwargs)
```

Loading and Reloading Modules

If you've written a Python program larger than just a few lines, you know that the import statement is used to import external modules (you can also use the from-import version). What you might not know already is that import delegates the actual work to a built-in function called _ _import_ _.

The trick is that you can call this function directly. This can be handy if you have the module name in a string variable, as in Example 1-4, which imports all modules whose names end with "-plugin":

Example 1-4. Using the _ _import_ _ Function to Load Named Modules

```
File: builtin-import-example-1.py

import glob, os

modules = []

for module_file in glob.glob("*-plugin.py"):
    try:
        module_name, ext = os.path.splitext(os.path.basename(module_file))
        module = _ _import_ _(module_name)
        modules.append(module)
    except ImportError:
        pass # ignore broken modules

# say hello to all modules
for module in modules:
    module.hello()
```

example-plugin says hello

Note that the plug-in modules have hyphens. This means that you cannot import such a module using the ordinary import command, since you cannot have hyphens in Python identifiers.

Example 1-5 shows the plug-in used in Example 1-4.

Example 1-5. A Sample Plug-in

```
File: example-plugin.py

def hello():
    print "example-plugin says hello"
```

Example 1-6 shows how to get a function object, given that the module and function name are strings.

Example 1-6. Using the __import__ Function to Get a Named Function

File: builtin-import-example-2.py

```
def getfunctionbyname(module_name, function_name):
    module = __import__(module_name)
    return getattr(module, function_name)

print repr(getfunctionbyname("dumbdbm", "open"))
```

<function open at 794fa0>

You can also use this function to implement lazy module loading. In Example 1-7, the string module is imported when it is first used.

Example 1-7. Using the __import__ Function to Implement Lazy Import

File: builtin-import-example-3.py

```
class LazyImport:
    def __init__(self, module_name):
        self.module_name = module_name
        self.module = None
    def __getattr__(self, name):
        if self.module is None:
            self.module = __import__(self.module_name)
        return getattr(self.module, name)

string = LazyImport("string")

print string.lowercase
```

abcdefghijklmnopqrstuvwxyz

Python provides some basic support for reloading modules that you've already imported. Example 1-8 loads the *hello.py* file three times.

Example 1-8. Using the reload Function

File: builtin-reload-example-1.py

```
import hello
reload(hello)
reload(hello)
```

hello again, and welcome to the show
hello again, and welcome to the show
hello again, and welcome to the show

reload uses the module name associated with the module object, not the variable name. Even if you've renamed the original module, reload can still find it.

Note that when you reload a module, it is recompiled, and the new module replaces the old one in the module dictionary. However, if you have created instances of classes defined in that module, those instances will still use the old implementation.

Likewise, if you've used from-import to create references to module members in other modules, those references will not be updated.

Looking in Namespaces

The dir function returns a list of all members of a given module, class, instance, or other type. It's probably most useful when you're working with an interactive Python interpreter, but can also come in handy in other situations. Example 1-9 shows the dir function in use.

Example 1-9. Using the dir Function

```
File: builtin-dir-example-1.py

def dump(value):
    print value, "=>", dir(value)

import sys

dump(0)
dump(1.0)
dump(0.0j) # complex number
dump([]) # list
dump({}) # dictionary
dump("string")
dump(len) # function
dump(sys) # module

0 => []
1.0 => []
0j => ['conjugate', 'imag', 'real']
[] => ['append', 'count', 'extend', 'index', 'insert',
    'pop', 'remove', 'reverse', 'sort']
{} => ['clear', 'copy', 'get', 'has_key', 'items',
    'keys', 'update', 'values']
string => []
<built-in function len> => ['__doc__', '__name__', '__self__']
<module 'sys' (built-in)> => ['__doc__', '__name__',
    '__stderr__', '__stdin__', '__stdout__', 'argv',
    'builtin_module_names', 'copyright', 'dllhandle',
    'exc_info', 'exc_type', 'exec_prefix', 'executable',
...
```

In Example 1-10, the getmember function returns all class-level attributes and methods defined by a given class.

Example 1-10. Using the dir Function to Find All Members of a Class

File: builtin-dir-example-2.py

```
class A:
    def a(self):
        pass
    def b(self):
        pass

class B(A):
    def c(self):
        pass
    def d(self):
        pass

def getmembers(klass, members=None):
    # get a list of all class members, ordered by class
    if members is None:
        members = []
    for k in klass.__bases__:
        getmembers(k, members)
    for m in dir(klass):
        if m not in members:
            members.append(m)
    return members

print getmembers(A)
print getmembers(B)
print getmembers(IOError)

['__doc__', '__module__', 'a', 'b']
['__doc__', '__module__', 'a', 'b', 'c', 'd']
['__doc__', '__getitem__', '__init__', '__module__', '__str__']
```

Note that the getmembers function returns an ordered list. The earlier a name appears in the list, the higher up in the class hierarchy it's defined. If order doesn't matter, you can use a dictionary to collect the names instead of a list.

The vars function is similar, but it returns a dictionary containing the current value for each member. If you use vars without an argument, it returns a dictionary containing what's visible in the current local namespace, as shown in Example 1-11.

Example 1-11. Using the vars Function

File: builtin-vars-example-1.py

```
book = "library2"
pages = 250
scripts = 350
```

Example 1-11. Using the vars Function (continued)

```
print "the %(book)s book contains more than %(scripts)s scripts" % vars()
```

the library book contains more than 350 scripts

Checking an Object's Type

Python is a dynamically typed language, which means that a given variable can be bound to values of different types on different occasions. In the following example, the same function is called with an integer, a floating point value, and a string:

```
def function(value):
    print value
function(1)
function(1.0)
function("one")
```

The type function (shown in Example 1-12) allows you to check what type a variable has. This function returns a *type descriptor*, which is a unique object for each type provided by the Python interpreter.

Example 1-12. Using the type Function

```
File: builtin-type-example-1.py
```

```
def dump(value):
    print type(value), value

dump(1)
dump(1.0)
dump("one")
```

<type 'int'> 1
<type 'float'> 1.0
<type 'string'> one

Each type has a single corresponding type object, which means that you can use the is operator (object identity) to do type testing (as shown in Example 1-13).

Example 1-13. Using the type Function with Filenames and File Objects

```
File: builtin-type-example-2.py
```

```
def load(file):
    if isinstance(file, type("")):
        file = open(file, "rb")
    return file.read()

print len(load("samples/sample.jpg")), "bytes"
print len(load(open("samples/sample.jpg", "rb"))), "bytes"
```

Example 1-13. Using the type Function with Filenames and File Objects (continued)

```
4672 bytes
4672 bytes
```

The callable function, shown in Example 1-14, checks if an object can be called (either directly or via `apply`). It returns true for functions, methods, lambda expressions, classes, and class instances that define the _ _call_ _ method.

Example 1-14. Using the callable Function

```
File: builtin-callable-example-1.py

def dump(function):
    if callable(function):
        print function, "is callable"
    else:
        print function, "is *not* callable"

class A:
    def method(self, value):
        return value

class B(A):
    def _ _call_ _(self, value):
        return value

a = A()
b = B()

dump(0) # simple objects
dump("string")
dump(callable)
dump(dump) # function

dump(A) # classes
dump(B)
dump(B.method)

dump(a) # instances
dump(b)
dump(b.method)

0 is *not* callable
string is *not* callable
<built-in function callable> is callable
<function dump at 8ca320> is callable
A is callable
B is callable
<unbound method A.method> is callable
<A instance at 8caa10> is *not* callable
<B instance at 8cab00> is callable
<method A.method of B instance at 8cab00> is callable
```

Note that the class objects (*A* and *B*) are both callable; if you call them, they create new objects. However, instances of class *A* are not callable, since that class doesn't have a _ _call_ _ method.

You'll find functions to check if an object is of any of the built-in number, sequence, or dictionary types in the operator module. However, since it's easy to create a class that implements (for example, the basic sequence methods), it's usually a bad idea to use explicit type testing on such objects.

Things get even more complicated when it comes to classes and instances. Python doesn't treat classes as types per se; instead, all classes belong to a special class type, and all class instances belong to a special instance type.

This means that you cannot use type to test if an instance belongs to a given class; all instances have the same type! To solve this, you can use the isinstance function, which checks if an object is an instance of a given class (or of a subclass to it). Example 1-15 illustrates the isinstance function.

Example 1-15. Using the isinstance Function

```
File: builtin-isinstance-example-1.py

class A:
    pass

class B:
    pass

class C(A):
    pass

class D(A, B):
    pass

def dump(object):
    print object, "=>",
    if isinstance(object, A):
        print "A",
    if isinstance(object, B):
        print "B",
    if isinstance(object, C):
        print "C",
    if isinstance(object, D):
        print "D",
    print

a = A()
b = B()
c = C()
d = D()
```

Example 1-15. Using the isinstance Function (continued)

```
dump(a)
dump(b)
dump(c)
dump(d)
dump(0)
dump("string")
```

```
<A instance at 8ca6d0> => A
<B instance at 8ca750> => B
<C instance at 8ca780> => A C
<D instance at 8ca7b0> => A B D
0 =>
string =>
```

The issubclass function is similar, but it instead checks whether a class object is the same as a given class, or is a subclass of it. The issubclass function is shown in Example 1-16.

Note that while isinstance accepts any kind of object, the issubclass function raises a *TypeError* exception if you use it on something that is not a class object.

Example 1-16. Using the issubclass Function

```
File: builtin-issubclass-example-1.py

class A:
    pass

class B:
    pass

class C(A):
    pass

class D(A, B):
    pass

def dump(object):
    print object, "=>",
    if issubclass(object, A):
        print "A",
    if issubclass(object, B):
        print "B",
    if issubclass(object, C):
        print "C",
    if issubclass(object, D):
        print "D",
    print

dump(A)
dump(B)
dump(C)
```

Example 1-16. Using the issubclass Function (continued)

```
dump(D)
dump(0)
dump("string")
```

```
A => A
B => B
C => A C
D => A B D
0 =>
Traceback (innermost last):
  File "builtin-issubclass-example-1.py", line 29, in ?
  File "builtin-issubclass-example-1.py", line 15, in dump
TypeError: arguments must be classes
```

Evaluating Python Expressions

Python provides several ways to interact with the interpreter from within a program. For example, the eval function evaluates a string as if it were a Python expression. You can pass it a literal, simple expression, or use built-in functions, as shown in Example 1-17.

Example 1-17. Using the eval Function

```
File: builtin-eval-example-1.py
```

```
def dump(expression):
    result = eval(expression)
    print expression, "=>", result, type(result)
```

```
dump("1")
dump("1.0")
dump("'string'")
dump("1.0 + 2.0")
dump("'*' * 10")
dump("len('world')")
```

```
1 => 1 <type 'int'>
1.0 => 1.0 <type 'float'>
'string' => string <type 'string'>
1.0 + 2.0 => 3.0 <type 'float'>
'*' * 10 => ********** <type 'string'>
len('world') => 5 <type 'int'>
```

If you cannot trust the source from which you got the string, you may get into trouble using eval. For example, someone might use the built-in _ _import_ _ function to load the os module, and then remove files on your disk (as shown in Example 1-18).

Example 1-18. Using the eval Function to Execute Arbitrary Commands

File: builtin-eval-example-2.py

```
print eval("__import__('os').getcwd()")
print eval("__import__('os').remove('file')")
```

```
/home/fredrik/librarybook
Traceback (innermost last):
  File "builtin-eval-example-2", line 2, in ?
  File "<string>", line 0, in ?
os.error: (2, 'No such file or directory')
```

Note that you get an *os.error* exception, which means that *Python actually tried to remove the file!*

Luckily, there's a way around this problem. You can pass a second argument to eval, which should contain a dictionary defining the namespace in which the expression is evaluated. Let's pass in an empty namespace:

```
>>> print eval("__import__('os').remove('file')", {})
Traceback (innermost last):
  File "<stdin>", line 1, in ?
  File "<string>", line 0, in ?
os.error: (2, 'No such file or directory')
```

Hmm. We still end up with an *os.error* exception.

The reason for this is that Python looks in the dictionary before it evaluates the code, and if it doesn't find a variable named __builtins__ in there (note the plural form), it adds one:

```
>>> namespace = {}
>>> print eval("__import__('os').remove('file')", namespace)
Traceback (innermost last):
  File "<stdin>", line 1, in ?
  File "<string>", line 0, in ?
os.error: (2, 'No such file or directory')
>>> namespace.keys()
['__builtins__']
```

If you print the contents of the namespace variable, you'll find that they contain the full set of built-in functions.

The solution to this little dilemma isn't far away: since Python doesn't add this item if it is already there, simply add a dummy item called __builtins__ to the namespace before calling eval, as shown in Example 1-19.

Example 1-19. Using the eval Function to Evaluate Arbitrary Strings Safely

```
File: builtin-eval-example-3.py

print eval("__import__('os').getcwd()", {})
print eval("__import__('os').remove('file')", {"__builtins__": {}})

/home/fredrik/librarybook
Traceback (innermost last):
  File "builtin-eval-example-3.py", line 2, in ?
  File "<string>", line 0, in ?
NameError: __import__
```

Note that this doesn't protect you from CPU or memory-resource attacks (for example, something like eval("'*'*1000000*2*2*2*2*2*2*2*2") will most likely cause your program to run out of memory after a while).

Compiling and Executing Code

The eval function only works for simple expressions. To handle larger blocks of code, use the compile and exec functions (as demonstrated in Example 1-20).

Example 1-20. Using the compile Function to Check Syntax

```
File: builtin-compile-example-1.py

NAME = "script.py"

BODY = """
prnt 'owl-stretching time'
"""

try:
    compile(BODY, NAME, "exec")
except SyntaxError, v:
    print "syntax error:", v, "in", NAME

# syntax error: invalid syntax in script.py
```

When successful, the compile function returns a code object, which you can execute with the exec statement, as in Example 1-21.

Example 1-21. Compiling and Executing Compiled Code

```
File: builtin-compile-example-2.py

BODY = """
print 'the ant, an introduction'
"""

code = compile(BODY, "<script>", "exec")

print code
```

Example 1-21. Compiling and Executing Compiled Code (continued)

```
exec code
```

**<code object ? at 8c6be0, file "<script>", line 0>
the ant, an introduction**

To generate code on the fly, use the class shown in the Example 1-22. Use the
write method to add statements, and the methods indent and dedent to add struc-
ture. The class will take care of the rest.

Example 1-22. A Simple Code Generator Tool

```
File: builtin-compile-example-3.py

import sys, string

class CodeGeneratorBackend:
    "Simple code generator for Python"

    def begin(self, tab="\t"):
        self.code = []
        self.tab = tab
        self.level = 0

    def end(self):
        self.code.append("") # make sure there's a newline at the end
        return compile(string.join(self.code, "\n"), "<code>", "exec")

    def write(self, string):
        self.code.append(self.tab * self.level + string)

    def indent(self):
        self.level = self.level + 1
        # in 2.0 and later, this can be written as: self.level += 1

    def dedent(self):
        if self.level == 0:
            raise SyntaxError, "internal error in code generator"
        self.level = self.level - 1
        # or: self.level -= 1

#
# try it out!

c = CodeGeneratorBackend()
c.begin()
c.write("for i in range(5):")
c.indent()
c.write("print 'code generation made easy!'")
c.dedent()
exec c.end()
```

code generation made easy!

Example 1-22. A Simple Code Generator Tool (continued)

```
code generation made easy!
code generation made easy!
code generation made easy!
code generation made easy!
```

Python also provides a function called execfile, a shortcut for loading code from a file, compiling it, and executing it. Example 1-23 shows how to use and emulate this function.

Example 1-23. Using the execfile Function

```
File: builtin-execfile-example-1.py

execfile("hello.py")

def EXECFILE(filename, locals=None, globals=None):
    exec compile(open(filename).read(), filename, "exec") in locals, globals

EXECFILE("hello.py")
```

```
hello again, and welcome to the show
hello again, and welcome to the show
```

The contents of the *hello.py* file used Example 1-23 are shown in Example 1-24.

Example 1-24. The hello.py Script

```
File: hello.py

print "hello again, and welcome to the show"
```

Overloading Functions from the _ _builtin_ _ Module

Since Python does not look among the built-in functions until *after* it has checked the local and module namespace, there may be situations in which you need to explicitly refer to the _ _builtin_ _ module. For instance, the script in Example 1-25 overloads the open function with a version that opens an ordinary file and checks that it starts with a "magic" string. To be able to use the original open function, the script explicitly refers to the function using the module name.

Example 1-25. Explicitly Accessing Functions in the _ _builtin_ _ Module

```
File: builtin-open-example-1.py

def open(filename, mode="rb"):
    import _ _builtin_ _
    file = _ _builtin_ _.open(filename, mode)
    if file.read(5) not in ("GIF87", "GIF89"):
        raise IOError, "not a GIF file"
```

Example 1-25. Explicitly Accessing Functions in the _ _builtin_ _ Module (continued)

```
    file.seek(0)
    return file

fp = open("samples/sample.gif")
print len(fp.read()), "bytes"

fp = open("samples/sample.jpg")
print len(fp.read()), "bytes"

3565 bytes
Traceback (innermost last):
  File "builtin-open-example-1.py", line 12, in ?
  File "builtin-open-example-1.py", line 5, in open
IOError: not a GIF file
```

The exceptions Module

The exceptions module provides the standard exception hierarchy. It's automatically imported when Python starts, and the exceptions are added to the _ _builtin_ _ module. In other words, you usually don't need to import this module.

This is a Python module in 1.5.2, and a built-in module in 2.0 and later.

The following standard exceptions are defined by this module:

- *Exception* is used as a base class for all exceptions. It's strongly recommended (but not yet required) that user exceptions are derived from this class too.

- *SystemExit(Exception)* is raised by the sys.exit function. If it propagates to the top level without being caught by a try-except clause, the interpreter is terminated without a traceback message.

- *StandardError(Exception)* is used as a base class for all standard exceptions (except *SystemExit*, that is).

- *KeyboardInterrupt(StandardError)* is raised when the user presses Control-C (or any other interrupt key). Note that this may cause strange errors if you use "catch all" try-except statements.

- *ImportError(StandardError)* is raised when Python fails to import a module.

- *EnvironmentError* is used as a base class for exceptions that can be caused by the interpreter's environment (that is, they're usually not caused by bugs in the program).

- *IOError(EnvironmentError)* is used to flag I/O-related errors.

- *OSError(EnvironmentError)* is used to flag errors by the os module.

- *WindowsError(OSError)* is used to flag Windows-specific errors from the os module.

- *NameError(StandardError)* is raised when Python fails to find a global or local name.

- *UnboundLocalError(NameError)* is raised if your program attempts to access a local variable before it has been assigned a value. This exception is only used in 2.0 and later; earlier versions raise a plain *NameError* exception instead.

- *AttributeError(StandardError)* is raised when Python fails to find (or assign to) an instance attribute, a method, a module function, or any other qualified name.

- *SyntaxError(StandardError)* is raised when the compiler stumbles upon a syntax error.

- (2.0 and later) *IndentationError(SyntaxError)* is raised for syntax errors caused by bad indentation. This exception is only used in 2.0 and later; earlier versions raise a plain *SyntaxError* exception instead.

- (2.0 and later) *TabError(IndentationError)* is raised by the interpreter when the *-tt* option is used to check for inconsistent indentation. This exception is only used in 2.0 and later; earlier versions raise a plain *SyntaxError* exception instead.

- *TypeError(StandardError)* is raised when an operation cannot be applied to an object of the given type.

- *AssertionError(StandardError)* is raised when an assert statement fails (if the expression is false, that is).

- *LookupError(StandardError)* is used as a base class for exceptions raised when a sequence or dictionary type doesn't contain a given index or key.

- *IndexError(LookupError)* is raised by sequence objects when the given index doesn't exist.

- *KeyError(LookupError)* is raised by dictionary objects when the given key doesn't exist.

- *ArithmeticError(StandardError)* is used as a base class for exceptions that are math-related.

- *OverflowError(ArithmeticError)* is raised when an operations overflows (for example, when an integer is too large to fit in the given type).

- *ZeroDivisionError(ArithmeticError)* is raised when you try to divide a number by zero.

- *FloatingPointError(ArithmeticError)* is raised when a floating point operation fails.

- *ValueError(StandardError)* is raised if an argument has the right type, but an invalid value.

- (2.0 and later) *UnicodeError(ValueError)* is raised for type problems related to the Unicode string type. This is only used in 2.0 and later.

- *RuntimeError(StandardError)* is used for various run-time problems, including attempts to get outside the box when running in restricted mode, unexpected hardware problems, etc.

- *NotImplementedError(RuntimeError)* can be used to flag functions that hasn't been implemented yet, or methods that should be overridden.

- *SystemError(StandardError)* is raised if the interpreter messes up, and knows about it. The exception value contains a more detailed description (usually something cryptic, like "eval_code2: NULL globals" or so). I cannot recall ever seeing this exception in over five years of full-time Python programming, but maybe that's just me.

- *MemoryError(StandardError)* is raised when the interpreter runs out of memory. Note that this only happens when the underlying memory allocation routines complain; you can often send your poor computer into a mindless swapping frenzy before that happens.

You can create your own exception classes. Just inherit from the built-in *Exception* class (or a proper standard exception), and override the constructor and/or _ _str_ _ method as necessary. Example 1-26 shows the exceptions module.

Example 1-26. Using the exceptions Module

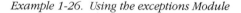

```
File: exceptions-example-1.py

# python imports this module by itself, so the following
# line isn't really needed
# import exceptions

class HTTPError(Exception):
    # indicates an HTTP protocol error
    def _ _init_ _(self, url, errcode, errmsg):
        self.url = url
        self.errcode = errcode
        self.errmsg = errmsg
    def _ _str_ _(self):
        return (
            "<HTTPError for %s: %s %s>" %
            (self.url, self.errcode, self.errmsg)
            )

try:
```

```
        raise HTTPError("http://www.python.org/foo", 200, "Not Found")
except HTTPError, error:
    print "url", "=>", error.url
    print "errcode", "=>", error.errcode
    print "errmsg", "=>", error.errmsg
    raise # reraise exception
```

```
url => http://www.python.org/foo
errcode => 200
errmsg => Not Found
Traceback (innermost last):
  File "exceptions-example-1", line 16, in ?
HTTPError: <HTTPError for http://www.python.org/foo: 200 Not Found>
```

The os Module

The os module provides a unified interface to many operating system functions.

Most of the functions in this module are implemented by platform-specific modules, such as posix or nt. The os module automatically loads the right implementation module when it is first imported.

Working with Files

The built-in open function lets you create, open, and modify files, as shown in Example 1-27. This module adds those extra functions you need to rename and remove files.

Example 1-27. Using the os Module to Rename and Remove Files

```
File: os-example-3.py

import os
import string

def replace(file, search_for, replace_with):
    # replace strings in a text file

    back = os.path.splitext(file)[0] + ".bak"
    temp = os.path.splitext(file)[0] + ".tmp"

    try:
        # remove old temp file, if any
        os.remove(temp)
    except os.error:
        pass

    fi = open(file)
    fo = open(temp, "w")

    for s in fi.readlines():
        fo.write(string.replace(s, search_for, replace_with))
```

Example 1-27. Using the os Module to Rename and Remove Files (continued)

```
    fi.close()
    fo.close()

    try:
        # remove old backup file, if any
        os.remove(back)
    except os.error:
        pass

    # rename original to backup...
    os.rename(file, back)

    # ...and temporary to original
    os.rename(temp, file)

#
# try it out!

file = "samples/sample.txt"

replace(file, "hello", "tjena")
replace(file, "tjena", "hello")
```

Working with Directories

The os module also contains many functions that work on entire directories.

The listdir function returns a list of all filenames in a given directory, as shown in Example 1-28. The current and parent directory markers used on Unix and Windows (. and ..) are not included in this list.

Example 1-28. Using the os Module to List the Files in a Directory

```
File: os-example-5.py

import os

for file in os.listdir("samples"):
    print file

sample.au
sample.jpg
sample.wav
...
```

The getcwd and chdir functions are used to get and set the current directory, as shown in Example 1-29.

Example 1-29. Using the os Module to Change the Working Directory

```
File: os-example-4.py

import os

# where are we?
cwd = os.getcwd()
print "1", cwd

# go down
os.chdir("samples")
print "2", os.getcwd()

# go back up
os.chdir(os.pardir)
print "3", os.getcwd()
```

1 /ematter/librarybook
2 /ematter/librarybook/samples
3 /ematter/librarybook

The `makedirs` and `removedirs` functions are used to create and remove directory hierarchies, as shown in Example 1-30.

Example 1-30. Using the os Module to Create and Remove Multiple Directory Levels

```
File: os-example-6.py

import os

os.makedirs("test/multiple/levels")

fp = open("test/multiple/levels/file", "w")
fp.write("inspector praline")
fp.close()

# remove the file
os.remove("test/multiple/levels/file")

# and all empty directories above it
os.removedirs("test/multiple/levels")
```

Note that `removedirs` removes all empty directories along the given path, starting with the last directory in the given pathname. In contrast, the `mkdir` and `rmdir` functions can only handle a single directory level, as shown in Example 1-31.

Example 1-31. Using the os Module to Create and Remove Directories

```
File: os-example-7.py

import os

os.mkdir("test")
```

Example 1-31. Using the os Module to Create and Remove Directories (continued)

```
os.rmdir("test")

os.rmdir("samples") # this will fail
```

```
Traceback (innermost last):
  File "os-example-7", line 6, in ?
OSError: [Errno 41] Directory not empty: 'samples'
```

To remove non-empty directories, you can use the rmtree function in the shutil module.

Working with File Attributes

The stat function fetches information about an existing file, as demonstrated in Example 1-32. It returns a 9-tuple which contains the size, inode change timestamp, modification timestamp, and access privileges.

Example 1-32. Using the os Module to Get Information About a File

```
File: os-example-1.py

import os
import time

file = "samples/sample.jpg"

def dump(st):
    mode, ino, dev, nlink, uid, gid, size, atime, mtime, ctime = st
    print "- size:", size, "bytes"
    print "- owner:", uid, gid
    print "- created:", time.ctime(ctime)
    print "- last accessed:", time.ctime(atime)
    print "- last modified:", time.ctime(mtime)
    print "- mode:", oct(mode)
    print "- inode/dev:", ino, dev

#
# get stats for a filename

st = os.stat(file)

print "stat", file
dump(st)
print

#
# get stats for an open file

fp = open(file)

st = os.fstat(fp.fileno())
```

Example 1-32. Using the os Module to Get Information About a File (continued)

```
print "fstat", file
dump(st)

stat samples/sample.jpg
- size: 4762 bytes
- owner: 0 0
- created: Tue Sep 07 22:45:58 1999
- last accessed: Sun Sep 19 00:00:00 1999
- last modified: Sun May 19 01:42:16 1996
- mode: 0100666
- inode/dev: 0 2

fstat samples/sample.jpg
- size: 4762 bytes
- owner: 0 0
- created: Tue Sep 07 22:45:58 1999
- last accessed: Sun Sep 19 00:00:00 1999
- last modified: Sun May 19 01:42:16 1996
- mode: 0100666
- inode/dev: 0 0
```

Some fields don't make sense on non-Unix platforms; for example, the (inode, dev) tuple provides a unique identity for each file on Unix, but may contain arbitrary data on other platforms.

The stat module contains a number of useful constants and helper functions for dealing with the members of the stat tuple. Some of these are shown in the examples that follow.

You can modify the mode and time fields using the chmod and utime functions, as shown in Example 1-33.

Example 1-33. Using the os Module to Change a File's Privileges and Timestamps

```
File: os-example-2.py

import os
import stat, time

infile = "samples/sample.jpg"
outfile = "out.jpg"

# copy contents
fi = open(infile, "rb")
fo = open(outfile, "wb")

while 1:
    s = fi.read(10000)
    if not s:
        break
    fo.write(s)
```

Example 1-33. Using the os Module to Change a File's Privileges and Timestamps (continued)

```
fi.close()
fo.close()

# copy mode and timestamp
st = os.stat(infile)
os.chmod(outfile, stat.S_IMODE(st[stat.ST_MODE]))
os.utime(outfile, (st[stat.ST_ATIME], st[stat.ST_MTIME]))

print "original", "=>"
print "mode", oct(stat.S_IMODE(st[stat.ST_MODE]))
print "atime", time.ctime(st[stat.ST_ATIME])
print "mtime", time.ctime(st[stat.ST_MTIME])

print "copy", "=>"
st = os.stat(outfile)
print "mode", oct(stat.S_IMODE(st[stat.ST_MODE]))
print "atime", time.ctime(st[stat.ST_ATIME])
print "mtime", time.ctime(st[stat.ST_MTIME])

original =>
mode 0666
atime Thu Oct 14 15:15:50 1999
mtime Mon Nov 13 15:42:36 1995
copy =>
mode 0666
atime Thu Oct 14 15:15:50 1999
mtime Mon Nov 13 15:42:36 1995
```

Working with Processes

The system function runs a new command under the current process, and waits for it to finish, as shown in Example 1-34.

Example 1-34. Using the os Module to Run an Operating System Command

```
File: os-example-8.py

import os

if os.name == "nt":
    command = "dir"
else:
    command = "ls -l"

os.system(command)

-rwxrw-r--   1 effbot    effbot           76 Oct  9 14:17 README
-rwxrw-r--   1 effbot    effbot         1727 Oct  7 19:00 SimpleAsyncHTTP.py
-rwxrw-r--   1 effbot    effbot          314 Oct  7 20:29 aifc-example-1.py
-rwxrw-r--   1 effbot    effbot          259 Oct  7 20:38 anydbm-example-1.py
...
```

The command is run via the operating system's standard shell, and returns the shell's exit status. Under Windows 95/98, the shell is usually command.com, whose exit status is always 0.

Since os.system passes the command on to the shell as is, it can be dangerous to use if you don't check the arguments carefully (consider running os.system("viewer %s" % file) with the file variable set to "sample.jpg; rm -rf $HOME"). When unsure, it's usually better to use exec or spawn instead (explained later).

The exec function starts a new process, replacing the current one ("go to process," in other words). In Example 1-35, note that the "goodbye" message is never printed.

Example 1-35. Using the os Module to Start a New Process

```
File: os-exec-example-1.py

import os
import sys

program = "python"
arguments = ["hello.py"]

print os.execvp(program, (program,) + tuple(arguments))
print "goodbye"
```

hello again, and welcome to the show

Python provides a whole bunch of exec functions, with slightly varying behaviors. Example 1-35 uses execvp, which searches for the program along the standard path, passes the contents of the second argument tuple as individual arguments to that program, and runs it with the current set of environment variables. See the *Python Library Reference* for more information on the other seven ways to call this function.

Under Unix, you can call other programs from the current one by combining exec with two other functions, fork and wait, as shown in Example 1-36. The fork function makes a copy of the current process, and the wait function waits for a child process to finish.

Example 1-36. Using the os Module to Run Another Program (Unix)

```
File: os-exec-example-2.py

import os
import sys
```

Example 1-36. Using the os Module to Run Another Program (Unix) (continued)

```
def run(program, *args):
    pid = os.fork()
    if not pid:
        os.execvp(program, (program,) + args)
    return os.wait()[0]

run("python", "hello.py")

print "goodbye"
```

hello again, and welcome to the show
goodbye

The fork returns zero in the new process (the return from fork is the first thing that happens in that process!), and a non-zero process identifier in the original process. Or in other words, "not pid" is true only if we're in the new process.

The fork and wait functions are not available on Windows, but you can use the spawn function instead, as shown in Example 1-37. Unfortunately, there's no standard version of spawn that searches for an executable along the path, so you have to do that yourself.

Example 1-37. Using the os Module to Run Another Program (Windows)

```
File: os-spawn-example-1.py

import os
import string

def run(program, *args):
    # find executable
    for path in string.split(os.environ["PATH"], os.pathsep):
        file = os.path.join(path, program) + ".exe"
        try:
            return os.spawnv(os.P_WAIT, file, (file,) + args)
        except os.error:
            pass
    raise os.error, "cannot find executable"

run("python", "hello.py")

print "goodbye"
```

hello again, and welcome to the show
goodbye

You can also use spawn to run other programs in the background. Example 1-38 adds an optional mode argument to the run function; when set to os.P_NOWAIT, the script doesn't wait for the other program to finish. The default flag value os.P_WAIT tells spawn to wait until the new process is finished.

Other flags include os.P_OVERLAY, which makes spawn behave like exec, and os.P_DETACH, which runs the new process in the background, detached from both console and keyboard.

Example 1-38. Using the os Module to Run Another Program in the Background (Windows)

```
File: os-spawn-example-2.py

import os
import string

def run(program, *args, **kw):
    # find executable
    mode = kw.get("mode", os.P_WAIT)
    for path in string.split(os.environ["PATH"], os.pathsep):
        file = os.path.join(path, program) + ".exe"
        try:
            return os.spawnv(mode, file, (file,) + args)
        except os.error:
            pass
    raise os.error, "cannot find executable"

run("python", "hello.py", mode=os.P_NOWAIT)
print "goodbye"
```

goodbye
hello again, and welcome to the show

Example 1-39 provides a spawn method that works on either platform.

Example 1-39. Using Either spawn or fork/exec to Run Another Program

```
File: os-spawn-example-3.py

import os
import string

if os.name in ("nt", "dos"):
    exefile = ".exe"
else:
    exefile = ""

def spawn(program, *args):
    try:
        # possible 2.0 shortcut!
        return os.spawnvp(program, (program,) + args)
    except AttributeError:
        pass
    try:
        spawnv = os.spawnv
    except AttributeError:
```

Example 1-39. Using Either spawn or fork/exec to Run Another Program (continued)

```
        # assume it's unix
        pid = os.fork()
        if not pid:
            os.execvp(program, (program,) + args)
        return os.wait()[0]
    else:
        # got spawnv but no spawnp: go look for an executable
        for path in string.split(os.environ["PATH"], os.pathsep):
            file = os.path.join(path, program) + exefile
            try:
                return spawnv(os.P_WAIT, file, (file,) + args)
            except os.error:
                pass
        raise IOError, "cannot find executable"

#
# try it out!

spawn("python", "hello.py")

print "goodbye"
```

```
hello again, and welcome to the show
goodbye
```

Example 1-39 first attempts to call a function named spawnvp. If that doesn't exist
(it doesn't, in 2.0 and earlier), the function looks for a function named spawnv and
searches the path all by itself. As a last resort, it falls back on exec and fork.

Working with Daemon Processes

On Unix, you can also use fork to turn the current process into a background process (a "daemon"). Basically, you need to fork off a copy of the current process,
and terminate the original process, as shown in Example 1-40.

Example 1-40. Using the os Module to Run as Daemon (Unix)

```
File: os-example-14.py

import os
import time

pid = os.fork()
if pid:
    os._exit(0) # kill original

print "daemon started"
time.sleep(10)
print "daemon terminated"
```

It takes a bit more work to create a real daemon, however. First, call `setpgrp` to make the new process a "process group leader." Otherwise, signals sent to a (by that time) unrelated process group might cause problems in your daemon:

```
os.setpgrp()
```

It's also a good idea to remove the user mode mask, to make sure files created by the daemon actually get the mode flags specified by the program:

```
os.umask(0)
```

Then, you should redirect the *stdout/stderr* files, instead of just closing them (if you don't do this, you may get unexpected exceptions the day some of your code tries to write something to the console via *stdout* or *stderr*).

```
class NullDevice:
    def write(self, s):
        pass
sys.stdin.close()
sys.stdout = NullDevice()
sys.stderr = NullDevice()
```

In other words, while Python's `print` and C's `printf/fprintf` won't crash your program if the devices have been disconnected, `sys.stdout.write()` happily throws an *IOError* exception when the application runs as a daemon. But your program works just fine when running in the foreground...

By the way, the _exit function used in the previous examples terminates the current process. In contrast to `sys.exit`, this works also if the caller happens to catch the *SystemExit* exception, as shown in Example 1-41.

Example 1-41. Using the os Module to Exit the Current Process

```
File: os-example-9.py

import os
import sys

try:
    sys.exit(1)
except SystemExit, value:
    print "caught exit(%s)" % value

try:
    os._exit(2)
except SystemExit, value:
    print "caught exit(%s)" % value

print "bye!"

caught exit(1)
```

The os.path Module

The os.path module contains functions that deal with long filenames (pathnames) in various ways. To use this module, import the os module, and access this module as os.path.

Working with Filenames

The os.path module contains a number of functions that deal with long filenames in a platform independent way. In other words, you won't have to deal with forward and backward slashes, colons, and whatnot. Let's look at Example 1-42.

Example 1-42. Using the os.path Module to Handle Filename

```
File: os-path-example-1.py

import os

filename = "my/little/pony"

print "using", os.name, "..."
print "split", "=>", os.path.split(filename)
print "splitext", "=>", os.path.splitext(filename)
print "dirname", "=>", os.path.dirname(filename)
print "basename", "=>", os.path.basename(filename)
print "join", "=>", os.path.join(os.path.dirname(filename),
                                 os.path.basename(filename))

using nt ...
split => ('my/little', 'pony')
splitext => ('my/little/pony', '')
dirname => my/little
basename => pony
join => my/little\pony
```

Note that split only splits off a single item.

The os.path module also contains a number of functions that allow you to quickly figure out what a filename represents, as shown in Example 1-43.

Example 1-43. Using the os.path Module to Check What a Filename Represents

```
File: os-path-example-2.py

import os

FILES = (
    os.curdir,
    "/",
    "file",
    "/file",
    "samples",
```

Example 1-43. Using the os.path Module to Check What a Filename Represents (continued)

```
    "samples/sample.jpg",
    "directory/file",
    "../directory/file",
    "/directory/file"
    )

for file in FILES:
    print file, "=>",
    if os.path.exists(file):
        print "EXISTS",
    if os.path.isabs(file):
        print "ISABS",
    if os.path.isdir(file):
        print "ISDIR",
    if os.path.isfile(file):
        print "ISFILE",
    if os.path.islink(file):
        print "ISLINK",
    if os.path.ismount(file):
        print "ISMOUNT",
    print
```

```
. => EXISTS ISDIR
/ => EXISTS ISABS ISDIR ISMOUNT
file =>
/file => ISABS
samples => EXISTS ISDIR
samples/sample.jpg => EXISTS ISFILE
directory/file =>
../directory/file =>
/directory/file => ISABS
```

The expanduser function treats a username shortcut in the same way as most modern Unix shells (it doesn't work well on Windows), as shown in Example 1-44.

Example 1-44. Using the os.path Module to Insert the Username into a Filename

```
File: os-path-expanduser-example-1.py

import os

print os.path.expanduser("~/.pythonrc")

# /home/effbot/.pythonrc
```

The expandvars function inserts environment variables into a filename, as shown in Example 1-45.

Example 1-45. Using the os.path Module to Insert Variables into a Filename

```
File: os-path-expandvars-example-1.py

import os

os.environ["USER"] = "user"

print os.path.expandvars("/home/$USER/config")
print os.path.expandvars("$USER/folders")
```

/home/user/config
user/folders

Traversing a Filesystem

The walk function helps you find all files in a directory tree (as Example 1-46 demonstrates). It takes a directory name, a callback function, and a data object that is passed on to the callback.

Example 1-46. Using the os.path Module to Traverse a Filesystem

```
File: os-path-walk-example-1.py

import os

def callback(arg, directory, files):
    for file in files:
        print os.path.join(directory, file), repr(arg)

os.path.walk(".", callback, "secret message")
```

./aifc-example-1.py 'secret message'
./anydbm-example-1.py 'secret message'
./array-example-1.py 'secret message'
...
./samples 'secret message'
./samples/sample.jpg 'secret message'
./samples/sample.txt 'secret message'
./samples/sample.zip 'secret message'
./samples/articles 'secret message'
./samples/articles/article-1.txt 'secret message'
./samples/articles/article-2.txt 'secret message'
...

The walk function has a somewhat obscure user interface (maybe it's just me, but I can never remember the order of the arguments). The index function in Example 1-47 returns a list of filenames instead, which lets you use a straightforward for-in loop to process the files.

Example 1-47. Using os.listdir to Traverse a Filesystem

File: os-path-walk-example-2.py

```
import os

def index(directory):
    # like os.listdir, but traverses directory trees
    stack = [directory]
    files = []
    while stack:
        directory = stack.pop()
        for file in os.listdir(directory):
            fullname = os.path.join(directory, file)
            files.append(fullname)
            if os.path.isdir(fullname) and not os.path.islink(fullname):
                stack.append(fullname)
    return files

for file in index("."):
    print file
```

.\aifc-example-1.py
.\anydbm-example-1.py
.\array-example-1.py
...

If you don't want to list all files (for performance or memory reasons), Example 1-48 uses a different approach. Here, the *DirectoryWalker* class behaves like a sequence object, returning one file at a time:

Example 1-48. Using DirectoryWalker to Traverse a Filesystem

File: os-path-walk-example-3.py

```
import os

class DirectoryWalker:
    # a forward iterator that traverses a directory tree

    def __init__(self, directory):
        self.stack = [directory]
        self.files = []
        self.index = 0

    def __getitem__(self, index):
        while 1:
            try:
                file = self.files[self.index]
                self.index = self.index + 1
            except IndexError:
                # pop next directory from stack
                self.directory = self.stack.pop()
                self.files = os.listdir(self.directory)
```

Example 1-48. Using DirectoryWalker to Traverse a Filesystem (continued)

```
                self.index = 0
        else:
            # got a filename
            fullname = os.path.join(self.directory, file)
            if os.path.isdir(fullname) and not os.path.islink(fullname):
                self.stack.append(fullname)
            return fullname

for file in DirectoryWalker("."):
    print file
```

.\aifc-example-1.py
.\anydbm-example-1.py
.\array-example-1.py
...

Note the *DirectoryWalker* class doesn't check the index passed to the
_ _getitem_ _ method. This means that it won't work properly if you access the
sequence members out of order.

Finally, if you're interested in the file sizes or timestamps, Example 1-49 demonstrates a version of the class that returns both the filename and the tuple returned
from os.stat. This version saves one or two stat calls for each file (both
os.path.isdir and os.path.islink uses stat), and runs quite a bit faster on some
platforms.

Example 1-49. Using DirectoryStatWalker to Traverse a Filesystem

File: os-path-walk-example-4.py

```
import os, stat

class DirectoryStatWalker:
    # a forward iterator that traverses a directory tree, and
    # returns the filename and additional file information

    def _ _init_ _(self, directory):
        self.stack = [directory]
        self.files = []
        self.index = 0

    def _ _getitem_ _(self, index):
        while 1:
            try:
                file = self.files[self.index]
                self.index = self.index + 1
            except IndexError:
                # pop next directory from stack
                self.directory = self.stack.pop()
                self.files = os.listdir(self.directory)
                self.index = 0
```

Example 1-49. Using DirectoryStatWalker to Traverse a Filesystem (continued)

```
        else:
            # got a filename
            fullname = os.path.join(self.directory, file)
            st = os.stat(fullname)
            mode = st[stat.ST_MODE]
            if stat.S_ISDIR(mode) and not stat.S_ISLNK(mode):
                self.stack.append(fullname)
            return fullname, st

for file, st in DirectoryStatWalker("."):
    print file, st[stat.ST_SIZE]
```

```
.\aifc-example-1.py 336
.\anydbm-example-1.py 244
.\array-example-1.py 526
```

The stat Module

The stat module, shown in Example 1-50, contains a number of constants and test functions that can be used with the os.stat function.

Example 1-50. Using the stat Module

```
File: stat-example-1.py

import stat
import os, time

st = os.stat("samples/sample.txt")

print "mode", "=>", oct(stat.S_IMODE(st[stat.ST_MODE]))

print "type", "=>",
if stat.S_ISDIR(st[stat.ST_MODE]):
    print "DIRECTORY",
if stat.S_ISREG(st[stat.ST_MODE]):
    print "REGULAR",
if stat.S_ISLNK(st[stat.ST_MODE]):
    print "LINK",
print

print "size", "=>", st[stat.ST_SIZE]

print "last accessed", "=>", time.ctime(st[stat.ST_ATIME])
print "last modified", "=>", time.ctime(st[stat.ST_MTIME])
print "inode changed", "=>", time.ctime(st[stat.ST_CTIME])
```

```
mode => 0664
type => REGULAR
size => 305
last accessed => Sun Oct 10 22:12:30 1999
```

Example 1-50. Using the stat Module (continued)

```
last modified => Sun Oct 10 18:39:37 1999
inode changed => Sun Oct 10 15:26:38 1999
```

The string Module

The string module contains a number of functions to process standard Python strings, as shown in Example 1-51.

Example 1-51. Using the string Module

```
File: string-example-1.py

import string

text = "Monty Python's Flying Circus"

print "upper", "=>", string.upper(text)
print "lower", "=>", string.lower(text)
print "split", "=>", string.split(text)
print "join", "=>", string.join(string.split(text), "+")
print "replace", "=>", string.replace(text, "Python", "Java")
print "find", "=>", string.find(text, "Python"), string.find(text, "Java")
print "count", "=>", string.count(text, "n")

upper => MONTY PYTHON'S FLYING CIRCUS
lower => monty python's flying circus
split => ['Monty', "Python's", 'Flying', 'Circus']
join => Monty+Python's+Flying+Circus
replace => Monty Java's Flying Circus
find => 6 -1
count => 3
```

In Python 1.5.2 and earlier, the string module uses functions from the strop implementation module where possible.

In Python 1.6 and later, most string operations are made available as string methods as well, as shown in Example 1-52. Many of the functions in the string module are simply wrapper functions that call the corresponding string method.

Example 1-52. Using string Methods Instead of string Module Functions

```
File: string-example-2.py

text = "Monty Python's Flying Circus"

print "upper", "=>", text.upper()
print "lower", "=>", text.lower()
print "split", "=>", text.split()
print "join", "=>", "+".join(text.split())
print "replace", "=>", text.replace("Python", "Perl")
print "find", "=>", text.find("Python"), text.find("Perl")
```

Example 1-52. Using string Methods Instead of string Module Functions (continued)

```
print "count", "=>", text.count("n")
```

```
upper => MONTY PYTHON'S FLYING CIRCUS
lower => monty python's flying circus
split => ['Monty', "Python's", 'Flying', 'Circus']
join => Monty+Python's+Flying+Circus
replace => Monty Perl's Flying Circus
find => 6 -1
count => 3
```

In addition to the string-manipulation capabilities offered by string, the module also contains a number of functions that convert strings to other types (as Example 1-53 demonstrates).

Example 1-53. Using the string Module to Convert Strings to Numbers

```
File: string-example-3.py

import string

print int("4711"),
print string.atoi("4711"),
print string.atoi("11147", 8), # octal
print string.atoi("1267", 16), # hexadecimal
print string.atoi("3mv", 36) # whatever...

print string.atoi("4711", 0),
print string.atoi("04711", 0),
print string.atoi("0x4711", 0)

print float("4711"),
print string.atof("1"),
print string.atof("1.23e5")
```

```
4711 4711 4711 4711 4711
4711 2505 18193
4711.0 1.0 123000.0
```

In most cases (especially if you're using 1.6 or later), you can use the int and float functions instead of their string module counterparts.

The atoi function takes an optional second argument, which specifices the number base. If the base is 0, the function looks at the first few characters before attempting to interpret the value: if "0x," the base is set to 16 (hexadecimal), and if "0," the base is set to 8 (octal). The default is base 10 (decimal), just as if you hadn't provided an extra argument.

In 1.6 and later, int also accepts a second argument, just like atoi. Unlike the string versions, int and float accept Unicode strings.

The re Module

"Some people, when confronted with a problem, think
'I know, I'll use regular expressions.' Now they
have two problems."
—Jamie Zawinski, on *comp.lang.emacs*

The re module provides a set of powerful regular expression facilities, which allows you to quickly check whether a given string *matches* a given pattern (using the match function), or *contains* such a pattern (using the search function). A regular expression is a string pattern written in a compact (and quite cryptic) syntax.

The match function attempts to match a pattern against the beginning of the given string, as shown in Example 1-54. If the pattern matches anything at all (including an empty string, if the pattern allows that!), match returns a *match object*. The group method can be used to find out what matched.

Example 1-54. Using the re Module to Match Strings

```
File: re-example-1.py

import re

text = "The Attila the Hun Show"

# a single character
m = re.match(".", text)
if m: print repr("."), "=>", repr(m.group(0))

# any string of characters
m = re.match(".*", text)
if m: print repr(".*"), "=>", repr(m.group(0))

# a string of letters (at least one)
m = re.match("\w+", text)
if m: print repr("\w+"), "=>", repr(m.group(0))

# a string of digits
m = re.match("\d+", text)
if m: print repr("\d+"), "=>", repr(m.group(0))

 '.' => 'T'
'.*' => 'The Attila the Hun Show'
'\\w+' => 'The'
```

You can use parentheses to mark regions in the pattern. If the pattern matched, the group method can be used to extract the contents of these regions, as shown in Example 1-55. group(1) returns the contents of the first group, group(2) returns the contents of the second, and so on. If you pass several group numbers to the group function, it returns a tuple.

Example 1-55. Using the re Module to Extract Matching Substrings

```
File: re-example-2.py

import re

text ="10/15/99"

m = re.match("(\d{2})/(\d{2})/(\d{2,4})", text)
if m:
    print m.group(1, 2, 3)
```

('10', '15', '99')

The `search` function searches for the pattern inside the string, as shown in Example 1-56. It basically tries the pattern at every possible character position, starting from the left, and returns a match object as soon it has found a match. If the pattern doesn't match anywhere, it returns *None*.

Example 1-56. Using the re Module to Search for Substrings

```
File: re-example-3.py

import re

text = "Example 3: There is 1 date 10/25/95 in here!"

m = re.search("(\d{1,2})/(\d{1,2})/(\d{2,4})", text)

print m.group(1), m.group(2), m.group(3)

month, day, year = m.group(1, 2, 3)
print month, day, year

date = m.group(0)
print date
```

10 25 95
10 25 95
10/25/95

The `sub` function used in Example 1-57 can be used to replace patterns with another string.

Example 1-57. Using the re Module to Replace Substrings

```
File: re-example-4.py

import re

text = "you're no fun anymore..."

# literal replace (string.replace is faster)
print re.sub("fun", "entertaining", text)
```

Example 1-57. Using the re Module to Replace Substrings (continued)

```
# collapse all non-letter sequences to a single dash
print re.sub("[^\w]+", "-", text)

# convert all words to beeps
print re.sub("\S+", "-BEEP-", text)
```

you're no entertaining anymore...
you-re-no-fun-anymore-
-BEEP- -BEEP- -BEEP- -BEEP-

You can also use `sub` to replace patterns via a `callback` function. Example 1-58 shows how to precompile patterns.

Example 1-58. Using the re Module to Replace Substrings via the callback Function

```
File: re-example-5.py

import re
import string

text = "a line of text\\012another line of text\\012etc..."

def octal(match):
    # replace octal code with corresponding ASCII character
    return chr(string.atoi(match.group(1), 8))

octal_pattern = re.compile(r"\\(\d\d\d)")

print text
print octal_pattern.sub(octal, text)
```

a line of text
another line of text
etc...
a line of text
another line of text
etc...

If you don't compile, the `re` module caches compiled versions for you, so you usually don't have to compile regular expressions in small scripts. In Python 1.5.2, the cache holds 20 patterns. In 2.0, the cache size has been increased to 100 patterns.

Finally, Example 1-59 matches a string against a list of patterns. The list of patterns are combined into a single pattern, and precompiled to save time.

Example 1-59. Using the re Module to Match Against One of Many Patterns

```
File: re-example-6.py

import re, string
```

Example 1-59. Using the re Module to Match Against One of Many Patterns (continued)

```
def combined_pattern(patterns):
    p = re.compile(
        string.join(map(lambda x: "("+x+")", patterns), "|")
        )
    def fixup(v, m=p.match, r=range(0,len(patterns))):
        try:
            regs = m(v).regs
        except AttributeError:
            return None # no match, so m.regs will fail
        else:
            for i in r:
                if regs[i+1] != (-1, -1):
                    return i
    return fixup

#
# try it out!

patterns = [
    r"\d+",
    r"abc\d{2,4}",
    r"p\w+"
]

p = combined_pattern(patterns)

print p("129391")
print p("abc800")
print p("abc1600")
print p("python")
print p("perl")
print p("tcl")

0
1
1
2
2
None
```

The math Module

The math module implements a number of mathematical operations for floating-point numbers. The functions are generally thin wrappers around the platform C library functions of the same name, so results may vary slightly across platforms in normal cases, or vary a lot in exceptional cases. Example 1-60 demonstrates the use of the math module.

Example 1-60. Using the math Module

```
File: math-example-1.py

import math

print "e", "=>", math.e
print "pi", "=>", math.pi
print "hypot", "=>", math.hypot(3.0, 4.0)

# and many others...

e => 2.71828182846
pi => 3.14159265359
hypot => 5.0
```

See the *Python Library Reference* for a full list of functions.

The cmath Module

The cmath module shown in Example 1-61 contains a number of mathematical operations for complex numbers.

Example 1-61. Using the cmath Module

```
File: cmath-example-1.py

import cmath

print "pi", "=>", cmath.pi
print "sqrt(-1)", "=>", cmath.sqrt(-1)

pi => 3.14159265359
sqrt(-1) => 1j
```

See the *Python Library Reference* for a full list of functions.

The operator Module

The operator module provides a "functional" interface to the standard operators in Python. The functions in this module can be used instead of some lambda constructs, when processing data with functions like map and filter. They are also quite popular among people who like to write obscure code, for obvious reasons. The operator module is demonstrated in Example 1-62.

Example 1-62. Using the operator Module

```
File: operator-example-1.py

import operator
```

Example 1-62. Using the operator Module (continued)

```
sequence = 1, 2, 4

print "add", "=>", reduce(operator.add, sequence)
print "sub", "=>", reduce(operator.sub, sequence)
print "mul", "=>", reduce(operator.mul, sequence)
print "concat", "=>", operator.concat("spam", "egg")
print "repeat", "=>", operator.repeat("spam", 5)
print "getitem", "=>", operator.getitem(sequence, 2)
print "indexOf", "=>", operator.indexOf(sequence, 2)
print "sequenceIncludes", "=>", operator.sequenceIncludes(sequence, 3)

add => 7
sub => -5
mul => 8
concat => spamegg
repeat => spamspamspamspamspam


getitem => 4
indexOf => 1
sequenceIncludes => 0
```

Example 1-63 shows some operator functions that can be used to check object types.

Example 1-63. Using the operator Module for Type Checking

```
File: operator-example-2.py

import operator
import UserList

def dump(data):
    print type(data), "=>",
    if operator.isCallable(data):
        print "CALLABLE",
    if operator.isMappingType(data):
        print "MAPPING",
    if operator.isNumberType(data):
        print "NUMBER",
    if operator.isSequenceType(data):
        print "SEQUENCE",
    print

dump(0)
dump("string")
dump("string"[0])
dump([1, 2, 3])
dump((1, 2, 3))
dump({"a": 1})
dump(len) # function
dump(UserList) # module
```

Example 1-63. Using the operator Module for Type Checking (continued)

```
dump(UserList.UserList) # class
dump(UserList.UserList()) # instance

<type 'int'> => NUMBER
<type 'string'> => SEQUENCE
<type 'string'> => SEQUENCE
<type 'list'> => SEQUENCE
<type 'tuple'> => SEQUENCE
<type 'dictionary'> => MAPPING
<type 'builtin_function_or_method'> => CALLABLE
<type 'module'> =>
<type 'class'> => CALLABLE
<type 'instance'> => MAPPING NUMBER SEQUENCE
```

Note that the operator module doesn't handle object instances in a normal fashion. Be careful when you use the isNumberType, isMappingType, and isSequence-Type functions. It's easy to make your code less flexible than it has to be.

Also, note that a string sequence member (a character) is also a sequence. If you're writing a recursive function that uses isSequenceType to traverse an object tree, you better not pass it an ordinary string (or anything containing one).

The copy Module

The copy module contains two functions that are used to copy objects, as shown in Example 1-64.

copy(object) ⇒ object creates a "shallow" copy of the given object. In this context, shallow means that the object itself is copied, but if the object is a container, the members will still refer to the original member objects.

Example 1-64. Using the copy Module to Copy Objects

```
File: copy-example-1.py

import copy

a = [[1],[2],[3]]
b = copy.copy(a)

print "before", "=>"
print a
print b

# modify original
a[0][0] = 0
a[1] = None

print "after", "=>"
print a
```

Example 1-64. Using the copy Module to Copy Objects (continued)

```
print b
```

```
before =>
[[1], [2], [3]]
[[1], [2], [3]]
after =>
[[0], None, [3]]
[[0], [2], [3]]
```

You can also make shallow copies of lists using the [:] syntax (full slice), and you can make copies of dictionaries using the copy method.

In contrast, deepcopy(object) ⇒ object creates a "deep" copy of the given object, as shown in Example 1-65. If the object is a container, all members are copied as well, recursively.

Example 1-65. Using the copy Module to Copy Collections

```
File: copy-example-2.py

import copy

a = [[1],[2],[3]]
b = copy.deepcopy(a)

print "before", "=>"
print a
print b

# modify original
a[0][0] = 0
a[1] = None

print "after", "=>"
print a
print b

before =>
[[1], [2], [3]]
[[1], [2], [3]]
after =>
[[0], None, [3]]
[[1], [2], [3]]
```

The sys Module

The sys module provides a number of functions and variables that can be used to manipulate different parts of the Python runtime environment.

Working with Command-line Arguments

The argv list contains the arguments that were passed to the script, when the interpreter was started, as shown in Example 1-66. The first item contains the name of the script itself.

Example 1-66. Using the sys Module to Get Script Arguments

```
File: sys-argv-example-1.py

import sys

print "script name is", sys.argv[0]

if len(sys.argv) > 1:
    print "there are", len(sys.argv)-1, "arguments:"
    for arg in sys.argv[1:]:
        print arg
else:
    print "there are no arguments!"
```

```
script name is sys-argv-example-1.py
there are no arguments!
```

If you read the script from standard input (like "python < sys-argv-example-1.py"), the script name is set to an empty string. If you pass in the program as a string (using the –c option), the script name is set to "–c."

Working with Modules

The path list contains a list of directory names in which Python looks for extension modules (Python source modules, compiled modules, or binary extensions). When you start Python, this list is initialized from a mixture of built-in rules, the contents of the PYTHONPATH environment variable, and the registry contents (on Windows). But since it's an ordinary list, you can also manipulate it from within the program, as Example 1-67 shows.

Example 1-67. Using the sys Module to Manipulate the Module Search Path

```
File: sys-path-example-1.py

import sys

print "path has", len(sys.path), "members"
```

Example 1-67. Using the sys Module to Manipulate the Module Search Path (continued)

```
# add the sample directory to the path
sys.path.insert(0, "samples")
import sample

# nuke the path
sys.path = []
import random # oops!
```

path has 7 members
this is the sample module!
Traceback (innermost last):
  File "sys-path-example-1.py", line 11, in ?
    import random # oops!
ImportError: No module named random

Example 1-68 demonstrates the builtin_module_names list, which contains the names of all modules built into the Python interpreter.

Example 1-68. Using the sys Module to Find Built-in Modules

```
File: sys-builtin-module-names-example-1.py

import sys

def dump(module):
    print module, "=>",
    if module in sys.builtin_module_names:
        print "<BUILTIN>"
    else:
        module = __import__(module)
        print module.__file__

dump("os")
dump("sys")
dump("string")
dump("strop")
dump("zlib")
```

os => C:\python\lib\os.pyc
sys => <BUILTIN>
string => C:\python\lib\string.pyc
strop => <BUILTIN>
zlib => C:\python\zlib.pyd

The modules dictionary contains all loaded modules. The import statement checks this dictionary before it actually loads something from disk.

As you can see from Example 1-69, Python loads quite a bunch of modules before handing control over to your script.

Example 1-69. Using the sys Module to Find Imported Modules

```
File: sys-modules-example-1.py

import sys

print sys.modules.keys()

['os.path', 'os', 'exceptions', '_ _main_ _', 'ntpath', 'strop', 'nt',
'sys', '_ _builtin_ _', 'site', 'signal', 'UserDict', 'string', 'stat']
```

Working with Reference Counts

The getrefcount function (shown in Example 1-70) returns the reference count for a given object—that is, the number of places where this variable is used. Python keeps track of this value, and when it drops to 0, the object is destroyed.

Example 1-70. Using the sys Module to Find the Reference Count

```
File: sys-getrefcount-example-1.py

import sys

variable = 1234

print sys.getrefcount(0)
print sys.getrefcount(variable)
print sys.getrefcount(None)

50
3
192
```

Note that this value is always larger than the actual count, since the function itself hangs on to the object while determining the value.

Checking the Host Platform

Example 1-71 shows the platform variable, which contains the name of the host platform.

Example 1-71. Using the sys Module to Find the Current Platform

```
File: sys-platform-example-1.py

import sys

#
# emulate "import os.path" (sort of)...

if sys.platform == "win32":
    import ntpath
```

Example 1-71. Using the sys Module to Find the Current Platform (continued)

```
    pathmodule = ntpath
elif sys.platform == "mac":
    import macpath
    pathmodule = macpath
else:
    # assume it's a posix platform
    import posixpath
    pathmodule = posixpath

print pathmodule
```

Typical platform names are `win32` for Windows 9X/NT and `mac` for Macintosh. For Unix systems, the platform name is usually derived from the output of the "uname -r" command, such as `irix6`, `linux2`, or `sunos5` (Solaris).

Tracing the Program

The `setprofiler` function allows you to install a profiling function. This is called every time a function or method is called, at every return (explicit or implied), and for each exception. Let's look at Example 1-72.

Example 1-72. Using the sys Module to Install a Profiler Function

```
File: sys-setprofiler-example-1.py

import sys

def test(n):
    j = 0
    for i in range(n):
        j = j + i
    return n

def profiler(frame, event, arg):
    print event, frame.f_code.co_name, frame.f_lineno, "->", arg

# profiler is activated on the next call, return, or exception
sys.setprofile(profiler)

# profile this function call
test(1)

# disable profiler
sys.setprofile(None)

# don't profile this call
test(2)

call test 3 -> None
return test 7 -> 1
```

The `profile` module provides a complete profiler framework, based on this function.

The `settrace` function in Example 1-73 is similar, but the `trace` function is called for each new line:

Example 1-73. Using the sys Module to Install a trace Function

```
File: sys-settrace-example-1.py

import sys

def test(n):
    j = 0
    for i in range(n):
        j = j + i
    return n

def tracer(frame, event, arg):
    print event, frame.f_code.co_name, frame.f_lineno, "->", arg
    return tracer

# tracer is activated on the next call, return, or exception
sys.settrace(tracer)

# trace this function call
test(1)

# disable tracing
sys.settrace(None)

# don't trace this call
test(2)

call test 3 -> None
line test 3 -> None
line test 4 -> None
line test 5 -> None
line test 5 -> None
line test 6 -> None
line test 5 -> None
line test 7 -> None
return test 7 -> 1
```

The `pdb` module provides a complete debugger framework, based on the tracing facilities offered by this function.

Working with Standard Input and Output

The `stdin`, `stdout`, and `stderr` variables contain stream objects corresponding to the standard I/O streams. You can access them directly if you need better control over the output than `print` can give you. You can also *replace* them, if you want to redirect output and input to some other device, or process them in some non-standard way, as shown in Example 1-74.

Example 1-74. Using the sys Module to Redirect Output

```
File: sys-stdout-example-1.py

import sys
import string

class Redirect:

    def __init__(self, stdout):
        self.stdout = stdout

    def write(self, s):
        self.stdout.write(string.lower(s))

# redirect standard output (including the print statement)
old_stdout = sys.stdout
sys.stdout = Redirect(sys.stdout)

print "HEJA SVERIGE",
print "FRISKT HUM\303\226R"

# restore standard output
sys.stdout = old_stdout

print "M\303\205\303\205\303\205\303\205L!"
```

```
heja sverige friskt hum\303\266r
M\303\205\303\205\303\205\303\205L!
```

An object that implements the `write` method is all it takes to redirect output.

(Unless it's a C type instance, that is: Python uses an integer attribute called `soft-space` to control spacing, and adds it to the object if it isn't there. You don't have to bother if you're using Python objects, but if you need to redirect to a C type, you should make sure that type supports the `softspace` attribute.)

Exiting the Program

When you reach the end of the main program, the interpreter is automatically terminated. If you need to exit in midflight, you can call the `sys.exit` function, which takes an optional integer value that is returned to the calling program. It is demonstrated in Example 1-75.

Example 1-75. Using the sys Module to Exit the Program

File: sys-exit-example-1.py

```
import sys

print "hello"

sys.exit(1)

print "there"
```

hello

It may not be obvious, but `sys.exit` doesn't exit at once. Instead, it raises a *SystemExit* exception. This means that you can trap calls to `sys.exit` in your main program, as Example 1-76 shows.

Example 1-76. Catching the sys.exit Call

File: sys-exit-example-2.py

```
import sys

print "hello"

try:
    sys.exit(1)
except SystemExit:
    pass

print "there"
```

hello
there

If you want to clean things up after yourself, you can install an "exit handler," which is a function that is automatically called on the way out. This is shown in Example 1-77.

Example 1-77. Catching the sys.exit Call Another Way

File: sys-exitfunc-example-1.py

```
import sys

def exitfunc():
    print "world"

sys.exitfunc = exitfunc

print "hello"
sys.exit(1)
print "there" # never printed
```

Example 1-77. Catching the sys.exit Call Another Way (continued)

hello
world

In Python 2.0, you can use the `atexit` module to register more than one exit handler.

The atexit Module

(2.0 only) The `atexit` module allows you to register one or more functions that are called when the interpreter is terminated.

To register a function, simply call the `register` function, as shown in Example 1-78. You can also add one or more extra arguments, which are passed as arguments to the `exit` function.

Example 1-78. Using the atexit Module

```
File: atexit-example-1.py

import atexit

def exit(*args):
    print "exit", args

# register two exit handler
atexit.register(exit)
atexit.register(exit, 1)
atexit.register(exit, "hello", "world")
```

exit ('hello', 'world')
exit (1,)
exit ()

This module is a straightforward wrapper for the `sys.exitfunc` hook.

The time Module

The `time` module provides a number of functions that deal with dates and the time within a day. It's a thin layer on top of the C runtime library.

A given date and time can either be represented as a floating-point value (the number of seconds since a reference date, usually January 1, 1970), or as a time tuple.

Getting the Current Time

Example 1-79 shows how you can use the time module to get the current time.

Example 1-79. Using the time Module to Get the Current Time

```
File: time-example-1.py

import time

now = time.time()

print now, "seconds since", time.gmtime(0)[:6]
print
print "or in other words:"
print "- local time:", time.localtime(now)
print "- utc:", time.gmtime(now)
```

```
937758359.77 seconds since (1970, 1, 1, 0, 0, 0)

or in other words:
- local time: (1999, 9, 19, 18, 25, 59, 6, 262, 1)
- utc: (1999, 9, 19, 16, 25, 59, 6, 262, 0)
```

The tuple returned by localtime and gmtime contains the year, month, day, hour, minute, second, day of the week, day of the year, daylight savings flag. The year number is four digits, the day of week begins with 0 for Monday, and January 1 is day number 1.

Converting Time Values to Strings

You can of course use standard string-formatting operators to convert a time tuple to a string, but the time module also provides a number of standard conversion functions, as Example 1-80 illustrates.

Example 1-80. Using the time Module to Format Dates and Times

```
File: time-example-2.py

import time

now = time.localtime(time.time())

print time.asctime(now)
print time.strftime("%y/%m/%d %H:%M", now)
print time.strftime("%a %b %d", now)
print time.strftime("%c", now)
print time.strftime("%I %p", now)
print time.strftime("%Y-%m-%d %H:%M:%S %Z", now)

# do it by hand...
year, month, day, hour, minute, second, weekday, yearday, daylight = now
```

Example 1-80. Using the time Module to Format Dates and Times (continued)

```
print "%04d-%02d-%02d" % (year, month, day)
print "%02d:%02d:%02d" % (hour, minute, second)
print ("MON", "TUE", "WED", "THU", "FRI", "SAT", "SUN")[weekday], yearday
```

```
Sun Oct 10 21:39:24 1999
99/10/10 21:39
Sun Oct 10
Sun Oct 10 21:39:24 1999
09 PM
1999-10-10 21:39:24 CEST
1999-10-10
21:39:24
SUN 283
```

Converting Strings to Time Values

On some platforms, the `time` module contains a `strptime` function, which is pretty
much the opposite of `strftime`. Given a string and a pattern, it returns the corresponding time tuple, as shown in Example 1-81.

Example 1-81. Using the time.strptime Function to Parse Dates and Times

```
File: time-example-6.py

import time

# make sure we have a strptime function!
try:
    strptime = time.strptime
except AttributeError:
    from strptime import strptime

print strptime("31 Nov 00", "%d %b %y")
print strptime("1 Jan 70 1:30pm", "%d %b %y %I:%M%p")
```

The `time.strptime` function is currently only made available by Python if it's provided by the platform's C libraries. For platforms that don't have a standard implementation (this includes Windows), Example 1-82 offers a partial replacement.

Example 1-82. A strptime Implementation

```
File: strptime.py

import re
import string

MONTHS = ["Jan", "Feb", "Mar", "Apr", "May", "Jun", "Jul", "Aug",
          "Sep", "Oct", "Nov", "Dec"]

SPEC = {
    # map formatting code to a regular expression fragment
```

Example 1-82. A strptime Implementation (continued)

```
    "%a": "(?P<weekday>[a-z]+)",
    "%A": "(?P<weekday>[a-z]+)",
    "%b": "(?P<month>[a-z]+)",
    "%B": "(?P<month>[a-z]+)",
    "%C": "(?P<century>\d\d?)",
    "%d": "(?P<day>\d\d?)",
    "%D": "(?P<month>\d\d?)/(?P<day>\d\d?)/(?P<year>\d\d)",
    "%e": "(?P<day>\d\d?)",
    "%h": "(?P<month>[a-z]+)",
    "%H": "(?P<hour>\d\d?)",
    "%I": "(?P<hour12>\d\d?)",
    "%j": "(?P<yearday>\d\d?\d?)",
    "%m": "(?P<month>\d\d?)",
    "%M": "(?P<minute>\d\d?)",
    "%p": "(?P<ampm12>am|pm)",
    "%R": "(?P<hour>\d\d?):(?P<minute>\d\d?)",
    "%S": "(?P<second>\d\d?)",
    "%T": "(?P<hour>\d\d?):(?P<minute>\d\d?):(?P<second>\d\d?)",
    "%U": "(?P<week>\d\d)",
    "%w": "(?P<weekday>\d)",
    "%W": "(?P<weekday>\d\d)",
    "%y": "(?P<year>\d\d)",
    "%Y": "(?P<year>\d\d\d\d)",
    "%%": "%"
}


class TimeParser:
    def __init__(self, format):
        # convert strptime format string to regular expression
        format = string.join(re.split("(?:\s|%t|%n)+", format))
        pattern = []
        try:
            for spec in re.findall("%\w|%%|.", format):
                if spec[0] == "%":
                    spec = SPEC[spec]
                pattern.append(spec)
        except KeyError:
            raise ValueError, "unknown specificer: %s" % spec
        self.pattern = re.compile("(?i)" + string.join(pattern, ""))
    def match(self, daytime):
        # match time string
        match = self.pattern.match(daytime)
        if not match:
            raise ValueError, "format mismatch"
        get = match.groupdict().get
        tm = [0] * 9
        # extract date elements
        y = get("year")
        if y:
            y = int(y)
            if y < 68:
                y = 2000 + y
```

Example 1-82. A strptime Implementation (continued)

```
            elif y < 100:
                y = 1900 + y
            tm[0] = y
        m = get("month")
        if m:
            if m in MONTHS:
                m = MONTHS.index(m) + 1
            tm[1] = int(m)
        d = get("day")
        if d: tm[2] = int(d)
        # extract time elements
        h = get("hour")
        if h:
            tm[3] = int(h)
        else:
            h = get("hour12")
            if h:
                h = int(h)
                if string.lower(get("ampm12", "")) == "pm":
                    h = h + 12
                tm[3] = h
        m = get("minute")
        if m: tm[4] = int(m)
        s = get("second")
        if s: tm[5] = int(s)
        # ignore weekday/yearday for now
        return tuple(tm)

def strptime(string, format="%a %b %d %H:%M:%S %Y"):
    return TimeParser(format).match(string)

if __name__ == "__main__":
    # try it out
    import time
    print strptime("2000-12-20 01:02:03", "%Y-%m-%d %H:%M:%S")
    print strptime(time.ctime(time.time()))

(2000, 12, 20, 1, 2, 3, 0, 0, 0)
(2000, 11, 15, 12, 30, 45, 0, 0, 0)
```

Converting Time Values

Converting a time tuple back to a time value is pretty easy, at least as long as we're talking about local time. Just pass the time tuple to the mktime function, as shown in Example 1-83.

Example 1-83. Using the time Module to Convert a Local Time Tuple to a Time Integer

```
File: time-example-3.py

import time

t0 = time.time()
tm = time.localtime(t0)

print tm

print t0
print time.mktime(tm)

(1999, 9, 9, 0, 11, 8, 3, 252, 1)
936828668.16
936828668.0
```

Unfortunately, there's no function in the 1.5.2 standard library that converts UTC time tuples *back* to time values (neither in Python nor in the underlying C libraries). Example 1-84 provides a Python implementation of such a function, called timegm.

Example 1-84. Converting a UTC Time Tuple to a Time Integer

```
File: time-example-4.py

import time

def _d(y, m, d, days=(0,31,59,90,120,151,181,212,243,273,304,334,365)):
    # map a date to the number of days from a reference point
    return (((y - 1901)*1461)/4 + days[m-1] + d +
        ((m > 2 and not y % 4 and (y % 100 or not y % 400)) and 1))

def timegm(tm, epoch=_d(1970,1,1)):
    year, month, day, h, m, s = tm[:6]
    assert year >= 1970
    assert 1 <= month <= 12
    return (_d(year, month, day) - epoch)*86400 + h*3600 + m*60 + s

t0 = time.time()
tm = time.gmtime(t0)

print tm

print t0
print timegm(tm)

(1999, 9, 8, 22, 12, 12, 2, 251, 0)
936828732.48
936828732
```

In 1.6 and later, a similar function is available in the calendar module, as calendar.timegm.

Timing Things

The time module can be used to time the execution of a Python program, as Example 1-85 demonstrates. You can measure either "wall time" (real world time), or "process time" (amount of CPU time the process has consumed, thus far).

Example 1-85. Using the time Module to Benchmark an Algorithm

```
File: time-example-5.py

import time

def procedure():
    time.sleep(2.5)

# measure process time
t0 = time.clock()
procedure()
print time.clock() - t0, "seconds process time"

# measure wall time
t0 = time.time()
procedure()
print time.time() - t0, "seconds wall time"
```

0.0 seconds process time
2.50903499126 seconds wall time

Not all systems can measure the true process time. On such systems (including Windows), clock usually measures the wall time since the program was started.

The process time has limited precision. On many systems, it wraps around after just over 30 minutes.

Also, see the timing module, which measures the wall time between two events.

The types Module

The types module contains type objects for all object types defined by the standard interpreter, as Example 1-86 demonstrates. All objects of the same type share a single type object. You can use is to test if an object has a given type.

Example 1-86. Using the types Module

```
File: types-example-1.py

import types

def check(object):
    print object,
```

Example 1-86. Using the types Module (continued)

```
    if type(object) is types.IntType:
        print "INTEGER",
    if type(object) is types.FloatType:
        print "FLOAT",
    if type(object) is types.StringType:
        print "STRING",
    if type(object) is types.ClassType:
        print "CLASS",
    if type(object) is types.InstanceType:
        print "INSTANCE",
    print

check(0)
check(0.0)
check("0")

class A:
    pass

class B:
    pass

check(A)
check(B)

a = A()
b = B()

check(a)
check(b)

0 INTEGER
0.0 FLOAT
0 STRING
A CLASS
B CLASS
<A instance at 796960> INSTANCE
<B instance at 796990> INSTANCE
```

Note that all classes have the same type, as do all instances. To test what class hierarchy a class or an instance belongs to, use the built-in `issubclass` and `isinstance` functions.

The `types` module destroys the current exception state when it is first imported. In other words, don't import it (or *any* module that imports it!) from within an exception handler.

The gc Module

(Optional, 2.0 and later) The gc module provides an interface to the built-in cyclic garbage collector.

Python uses reference counting to keep track of when to get rid of objects; as soon as the last reference to an object goes away, the object is destroyed.

Starting with Version 2.0, Python also provides a cyclic garbage collector, which runs at regular intervals. This collector looks for data structures that point to themselves, and attempts to break the cycles. Example 1-87 shows this.

You can use the gc.collect function to force full collection. This function returns the number of objects destroyed by the collector.

Example 1-87. Using the gc Module to Collect Cyclic Garbage

```
File: gc-example-1.py

import gc

# create a simple object that links to itself
class Node:

    def __init__(self, name):
        self.name = name
        self.parent = None
        self.children = []

    def addchild(self, node):
        node.parent = self
        self.children.append(node)

    def __repr__(self):
        return "<Node %s at %x>" % (repr(self.name), id(self))

# set up a self-referencing structure
root = Node("monty")

root.addchild(Node("eric"))
root.addchild(Node("john"))
root.addchild(Node("michael"))

# remove our only reference
del root

print gc.collect(), "unreachable objects"
print gc.collect(), "unreachable objects"

12 unreachable objects
0 unreachable objects
```

If you're sure that your program doesn't create any self-referencing data structures, you can use the `gc.disable` function to disable collection. After calling this function, Python 2.0 works exactly like 1.5.2 and earlier.

2

More Standard Modules

> *"Now, imagine that your friend kept complaining that she didn't*
> *want to visit you since she found it too hard to climb up the drain*
> *pipe, and you kept telling her to use the friggin' stairs like*
> *everyone else . . . "*
> —eff-bot, June 1998

Overview

This chapter describes a number of modules that are used in many Python programs. It's perfectly possible to write large Python programs without using them,
but they can help you save a lot of time and effort.

Files and Streams

The `fileinput` module makes it easy to write different kinds of text filters. This
module provides a wrapper class, which lets you use a simple `for-in` statement to
loop over the contents of one or more text files.

The `StringIO` module (and the `cStringIO` variant) implements an in-memory file
object. You can use `StringIO` objects in many places where Python expects an
ordinary file object.

Type Wrappers

`UserDict`, `UserList`, and `UserString` are thin wrappers on top of the corresponding
built-in types. Unlike the built-in types, these wrappers can be subclassed. This
can come in handy if you need a class that works almost like a built-in type, but
has one or more extra methods.

Random Numbers

The random module provides a number of different random number generators. The whrandom module is similar, but it also allows you to create multiple generator objects.

Digests and Encryption Algorithms

The md5 and sha modules are used to calculate cryptographically strong message signatures (so-called "message digests").

The crypt module implements a DES-style one-way encryption. This module is usually only available on Unix systems.

The rotor module provides simple two-way encryption.

The fileinput Module

The fileinput module allows you to loop over the contents of one or more text files, as shown in Example 2-1.

Example 2-1. Using the fileinput Module to Loop Over a Text File

```
File: fileinput-example-1.py

import fileinput
import sys

for line in fileinput.input("samples/sample.txt"):
    sys.stdout.write("-> ")
    sys.stdout.write(line)
```

```
-> We will perhaps eventually be writing only small
-> modules which are identified by name as they are
-> used to build larger ones, so that devices like
-> indentation, rather than delimiters, might become
-> feasible for expressing local structure in the
-> source language.
->      -- Donald E. Knuth, December 1974
```

The fileinput module also allows you to get metainformation about the current line. This includes isfirstline, filename, and lineno, as Example 2-2 shows.

Example 2-2. Using the fileinput Module to Process Multiple Files

```
File: fileinput-example-2.py

import fileinput
import glob
import string, sys
```

Example 2-2. Using the fileinput Module to Process Multiple Files (continued)

```
for line in fileinput.input(glob.glob("samples/*.txt")):
    if fileinput.isfirstline(): # first in a file?
        sys.stderr.write("-- reading %s --\n" % fileinput.filename())
    sys.stdout.write(str(fileinput.lineno()) + " " + string.upper(line))
```

```
-- reading samples\sample.txt --
1 WE WILL PERHAPS EVENTUALLY BE WRITING ONLY SMALL
2 MODULES WHICH ARE IDENTIFIED BY NAME AS THEY ARE
3 USED TO BUILD LARGER ONES, SO THAT DEVICES LIKE
4 INDENTATION, RATHER THAN DELIMITERS, MIGHT BECOME
5 FEASIBLE FOR EXPRESSING LOCAL STRUCTURE IN THE
6 SOURCE LANGUAGE.
7     -- DONALD E. KNUTH, DECEMBER 1974
```

Processing text files in place is also easy. Just call the input function with the inplace keyword argument set to 1, and the module takes care of the rest. Example 2-3 demonstrates this.

Example 2-3. Using the fileinput Module to Convert CRLF to LF

```
File: fileinput-example-3.py

import fileinput, sys

for line in fileinput.input(inplace=1):
    # convert Windows/DOS text files to Unix files
    if line[-2:] == "\r\n":
        line = line[:-2] + "\n"
    sys.stdout.write(line)
```

The shutil Module

The shutil utility module contains some functions for copying files and directories. The copy function used in Example 2-4 copies a file in pretty much the same way as the Unix cp command.

Example 2-4. Using the shutil Module to Copy Files

```
File: shutil-example-1.py

import shutil
import os

for file in os.listdir("."):
    if os.path.splitext(file)[1] == ".py":
        print file
        shutil.copy(file, os.path.join("backup", file))

aifc-example-1.py
anydbm-example-1.py
```

Example 2-4. Using the shutil Module to Copy Files (continued)

array-example-1.py
...

The copytree function copies an entire directory tree (same as cp -r), and rmtree removes an entire tree (same as rm -r). These functions are illustrated in Example 2-5.

Example 2-5. Using the shutil Module to Copy and Remove Directory Trees

```
File: shutil-example-2.py

import shutil
import os

SOURCE = "samples"
BACKUP = "samples-bak"

# create a backup directory
shutil.copytree(SOURCE, BACKUP)

print os.listdir(BACKUP)

# remove it
shutil.rmtree(BACKUP)

print os.listdir(BACKUP)

['sample.wav', 'sample.jpg', 'sample.au', 'sample.msg', 'sample.tgz',
...
Traceback (most recent call last):
  File "shutil-example-2.py", line 17, in ?
    print os.listdir(BACKUP)
os.error: No such file or directory
```

The tempfile Module

The tempfile module in Example 2-6 allows you to quickly come up with unique names to use for temporary files.

Example 2-6. Using the tempfile Module to Create Filenames for Temporary Files

```
File: tempfile-example-1.py

import tempfile
import os

tempfile = tempfile.mktemp()

print "tempfile", "=>", tempfile

file = open(tempfile, "w+b")
```

Example 2-6. Using the tempfile Module to Create Filenames for Temporary Files (continued)

```
file.write("*" * 1000)
file.seek(0)
print len(file.read()), "bytes"
file.close()

try:
    # must remove file when done
    os.remove(tempfile)
except OSError:
    pass
```

tempfile => C:\TEMP\~160-1
1000 bytes

The TemporaryFile function picks a suitable name and opens the file, as shown in
Example 2-7. It also makes sure that the file is removed when it's closed. (On
Unix, you can remove an open file and have it disappear when the file is closed.
On other platforms, this is done via a special wrapper class.)

Example 2-7. Using the tempfile Module to Open Temporary Files

```
File: tempfile-example-2.py

import tempfile

file = tempfile.TemporaryFile()

for i in range(100):
    file.write("*" * 100)

file.close() # removes the file!
```

The StringIO Module

The stringio module shown in Example 2-8 implements an in-memory file object.
This object can be used as input or output to most functions that expect a standard file object.

Example 2-8. Using the StringIO Module to Read from a Static File

```
File: stringio-example-1.py

import StringIO

MESSAGE = "That man is depriving a village somewhere of a computer scientist."

file = StringIO.StringIO(MESSAGE)
```

Example 2-8. Using the StringIO Module to Read from a Static File (continued)

```
print file.read()
```

That man is depriving a village somewhere of a computer scientist.

The StringIO class implements memory file versions of all methods available for
built-in file objects, plus a `getvalue` method that returns the internal string value.
Example 2-9 demonstrates this method.

Example 2-9. Using the StringIO Module to Write to a Memory File

```
File: stringio-example-2.py

import StringIO

file = StringIO.StringIO()
file.write("This man is no ordinary man. ")
file.write("This is Mr. F. G. Superman.")

print file.getvalue()
```

This man is no ordinary man. This is Mr. F. G. Superman.

StringIO can be used to capture redirected output from the Python interpreter, as
shown in Example 2-10.

Example 2-10. Using the StringIO Module to Capture Output

```
File: stringio-example-3.py

import StringIO
import string, sys

stdout = sys.stdout

sys.stdout = file = StringIO.StringIO()

print """
According to Gbaya folktales, trickery and guile
are the best ways to defeat the python, king of
snakes, which was hatched from a dragon at the
world's start. -- National Geographic, May 1997
"""

sys.stdout = stdout

print string.upper(file.getvalue())
```

**ACCORDING TO GBAYA FOLKTALES, TRICKERY AND GUILE
ARE THE BEST WAYS TO DEFEAT THE PYTHON, KING OF
SNAKES, WHICH WAS HATCHED FROM A DRAGON AT THE
WORLD'S START. -- NATIONAL GEOGRAPHIC, MAY 1997**

The cStringIO Module

The cStringIO is an optional module, which contains a faster implementation of the StringIO module. It works exactly like the StringIO module, but it cannot be subclassed. Example 2-11 shows how cStringIO is used.

Example 2-11. Using the cStringIO Module

```
File: cstringio-example-1.py

import cStringIO

MESSAGE = "That man is depriving a village somewhere of a computer scientist."

file = cStringIO.StringIO(MESSAGE)

print file.read()
```

That man is depriving a village somewhere of a computer scientist.

To make your code as fast as possible, but also robust enough to run on older Python installations, you can fall back on the StringIO module if cStringIO is not available, as Example 2-12 does.

Example 2-12. Falling Back on the StringIO Module

```
File: cstringio-example-2.py

try:
    import cStringIO
    StringIO = cStringIO
except ImportError:
    import StringIO

print StringIO
```

<module 'StringIO' (built-in)>

The mmap Module

(New in 2.0) The mmap module provides an interface to the operating system's memory mapping functions, as shown in Example 2-13. The mapped region behaves like a string object, but data is read directly from the file.

Example 2-13. Using the mmap Module

```
File: mmap-example-1.py

import mmap
import os
```

Example 2-13. Using the mmap Module (continued)

```
filename = "samples/sample.txt"

file = open(filename, "r+")
size = os.path.getsize(filename)

data = mmap.mmap(file.fileno(), size)

# basics
print data
print len(data), size

# use slicing to read from the file
print repr(data[:10]), repr(data[:10])

# or use the standard file interface
print repr(data.read(10)), repr(data.read(10))
```

```
<mmap object at 008A2A10>
302 302
'We will pe' 'We will pe'
'We will pe' 'rhaps even'
```

Under Windows, the file must currently be opened for both reading and writing (r+, or w+), or the mmap call will fail.

Example 2-14 shows that memory mapped regions can be used instead of ordinary strings in many places, including regular expressions and many string operations.

Example 2-14. Using String Functions and Regular Expressions on a Mapped Region

```
File: mmap-example-2.py

import mmap
import os, string, re

def mapfile(filename):
    file = open(filename, "r+")
    size = os.path.getsize(filename)
    return mmap.mmap(file.fileno(), size)

data = mapfile("samples/sample.txt")

# search
index = data.find("small")
print index, repr(data[index-5:index+15])

# regular expressions work too!
m = re.search("small", data)
print m.start(), m.group()
```

```
43 'only small\015\012modules '
43 small
```

The UserDict Module

The UserDict module contains a dictionary class that can be subclassed (it's actually a Python wrapper for the built-in dictionary type).

Example 2-15 shows an enhanced dictionary class, which allows dictionaries to be "added" to each other and initialized using the keyword argument syntax.

Example 2-15. Using the UserDict Module

```
File: userdict-example-1.py

import UserDict

class FancyDict(UserDict.UserDict):

    def __init__(self, data = {}, **kw):
        UserDict.UserDict.__init__(self)
        self.update(data)
        self.update(kw)

    def __add__(self, other):
        dict = FancyDict(self.data)
        dict.update(b)
        return dict

a = FancyDict(a = 1)
b = FancyDict(b = 2)

print a + b

{'b': 2, 'a': 1}
```

The UserList Module

The UserList module contains a list class that can be subclassed (simply a Python wrapper for the built-in list type).

In Example 2-16, *AutoList* instances work just like ordinary lists, except that they allow you to insert items at the end by assigning to them.

Example 2-16. Using the UserList Module

```
File: userlist-example-1.py

import UserList

class AutoList(UserList.UserList):

    def __setitem__(self, i, item):
        if i == len(self.data):
            self.data.append(item)
```

Example 2-16. Using the UserList Module (continued)

```
        else:
            self.data[i] = item

list = AutoList()

for i in range(10):
    list[i] = i

print list
```

[0, 1, 2, 3, 4, 5, 6, 7, 8, 9]

The UserString Module

(New in 2.0) The UserString module contains two classes, *UserString* and *MutableString*. The former is a wrapper for the standard string type that can be subclassed, and the latter is a variation that allows you to modify the string in place.

Note that *MutableString* is not very efficient. Most operations are implemented using slicing and string concatenation. If performance is important, use lists of string fragments or the array module. Example 2-17 shows the UserString module.

Example 2-17. Using the UserString Module

```
File: userstring-example-1.py

import UserString

class MyString(UserString.MutableString):

    def append(self, s):
        self.data = self.data + s

    def insert(self, index, s):
        self.data = self.data[index:] + s + self.data[index:]

    def remove(self, s):
        self.data = self.data.replace(s, "")

file = open("samples/book.txt")
text = file.read()
file.close()

book = MyString(text)

for bird in ["gannet", "robin", "nuthatch"]:
    book.remove(bird)

print book
```

Example 2-17. Using the UserString Module (continued)

```
...
C: The one without the !
P: The one without the -!!! They've ALL got the !! It's a
Standard British Bird, the , it's in all the books!!!
...
```

The traceback Module

The traceback module in Example 2-18 allows you to print exception tracebacks inside your programs, just like the interpreter does when you don't catch an exception yourself.

Example 2-18. Using the traceback Module to Print a Traceback

```
File: traceback-example-1.py

# note! importing the traceback module messes up the
# exception state, so you better do that here and not
# in the exception handler
import traceback

try:
    raise SyntaxError, "example"
except:
    traceback.print_exc()

Traceback (innermost last):
  File "traceback-example-1.py", line 7, in ?
SyntaxError: example
```

Example 2-19 uses the StringIO module to put the traceback in a string.

Example 2-19. Using the traceback Module to Copy a Traceback to a String

```
File: traceback-example-2.py

import traceback
import StringIO

try:
    raise IOError, "an i/o error occurred"
except:
    fp = StringIO.StringIO()
    traceback.print_exc(file=fp)
    message = fp.getvalue()

    print "failure! the error was:", repr(message)

failure! the error was: 'Traceback (innermost last):
  File
"traceback-example-2.py", line 5, in ?
```

Example 2-19. Using the traceback Module to Copy a Traceback to a String (continued)

```
IOError: an i/o error
occurred
'
```

To format the traceback in a nonstandard way, use the `extract_tb` function to convert a traceback object to a list of stack entries, as Example 2-20 demonstrates.

Example 2-20. Using the traceback Module to Decode a Traceback Object

```
File: traceback-example-3.py

import traceback
import sys

def function():
    raise IOError, "an i/o error occurred"

try:
    function()
except:
    info = sys.exc_info()
    for file, lineno, function, text in traceback.extract_tb(info[2]):
        print file, "line", lineno, "in", function
        print "=>", repr(text)
    print "** %s: %s" % info[:2]

traceback-example-3.py line 8 in ?
=> 'function()'
traceback-example-3.py line 5 in function
=> 'raise IOError, "an i/o error occurred"'
** exceptions.IOError: an i/o error occurred
```

The errno Module

The errno module defines a number of symbolic error codes, such as ENOENT ("no such directory entry") and EPERM ("permission denied"). It also provides a dictionary mapping from platform-dependent numerical error codes to symbolic names. Example 2-21 shows how to use errno.

In most cases, the *IOError* exception provides a 2-tuple with the numerical error code and an explanatory string. If you need to distinguish between different error codes, use the symbolic names where possible.

Example 2-21. Using the errno Module

```
File: errno-example-1.py

import errno

try:
```

Example 2-21. Using the errno Module (continued)

```
    fp = open("no.such.file")
except IOError, (error, message):
    if error == errno.ENOENT:
        print "no such file"
    elif error == errno.EPERM:
        print "permission denied"
    else:
        print message
```

no such file

Example 2-22 is a bit contrived, but it shows how to use the errorcode dictionary to map from a numerical error code to the symbolic name.

Example 2-22. Using the errorcode Dictionary

File: errno-example-2.py

```
import errno

try:
    fp = open("no.such.file")
except IOError, (error, message):
    print error, repr(message)
    print errno.errorcode[error]

# 2 'No such file or directory'
# ENOENT
```

The getopt Module

The getopt module used in Example 2-23 contains functions to extract command-line options and arguments. It can handle both short and long option formats.

The second argument specifies the short options that should be allowed. A colon (:) after an option name means that option must have an additional argument.

Example 2-23. Using the getopt Module

File: getopt-example-1.py

```
import getopt
import sys

# simulate command-line invocation
sys.argv = ["myscript.py", "-l", "-d", "directory", "filename"]

# process options
opts, args = getopt.getopt(sys.argv[1:], "ld:")

long = 0
```

Example 2-23. Using the getopt Module (continued)

```
directory = None

for o, v in opts:
    if o == "-l":
        long = 1
    elif o == "-d":
        directory = v

print "long", "=", long
print "directory", "=", directory
print "arguments", "=", args
```

long = 1
directory = directory
arguments = ['filename']

To make getopt look for long options, as in Example 2-24, pass a list of option
descriptors as the third argument. If an option name ends with an equals sign (=),
that option must have an additional argument.

Example 2-24. Using the getopt Module to Handle Long Options

```
File: getopt-example-2.py

import getopt
import sys

# simulate command-line invocation
sys.argv = ["myscript.py", "--echo", "--printer", "lp01", "message"]

opts, args = getopt.getopt(sys.argv[1:], "ep:", ["echo", "printer="])

# process options
echo = 0
printer = None

for o, v in opts:
    if o in ("-e", "--echo"):
        echo = 1
    elif o in ("-p", "--printer"):
        printer = v

print "echo", "=", echo
print "printer", "=", printer
print "arguments", "=", args
```

echo = 1
printer = lp01
arguments = ['message']

The getpass Module

The `getpass` module provides a platform-independent way to enter a password in a command-line program, as Example 2-25 shows.

`getpass(prompt)` prints the prompt string, switches off keyboard echo, and reads a password. If the prompt argument is omitted, it prints "`Password: `".

`getuser()` gets the current username, if possible.

Example 2-25. Using the getpass Module

```
File: getpass-example-1.py

import getpass

usr = getpass.getuser()

pwd = getpass.getpass("enter password for user %s: " % usr)

print usr, pwd
```

```
enter password for user mulder:
mulder trustno1
```

The glob Module

The `glob` module generates lists of files matching given patterns, just like the Unix shell.

File patterns are similar to regular expressions, but simpler. An asterisk (*) matches zero or more characters, and a question mark (?) matches exactly one character. You can also use brackets to indicate character ranges, such as [0-9] for a single digit. All other characters match themselves.

`glob(pattern)` returns a list of all files matching a given pattern. The `glob` module is demonstrated in Example 2-26.

Example 2-26. Using the glob Module

```
File: glob-example-1.py

import glob

for file in glob.glob("samples/*.jpg"):
    print file
```

```
samples/sample.jpg
```

Note that `glob` returns full pathnames, unlike the `os.listdir` function. `glob` uses the `fnmatch` module to do the actual pattern matching.

The fnmatch Module

The `fnmatch` module matches filenames against a pattern, as Example 2-27 shows.

The pattern syntax is the same as that used in Unix shells. An asterisk (`*`) matches zero or more characters, and a question mark (`?`) matches exactly one character. You can also use brackets to indicate character ranges, such as `[0-9]` for a single digit. All other characters match themselves.

Example 2-27. Using the fnmatch Module to Match Files

```
File: fnmatch-example-1.py

import fnmatch
import os

for file in os.listdir("samples"):
    if fnmatch.fnmatch(file, "*.jpg"):
        print file
```

sample.jpg

In Example 2-28, the `translate` function converts a file pattern to a regular expression.

Example 2-28. Using the fnmatch Module to Convert a Pattern to a Regular Expression

```
File: fnmatch-example-2.py

import fnmatch
import os, re

pattern = fnmatch.translate("*.jpg")

for file in os.listdir("samples"):
    if re.match(pattern, file):
        print file

print "(pattern was %s)" % pattern
```

sample.jpg
(pattern was .*\.jpg$)

The `fnmatch` module is used by the `glob` and `find` modules.

The random Module

"Anyone who considers arithmetical methods of producing random digits is, of course, in a state of sin."
—John von Neumann, 1951

The random module contains a number of random number generators.

The basic random number generator (after an algorithm by Wichmann and Hill, 1982) can be accessed in several ways, as Example 2-29 shows.

Example 2-29. Using the random Module to Get Random Numbers

```
File: random-example-1.py

import random

for i in range(5):

    # random float: 0.0 <= number < 1.0
    print random.random(),

    # random float: 10 <= number < 20
    print random.uniform(10, 20),

    # random integer: 100 <= number <= 1000
    print random.randint(100, 1000),

    # random integer: even numbers in 100 <= number < 1000
    print random.randrange(100, 1000, 2)

0.946842713956 19.5910069381 709 172
0.573613195398 16.2758417025 407 120
0.363241598013 16.8079747714 916 580
0.602115173978 18.386796935 531 774
0.526767588533 18.0783794596 223 344
```

Note that the randint function can return the upper limit, while the other functions always return values smaller than the upper limit.

Example 2-30 shows how the choice function picks a random item from a sequence. It can be used with lists, tuples, or any other sequence (provided it can be accessed in random order, of course).

Example 2-30. Using the random Module for Random Items from a Sequence

```
File: random-example-2.py

import random

# random choice from a list
for i in range(5):
    print random.choice([1, 2, 3, 5, 9])
```

Example 2-30. Using the random Module for Random Items from a Sequence (continued)

```
2
3
1
9
1
```

In 2.0 and later, the shuffle function can be used to shuffle the contents of a list
(that is, generate a random permutation of a list in-place). Example 2-31 also
shows how to implement that function under 1.5.2 and earlier.

Example 2-31. Using the random Module to Shuffle a Deck of Cards

```
File: random-example-4.py

import random

try:
    # available in 2.0 and later
    shuffle = random.shuffle
except AttributeError:
    def shuffle(x):
        for i in xrange(len(x)-1, 0, -1):
            # pick an element in x[:i+1] with which to exchange x[i]
            j = int(random.random() * (i+1))
            x[i], x[j] = x[j], x[i]

cards = range(52)

shuffle(cards)

myhand = cards[:5]

print myhand
```

```
[4, 8, 40, 12, 30]
```

The random module also contains random generators with non-uniform distribution. Example 2-32 uses the gauss function to generate random numbers with a
gaussian distribution.

Example 2-32. Using the random Module for Gaussian Random Numbers

```
File: random-example-3.py

import random

histogram = [0] * 20

# calculate histogram for gaussian
# noise, using average=5, stddev=1
for i in range(1000):
    i = int(random.gauss(5, 1) * 2)
```

Example 2-32. Using the random Module for Gaussian Random Numbers (continued)

```
    histogram[i] = histogram[i] + 1

# print the histogram
m = max(histogram)
for v in histogram:
    print "*" * (v * 50 / m)

****
*********
************************
***********************************
*****************************************************
******************************************************
************************************
**************************
*************
***
*
```

See the *Python Library Reference* for more information on non-uniform generators.

 The random-number generators provided in the standard library are pseudo-random generators. While this might be good enough for many purposes—including simulations, numerical analysis, and games—it's definitely not good enough for cryptographic use.

The whrandom Module

The whrandom module, shown in Example 2-33, provides a pseudo-random number generator (based on an algorithm by Wichmann and Hill, 1982). Unless you need several generators that do not share internal state (for example, in a multithreaded application), it's better to use the functions in the random module instead.

Example 2-33. Using the whrandom Module

```
File: whrandom-example-1.py

import whrandom

# same as random
print whrandom.random()
print whrandom.choice([1, 2, 3, 5, 9])
print whrandom.uniform(10, 20)
print whrandom.randint(100, 1000)

0.113412062346
1
```

Example 2-33. Using the whrandom Module (continued)

```
16.8778954689
799
```

Example 2-34 shows how to create multiple generators by creating instances of the
whrandom class.

Example 2-34. Using the whrandom Module to Create Multiple Random Generators

```
File: whrandom-example-2.py

import whrandom

# initialize all generators with the same seed
rand1 = whrandom.whrandom(4,7,11)
rand2 = whrandom.whrandom(4,7,11)
rand3 = whrandom.whrandom(4,7,11)

for i in range(5):
    print rand1.random(), rand2.random(), rand3.random()

0.123993532536 0.123993532536 0.123993532536
0.180951499518 0.180951499518 0.180951499518
0.291924111809 0.291924111809 0.291924111809
0.952048889363 0.952048889363 0.952048889363
0.969794283643 0.969794283643 0.969794283643
```

The md5 Module

The md5 module is used to calculate message signatures (message digests).

The md5 algorithm calculates a strong 128-bit signature. This means that if two
strings are different, it's highly likely that their md5 signatures are different as well.
To put it another way, given an md5 digest, it's supposed to be nearly impossible
to come up with a string that generates that digest. Example 2-35 demonstrates the
md5 module.

Example 2-35. Using the md5 Module

```
File: md5-example-1.py

import md5

hash = md5.new()
hash.update("spam, spam, and eggs")

print repr(hash.digest())

 'L\005J\243\266\355\243u'\305r\203\267\020F\303'
```

Note that the checksum is returned as a binary string. Getting a hexadecimal or base64-encoded string is quite easy, though, as Example 2-36 shows.

Example 2-36. Using the md5 Module to Get a Hexadecimal or Base64-Encoded md5 Value

```
File: md5-example-2.py

import md5
import string
import base64

hash = md5.new()
hash.update("spam, spam, and eggs")

value = hash.digest()
print string.join(map(lambda v: "%02x" % ord(v), value), "")
# in 2.0, the above can be written as
# print hash.hexdigest()

print base64.encodestring(value)

4c054aa3b6eda37560c57283b71046c3
TAVKo7bto3VgxXKDtxBGww==
```

Example 2-37 shows how, among other things, the md5 checksum can be used for challenge-response authentication (but see the note on random numbers later).

Example 2-37. Using the md5 Module for Challenge-Response Authentication

```
File: md5-example-3.py

import md5
import string, random

def getchallenge():
    # generate a 16-byte long random string.  (note that the built-
    # in pseudo-random generator uses a 24-bit seed, so this is not
    # as good as it may seem...)
    challenge = map(lambda i: chr(random.randint(0, 255)), range(16))
    return string.join(challenge, "")

def getresponse(password, challenge):
    # calculate combined digest for password and challenge
    m = md5.new()
    m.update(password)
    m.update(challenge)
    return m.digest()

#
# server/client communication

# 1. client connects.  server issues challenge.

print "client:", "connect"
```

Example 2-37. Using the md5 Module for Challenge-Response Authentication (continued)

```
challenge = getchallenge()

print "server:", repr(challenge)

# 2. client combines password and challenge, and calculates
# the response.

client_response = getresponse("trustno1", challenge)

print "client:", repr(client_response)

# 3. server does the same, and compares the result with the
# client response.  the result is a safe login in which the
# password is never sent across the communication channel.

server_response = getresponse("trustno1", challenge)

if server_response == client_response:
    print "server:", "login ok"
```

client: connect
server: '\334\352\227Z#\272\273\212KG\330\265\032>\311o'
client: "1'\305\240-x\245\237\035\225A\254\233\337\225\001"
server: login ok

Example 2-38 offers a variation of md5, which can be used to sign messages sent over a public network, so that their integrity can be verified at the receiving end.

Example 2-38. Using the md5 Module for Data Integrity Checks

```
File: md5-example-4.py

import md5
import array

class HMAC_MD5:
    # keyed md5 message authentication

    def __init__(self, key):
        if len(key) > 64:
            key = md5.new(key).digest()
        ipad = array.array("B", [0x36] * 64)
        opad = array.array("B", [0x5C] * 64)
        for i in range(len(key)):
            ipad[i] = ipad[i] ^ ord(key[i])
            opad[i] = opad[i] ^ ord(key[i])
        self.ipad = md5.md5(ipad.tostring())
        self.opad = md5.md5(opad.tostring())

    def digest(self, data):
        ipad = self.ipad.copy()
        opad = self.opad.copy()
```

Example 2-38. Using the md5 Module for Data Integrity Checks (continued)

```
        ipad.update(data)
        opad.update(ipad.digest())
        return opad.digest()

#
# simulate server end

key = "this should be a well-kept secret"
message = open("samples/sample.txt").read()

signature = HMAC_MD5(key).digest(message)

# (send message and signature across a public network)

#
# simulate client end

key = "this should be a well-kept secret"

client_signature = HMAC_MD5(key).digest(message)

if client_signature == signature:
    print "this is the original message:"
    print
    print message
else:
    print "someone has modified the message!!!"
```

The copy method takes a snapshot of the internal object state. This allows you to
precalculate partial digests (such as the padded key, in Example 2-38).

For details on this algorithm, see *HMAC-MD5:Keyed-MD5 for Message Authentication (http://www.research.ibm.com/security/draft-ietf-ipsec-hmac-md5-00.txt)* by
Krawczyk, et al.

 Don't forget that the built-in psuedo-random number generator isn't
really good enough for encryption purposes. Be careful.

The sha Module

The sha module provides an alternative way to calculate message signatures, as
shown in Example 2-39. It's similar to the md5 module, but generates 160-bit signatures instead.

Example 2-39. Using the sha Module

```
File: sha-example-1.py

import sha

hash = sha.new()
hash.update("spam, spam, and eggs")

print repr(hash.digest())
print hash.hexdigest()
```

'\321\333\003\026I\331\272-j\303\247\240\345\343Tvq\364\346\311'
d1db031649d9ba2d6ac3a7a0e5e3547671f4e6c9

See the md5 examples for more ways to use sha signatures.

The crypt Module

(Optional) The crypt module implements one-way DES encryption. Unix systems use this encryption algorithm to store passwords, and this module is really only useful to generate or check such passwords.

Example 2-40 shows how to encrypt a password by calling crypt.crypt with the password string, plus a *salt,* which should consist of two random characters. You can now throw away the actual password, and just store the encrypted string.

Example 2-40. Using the crypt Module

```
File: crypt-example-1.py

import crypt

import random, string

def getsalt(chars = string.letters + string.digits):
    # generate a random 2-character 'salt'
    return random.choice(chars) + random.choice(chars)

print crypt.crypt("bananas", getsalt())
```

'py8UGrijma1j6'

To verify a given password, encrypt the new password using the two first characters from the encrypted string as the salt. If the result matches the encrypted string, the password is valid. Example 2-41 uses the pwd module to fetch the encrypted password for a given user.

Example 2-41. Using the crypt Module for Authentication

File: crypt-example-2.py

```
import pwd, crypt

def login(user, password):
    "Check if user would be able to log in using password"
    try:
        pw1 = pwd.getpwnam(user)[1]
        pw2 = crypt.crypt(password, pw1[:2])
        return pw1 == pw2
    except KeyError:
        return 0 # no such user

user = raw_input("username:")
password = raw_input("password:")

if login(user, password):
    print "welcome", user
else:
    print "login failed"
```

For other ways to implement authentication, see the description of the md5 module.

The rotor Module

(Optional) The rotor module implements a simple encryption algorithm, shown in Example 2-42, which is based on the WWII Enigma engine.

Example 2-42. Using the rotor Module

File: rotor-example-1.py

```
import rotor

SECRET_KEY = "spam"
MESSAGE = "the holy grail"

r = rotor.newrotor(SECRET_KEY)

encoded_message = r.encrypt(MESSAGE)
decoded_message = r.decrypt(encoded_message)

print "original:", repr(MESSAGE)
print "encoded message:", repr(encoded_message)
print "decoded message:", repr(decoded_message)

original: 'the holy grail'
encoded message: '\227\271\244\015\305sw\3340\337\252\237\340U'
decoded message: 'the holy grail'
```

The zlib Module

(Optional) The zlib module provides support for "zlib" compression. (This compression method is also known as "deflate.")

Example 2-43 shows how the compress and decompress functions take string arguments.

Example 2-43. Using the zlib Module to Compress a String

```
File: zlib-example-1.py

import zlib

MESSAGE = "life of brian"

compressed_message = zlib.compress(MESSAGE)
decompressed_message = zlib.decompress(compressed_message)

print "original:", repr(MESSAGE)
print "compressed message:", repr(compressed_message)
print "decompressed message:", repr(decompressed_message)

original: 'life of brian'
compressed message: 'x\234\313\311LKU\310OSH*\312L\314\003\000!\010\004\302'
decompressed message: 'life of brian'
```

The compression rate varies a lot, depending on the contents of the file, as you can see in Example 2-44.

Example 2-44. Using the zlib Module to Compress a Group of Files

```
File: zlib-example-2.py

import zlib
import glob

for file in glob.glob("samples/*"):

    indata = open(file, "rb").read()
    outdata = zlib.compress(indata, zlib.Z_BEST_COMPRESSION)

    print file, len(indata), "=>", len(outdata),
    print "%d%%" % (len(outdata) * 100 / len(indata))

samples\sample.au 1676 => 1109 66%
samples\sample.gz 42 => 51 121%
samples\sample.htm 186 => 135 72%
samples\sample.ini 246 => 190 77%
samples\sample.jpg 4762 => 4632 97%
samples\sample.msg 450 => 275 61%
samples\sample.sgm 430 => 321 74%
samples\sample.tar 10240 => 125 1%
```

Example 2-44. Using the zlib Module to Compress a Group of Files (continued)

```
samples\sample.tgz 155 => 159 102%
samples\sample.txt 302 => 220 72%
samples\sample.wav 13260 => 10992 82%
```

You can also compress or decompress data on the fly, which Example 2-45 demonstrates.

Example 2-45. Using the zlib Module to Decompress Streams

```
File: zlib-example-3.py

import zlib

encoder = zlib.compressobj()

data = encoder.compress("life")
data = data + encoder.compress(" of ")
data = data + encoder.compress("brian")
data = data + encoder.flush()

print repr(data)
print repr(zlib.decompress(data))
```

```
'x\234\313\311LKU\310OSH*\312L\314\003\000!\010\004\302'
'life of brian'
```

Example 2-46 shows how to make it a bit more convenient to read a compressed file, by wrapping a decoder object in a file-like wrapper.

Example 2-46. Emulating a File Object for Compressed Streams

```
File: zlib-example-4.py

import zlib
import string, StringIO

class ZipInputStream:

    def __init__(self, file):
        self.file = file
        self.__rewind()

    def __rewind(self):
        self.zip = zlib.decompressobj()
        self.pos = 0 # position in zipped stream
        self.offset = 0 # position in unzipped stream
        self.data = ""

    def __fill(self, bytes):
        if self.zip:
            # read until we have enough bytes in the buffer
            while not bytes or len(self.data) < bytes:
```

Example 2-46. Emulating a File Object for Compressed Streams (continued)

```
                self.file.seek(self.pos)
                data = self.file.read(16384)
                if not data:
                    self.data = self.data + self.zip.flush()
                    self.zip = None # no more data
                    break
                self.pos = self.pos + len(data)
                self.data = self.data + self.zip.decompress(data)

    def seek(self, offset, whence=0):
        if whence == 0:
            position = offset
        elif whence == 1:
            position = self.offset + offset
        else:
            raise IOError, "Illegal argument"
        if position < self.offset:
            raise IOError, "Cannot seek backwards"

        # skip forward, in 16k blocks
        while position > self.offset:
            if not self.read(min(position - self.offset, 16384)):
                break

    def tell(self):
        return self.offset

    def read(self, bytes = 0):
        self.__fill(bytes)
        if bytes:
            data = self.data[:bytes]
            self.data = self.data[bytes:]
        else:
            data = self.data
            self.data = ""
        self.offset = self.offset + len(data)
        return data

    def readline(self):
        # make sure we have an entire line
        while self.zip and "\n" not in self.data:
            self.__fill(len(self.data) + 512)
        i = string.find(self.data, "\n") + 1
        if i <= 0:
            return self.read()
        return self.read(i)

    def readlines(self):
        lines = []
        while 1:
            s = self.readline()
            if not s:
```

Example 2-46. Emulating a File Object for Compressed Streams (continued)

```
            break
        lines.append(s)
    return lines

#
# try it out

data = open("samples/sample.txt").read()
data = zlib.compress(data)

file = ZipInputStream(StringIO.StringIO(data))
for line in file.readlines():
    print line[:-1]
```

**We will perhaps eventually be writing only small
modules which are identified by name as they are
used to build larger ones, so that devices like
indentation, rather than delimiters, might become
feasible for expressing local structure in the
source language.**
   -- Donald E. Knuth, December 1974

The code Module

The code module provides a number of functions that can be used to emulate the
behavior of the standard interpreter's interactive mode.

The compile_command behaves like the built-in compile function, but does some
additional tests to make sure you pass it a complete Python statement.

In Example 2-47, we're compiling a program line by line, executing the resulting
code objects as soon as we manage to compile. The program looks like this:

```
a = (
  1,
  2,
  3
)
print a
```

Note that the tuple assignment cannot be properly compiled until we've reached
the second parenthesis.

Example 2-47. Using the code Module to Compile Statements

```
File: code-example-1.py

import code
import string

#
```

Example 2-47. Using the code Module to Compile Statements (continued)

```
SCRIPT = [
    "a = (",
    "  1,",
    "  2,",
    "  3 ",
    ")",
    "print a"
]

script = ""

for line in SCRIPT:
    script = script + line + "\n"
    co = code.compile_command(script, "<stdin>", "exec")
    if co:
        # got a complete statement.  execute it!
        print "-"*40
        print script,
        print "-"*40
        exec co
        script = ""
```

```
----------------------------------------
a = (
  1,
  2,
  3
)
----------------------------------------
----------------------------------------
print a
----------------------------------------
(1, 2, 3)
```

The *InteractiveConsole* class implements an interactive console, much like the one you get when you fire up the Python interpreter in interactive mode.

The console can be either active (it calls a function to get the next line) or passive (you call the push method when you have new data). The default is to use the built-in raw_input function. Overload the method with the same name if you prefer to use another input function. Example 2-48 shows how to use the code module to emulate the interactive interpreter.

Example 2-48. Using the code Module to Emulate the Interactive Interpreter

```
File: code-example-2.py

import code

console = code.InteractiveConsole()
console.interact()
```

Example 2-48. Using the code Module to Emulate the Interactive Interpreter (continued)

```
Python 1.5.2
Copyright 1991-1995 Stichting Mathematisch Centrum, Amsterdam
(InteractiveConsole)
>>> a = (
...     1,
...     2,
...     3
... )
>>> print a
(1, 2, 3)
```

The script in Example 2-49 defines a function called `keyboard`. It allows you to hand control over to the interactive interpreter at any point in your program.

Example 2-49. Using the code Module for Simple Debugging

```
File: code-example-3.py

def keyboard(banner=None):
    import code, sys

    # use exception trick to pick up the current frame
    try:
        raise None
    except:
        frame = sys.exc_info()[2].tb_frame.f_back

    # evaluate commands in current namespace
    namespace = frame.f_globals.copy()
    namespace.update(frame.f_locals)

    code.interact(banner=banner, local=namespace)

def func():
    print "START"
    a = 10
    keyboard()
    print "END"

func()

START
Python 1.5.2
Copyright 1991-1995 Stichting Mathematisch Centrum, Amsterdam
(InteractiveConsole)
>>> print a
10
>>> print keyboard
<function keyboard at 9032c8>
^Z
END
```

3

Threads and Processes

"Well, since you last asked us to stop, this thread has moved
from discussing languages suitable for professional programmers via
accidental users to computer-phobic users. A few more iterations can
make this thread really interesting . . . "
—eff-bot, June 1996

Overview

This chapter describes the thread-support modules provided with the standard Python interpreter. Note that thread support is optional and may not be available in your Python interpreter.

This chapter also covers some modules that allow you to run external processes on Unix and Windows systems.

Threads

When you run a Python program, execution starts at the top of the main module and proceeds downwards. Loops can be used to repeat portions of the program, and function and method calls transfer control to a different part of the program (but only temporarily).

With threads, your program can do several things at one time. Each thread has its own flow of control. While one thread might be reading data from a file, another thread can keep the screen updated.

To keep two threads from accessing the same internal data structure at the same time, Python uses a *global interpreter lock*. Only one thread at a time can execute Python code; Python automatically switches to the next thread after a short period of time, or when a thread does something that may take a while (like waiting for the next byte to arrive over a network socket, or reading data from a file).

The global lock isn't enough to avoid problems in your own programs, though. If multiple threads attempt to access the same data object, it may end up in an inconsistent state. Consider a simple cache:

```
def getitem(key):
    item = cache.get(key)
    if item is None:
        # not in cache; create a new one
        item = create_new_item(key)
        cache[key] = item
    return item
```

If two threads call the getitem function just after each other with the same missing key, they're likely to end up calling create_new_item twice with the same argument. While this may be okay in many cases, it can cause serious problems in others.

To avoid problems like this, you can use *lock objects* to synchronize threads. A lock object can only be owned by one thread at a time, and can thus be used to make sure that only one thread at a time is executing the code in the getitem body.

Processes

On most modern operating systems, each program runs in its own *process*. You usually start a new program/process by entering a command to the shell, or by selecting it in a menu. Python also allows you to start new programs from inside a Python program.

Most process-related functions are defined by the os module. See "Working with Processes" for the full story.

The threading Module

(Optional) The threading module is a higher-level interface for threading, demonstrated in Example 3-1. It's modeled after the Java thread facilities. Like the lower-level thread module, it's only available if your interpreter was built with thread support.

To create a new thread, subclass the *Thread* class and define the run method. To run such threads, create one or more instances of that class, and call the start method. Each instance's run method will execute in its own thread.

Example 3-1. Using the threading Module

```
File: threading-example-1.py

import threading
import time, random

class Counter:
    def __init__(self):
        self.lock = threading.Lock()
        self.value = 0

    def increment(self):
        self.lock.acquire() # critical section
        self.value = value = self.value + 1
        self.lock.release()
        return value

counter = Counter()

class Worker(threading.Thread):

    def run(self):
        for i in range(10):
            # pretend we're doing something that takes 10-100 ms
            value = counter.increment() # increment global counter
            time.sleep(random.randint(10, 100) / 1000.0)
            print self.getName(), "-- task", i, "finished", value

#
# try it

for i in range(10):
    Worker().start() # start a worker

Thread-1 -- task 0 finished 1
Thread-3 -- task 0 finished 3
Thread-7 -- task 0 finished 8
Thread-1 -- task 1 finished 7
Thread-4 -- task 0 Thread-5 -- task 0 finished 4
finished 5
Thread-8 -- task 0 Thread-6 -- task 0 finished 9
finished 6
...
Thread-6 -- task 9 finished 98
Thread-4 -- task 9 finished 99
Thread-9 -- task 9 finished 100
```

Example 3-1 also uses *Lock* objects to create a critical section inside the global counter object. If you remove the calls to `acquire` and `release`, it's pretty likely that the counter won't reach 100.

The Queue Module

The Queue module provides a thread-safe queue implementation, shown in Example 3-2. It provides a convenient way of moving Python objects between different threads.

Example 3-2. Using the Queue Module

```
File: queue-example-1.py

import threading
import Queue
import time, random

WORKERS = 2

class Worker(threading.Thread):

    def __init__(self, queue):
        self.__queue = queue
        threading.Thread.__init__(self)

    def run(self):
        while 1:
            item = self.__queue.get()
            if item is None:
                break # reached end of queue

            # pretend we're doing something that takes 10–100 ms
            time.sleep(random.randint(10, 100) / 1000.0)

            print "task", item, "finished"

#
# try it

queue = Queue.Queue(0)

for i in range(WORKERS):
    Worker(queue).start() # start a worker

for i in range(10):
    queue.put(i)

for i in range(WORKERS):
    queue.put(None) # add end-of-queue markers

task 1 finished
task 0 finished
task 3 finished
task 2 finished
task 4 finished
task 5 finished
```

Example 3-2. Using the Queue Module (continued)

```
task 7 finished
task 6 finished
task 9 finished
task 8 finished
```

Example 3-3 shows how you can limit the size of the queue. If the producer threads fill the queue, they will block until items are popped off the queue.

Example 3-3. Using the Queue Module with a Maximum Size

```
File: queue-example-2.py

import threading
import Queue

import time, random

WORKERS = 2

class Worker(threading.Thread):

    def _ _init_ _(self, queue):
        self._ _queue = queue
        threading.Thread._ _init_ _(self)

    def run(self):
        while 1:
            item = self._ _queue.get()
            if item is None:
                break # reached end of queue

            # pretend we're doing something that takes 10-100 ms
            time.sleep(random.randint(10, 100) / 1000.0)

            print "task", item, "finished"

#
# run with limited queue

queue = Queue.Queue(3)

for i in range(WORKERS):
    Worker(queue).start() # start a worker

for item in range(10):
    print "push", item
    queue.put(item)

for i in range(WORKERS):
    queue.put(None) # add end-of-queue markers

push 0
```

Example 3-3. Using the Queue Module with a Maximum Size (continued)

```
push 1
push 2
push 3
push 4
push 5
task 0 finished
push 6
task 1 finished
push 7
task 2 finished
push 8
task 3 finished
push 9
task 4 finished
task 6 finished
task 5 finished
task 7 finished
task 9 finished
task 8 finished
```

You can modify the behavior through subclassing. The class in Example 3-4 provides a simple priority queue. It expects all items added to the queue to be tuples, where the first member contains the priority (lower value means higher priority).

Example 3-4. Using the Queue Module to Implement a Priority Queue

```
File: queue-example-3.py

import Queue
import bisect

Empty = Queue.Empty

class PriorityQueue(Queue.Queue):
    "Thread-safe priority queue"

    def _put(self, item):
        # insert in order
        bisect.insort(self.queue, item)

#
# try it

queue = PriorityQueue(0)

# add items out of order
queue.put((20, "second"))
queue.put((10, "first"))
queue.put((30, "third"))

# print queue contents
try:
```

Example 3-4. Using the Queue Module to Implement a Priority Queue (continued)

```
    while 1:
        print queue.get_nowait()
except Empty:
    pass
```

third
second
first

Example 3-5 shows a simple stack implementation (last-in, first-out, instead of first-in, first-out).

Example 3-5. Using the Queue Module to Implement a Stack

```
File: queue-example-4.py

import Queue

Empty = Queue.Empty

class Stack(Queue.Queue):
    "Thread-safe stack"

    def _put(self, item):
        # insert at the beginning of queue, not at the end
        self.queue.insert(0, item)

    # method aliases
    push = Queue.Queue.put
    pop = Queue.Queue.get
    pop_nowait = Queue.Queue.get_nowait

#
# try it

stack = Stack(0)

# push items on stack
stack.push("first")
stack.push("second")
stack.push("third")

# print stack contents
try:
    while 1:
        print stack.pop_nowait()
except Empty:
    pass
```

third
second
first

The thread Module

(Optional) The thread module provides a low-level interface for threading, as shown in Example 3-6. It's only available if your interpreter is built with thread support. New code should use the higher-level interface in the threading module instead.

Example 3-6. Using the thread Module

```
File: thread-example-1.py

import thread
import time, random

def worker():
    for i in range(50):
        # pretend we're doing something that takes 10-100 ms
        time.sleep(random.randint(10, 100) / 1000.0)
        print thread.get_ident(), "-- task", i, "finished"

#
# try it out!

for i in range(2):
    thread.start_new_thread(worker, ())

time.sleep(1)

print "goodbye!"

311 -- task 0 finished
265 -- task 0 finished
265 -- task 1 finished
311 -- task 1 finished
...
265 -- task 17 finished
311 -- task 13 finished
265 -- task 18 finished
goodbye!
```

Note that when the main program exits, all threads are killed. The threading module doesn't have that problem.

The commands Module

(Unix only) The commands module contains a few convenience functions designed to make it easier to execute external commands under Unix. Example 3-7 demonstrates this module.

Example 3-7. Using the commands Module

```
File: commands-example-1.py

import commands

stat, output = commands.getstatusoutput("ls -lR")

print "status", "=>", stat
print "output", "=>", len(output), "bytes"

status => 0
output => 171046 bytes
```

The pipes Module

(Unix only) The pipes module shown in Example 3-8 contains support functions to create "conversion pipelines." You can create a pipeline consisting of a number of external utilities and use it on one or more files.

Example 3-8. Using the pipes Module

```
File: pipes-example-1.py

import pipes

t = pipes.Template()

# create a pipeline
t.append("sort", "--")
t.append("uniq", "--")

# filter some text
t.copy("samples/sample.txt", "")

Alan Jones (sensible party)
Kevin Phillips-Bong (slightly silly)
Tarquin Fin-tim-lin-bin-whin-bim-lin-bus-stop-F'tang-F'tang-Olã©-Biscuitbarrel
```

The popen2 Module

The popen2 module allows you to run an external command and access stdin and stdout (and possibly also stderr) as individual streams.

In Python 1.5.2 and earlier, this module is only supported on Unix. In 2.0, the functions are also implemented on Windows. Example 3-9 shows you how to sort strings using this module.

Example 3-9. Using the popen2 Module to Sort Strings

```
File: popen2-example-1.py

import popen2, string

fin, fout = popen2.popen2("sort")

fout.write("foo\n")
fout.write("bar\n")
fout.close()

print fin.readline(),
print fin.readline(),
fin.close()
```

bar
foo

Example 3-10 demonstrates how you can use this module to control an existing application.

Example 3-10. Using the popen2 Module to Control gnuchess

```
File: popen2-example-2.py

import popen2
import string

class Chess:
    "Interface class for chesstool-compatible programs"

    def __init__(self, engine = "gnuchessc"):
        self.fin, self.fout = popen2.popen2(engine)
        s = self.fin.readline()
        if s != "Chess\n":
            raise IOError, "incompatible chess program"

    def move(self, move):
        self.fout.write(move + "\n")
        self.fout.flush()
        my = self.fin.readline()
        if my == "Illegal move":
            raise ValueError, "illegal move"
        his = self.fin.readline()
        return string.split(his)[2]

    def quit(self):
        self.fout.write("quit\n")
        self.fout.flush()

#
# play a few moves
```

Example 3-10. Using the popen2 Module to Control gnuchess (continued)

```
g = Chess()

print g.move("a2a4")
print g.move("b2b3")

g.quit()
```

b8c6
e7e5

The signal Module

The signal module is used to install your own signal handlers, as Example 3-11 shows. When the interpreter sees a signal, the signal handler is executed as soon as possible.

Example 3-11. Using the signal Module

```
File: signal-example-1.py

import signal
import time

def handler(signo, frame):
    print "got signal", signo

signal.signal(signal.SIGALRM, handler)

# wake me up in two seconds
signal.alarm(2)

now = time.time()

time.sleep(200)

print "slept for", time.time() - now, "seconds"
```

got signal 14
slept for 1.99262607098 seconds

4

Data Representation

Overview

This chapter describes a number of modules that can be used to convert between
Python objects and other data representations. These modules are often used to
read and write foreign file formats and to store or transfer Python variables.

Binary Data

Python provides several support modules that help you decode and encode binary
data formats. The struct module can convert between binary data structures (like
C structs) and Python tuples. The array module wraps binary arrays of data (C
arrays) into a Python sequence object.

Self-Describing Formats

To pass data between different Python programs, you can marshal or pickle your
data.

The marshal module uses a simple self-describing format that supports most built-
in datatypes, including code objects. Python uses this format itself to store compiled code on disk (in PYC files).

The pickle module provides a more sophisticated format, which supports user-
defined classes, self-referencing data structures, and more. This module is available

in two versions; the basic `pickle` module is written in Python and is relatively slow, while `cPickle` is written in C and is usually as fast as `marshal`.

Output Formatting

The modules in this group supplement built-in formatting functions like `repr` and the `%` string formatting operator.

The `pprint` module can print almost any Python data structure in a nice, readable way (as readable as it can make things, that is).

The `repr` module provides a replacement for the built-in function with the same name. The version in this module applies tight limits on most things: it doesn't print more than 30 characters from each string, it doesn't print more than a few levels of deeply nested data structures, etc.

Encoded Binary Data

Python supports most common binary encodings, such as `base64`, `binhex` (a Macintosh format), `quoted printable`, and `uu` encoding.

The array Module

The `array` module implements an efficient array storage type. Arrays are similar to lists, but all items must be of the same primitive type. The type is defined when the array is created.

Examples 4-1 through 4-5 are simple ones. Example 4-1 creates an *array* object and copies the internal buffer to a string through the `tostring` method.

Example 4-1. Using the array Module to Convert Lists of Integers to Strings

```
File: array-example-1.py

import array

a = array.array("B", range(16)) # unsigned char
b = array.array("h", range(16)) # signed short

print a
print repr(a.tostring())

print b
print repr(b.tostring())
```

```
array('B', [0, 1, 2, 3, 4, 5, 6, 7, 8, 9, 10, 11, 12, 13, 14, 15])
'\000\001\002\003\004\005\006\007\010\011\012\013\014\015\016\017'
```

Example 4-1. Using the array Module to Convert Lists of Integers to Strings (continued)

```
array('h', [0, 1, 2, 3, 4, 5, 6, 7, 8, 9, 10, 11, 12, 13, 14, 15])
'\000\000\001\000\002\000\003\000\004\000\005\000\006\000\007\000
\010\000\011\000\012\000\013\000\014\000\015\000\016\000\017\000'
```

The *array* objects can be treated as ordinary lists to some extent, as Example 4-2 shows. You cannot concatenate arrays if they have different type codes, though.

Example 4-2. Using Arrays as Ordinary Sequences

```
File: array-example-2.py

import array

a = array.array("B", [1, 2, 3])

a.append(4)

a = a + a

a = a[2:-2]

print a
print repr(a.tostring())
for i in a:
    print i,
```

```
array('B', [3, 4, 1, 2])
'\003\004\001\002'
3 4 1 2
```

This module also provides a very efficient way to turn raw binary data into a sequence of integers (or floating point values, for that matter), as Example 4-3 demonstrates.

Example 4-3. Using Arrays to Convert Strings to Lists of Integers

```
File: array-example-3.py

import array

a = array.array("i", "fish license") # signed integer

print a
print repr(a.tostring())
print a.tolist()
```

```
array('i', [1752394086, 1667853344, 1702063717])
'fish license'
[1752394086, 1667853344, 1702063717]
```

Finally, Example 4-4 shows how to use this module to determine the endianess of the current platform.

Example 4-4. Using the array Module to Determine Platform Endianess

File: array-example-4.py

```
import array

def little_endian():
    return ord(array.array("i",[1]).tostring()[0])

if little_endian():
    print "little-endian platform (intel, alpha)"
else:
    print "big-endian platform (motorola, sparc)"
```

big-endian platform (motorola, sparc)

Python 2.0 and later provides a **sys.byteorder** attribute, which is set to either "little" or "big," as you can see in Example 4-5.

Example 4-5. Using the sys.byteorder Attribute to Determine Platform Endianess (Python 2.0)

File: sys-byteorder-example-1.py

```
import sys

# 2.0 and later
if sys.byteorder == "little":
    print "little-endian platform (intel, alpha)"
else:
    print "big-endian platform (motorola, sparc)"
```

big-endian platform (motorola, sparc)

The struct Module

The struct module shown in Example 4-6 contains functions to convert between binary strings and Python tuples. The pack function takes a format string and one or more arguments, and returns a binary string. The unpack function takes a string and returns a tuple.

Example 4-6. Using the struct Module

File: struct-example-1.py

```
import struct

# native byteorder
buffer = struct.pack("ihb", 1, 2, 3)
print repr(buffer)
print struct.unpack("ihb", buffer)

# data from a sequence, network byteorder
```

Example 4-6. Using the struct Module (continued)

```
data = [1, 2, 3]
buffer = apply(struct.pack, ("!ihb",) + tuple(data))
print repr(buffer)
print struct.unpack("!ihb", buffer)

# in 2.0, the apply statement can also be written as:
# buffer = struct.pack("!ihb", *data)
```

```
'\001\000\000\000\002\000\003'
(1, 2, 3)
'\000\000\000\001\000\002\003'
(1, 2, 3)
```

The xdrlib Module

The `xdrlib` module converts between Python datatypes and Sun's external data representation (XDR), as Example 4-7 illustrates.

Example 4-7. Using the xdrlib Module

```
File: xdrlib-example-1.py

import xdrlib

#
# create a packer and add some data to it

p = xdrlib.Packer()
p.pack_uint(1)
p.pack_string("spam")

data = p.get_buffer()

print "packed:", repr(data)

#
# create an unpacker and use it to decode the data

u = xdrlib.Unpacker(data)

print "unpacked:", u.unpack_uint(), repr(u.unpack_string())

u.done()
```

```
packed: '\000\000\000\001\000\000\000\004spam'
unpacked: 1 'spam'
```

The XDR format is used by Sun's remote procedure call (RPC) protocol. Example 4-8 is an incomplete (and rather contrived) example showing how to build an RPC request package.

Example 4-8. Using the xdrlib Module to Send an RPC Call Package

```
File: xdrlib-example-2.py

import xdrlib

# some constants (see the RPC specs for details)
RPC_CALL = 1
RPC_VERSION = 2

MY_PROGRAM_ID = 1234 # assigned by Sun
MY_VERSION_ID = 1000
MY_TIME_PROCEDURE_ID = 9999

AUTH_NULL = 0

transaction = 1

p = xdrlib.Packer()

# send a Sun RPC call package
p.pack_uint(transaction)
p.pack_enum(RPC_CALL)
p.pack_uint(RPC_VERSION)
p.pack_uint(MY_PROGRAM_ID)
p.pack_uint(MY_VERSION_ID)
p.pack_uint(MY_TIME_PROCEDURE_ID)
p.pack_enum(AUTH_NULL)
p.pack_uint(0)
p.pack_enum(AUTH_NULL)
p.pack_uint(0)

print repr(p.get_buffer())

'\000\000\000\001\000\000\000\001\000\000\000\002\000\000\004\322
\000\000\003\350\000\000\'\017\000\000\000\000\000\000\000\000\000
\000\000\000\000\000\000\000'
```

The marshal Module

The marshal module is used to serialize data—that is, convert data to and from character strings, so that they can be stored on file or sent over a network. Example 4-9 illustrates this.

The marshal module uses a simple self-describing data format. For each data item, the marshalled string contains a type code, followed by one or more type-specific fields. Integers are stored in little-endian order, strings are stored as length fields followed by the strings' contents (which can include null bytes), tuples are stored as length fields followed by the objects that make up each tuple, etc.

Example 4-9. Using the marshal Module to Serialize Data

```
File: marshal-example-1.py

import marshal

value = (
    "this is a string",
    [1, 2, 3, 4],
    ("more tuples", 1.0, 2.3, 4.5),
    "this is yet another string"
    )

data = marshal.dumps(value)

# intermediate format
print type(data), len(data)

print "-"*50
print repr(data)
print "-"*50

print marshal.loads(data)
```

```
<type 'string'> 118
--------------------------------------------------
'(\004\000\000\000s\020\000\000\000this is a string
[\004\000\000\000i\001\000\000\000i\002\000\000\000
i\003\000\000\000i\004\000\000\000(\004\000\000\000
s\013\000\000\000more tuplesf\0031.0f\0032.3f\0034.
5s\032\000\000\000this is yet another string'
--------------------------------------------------
('this is a string', [1, 2, 3, 4], ('more tuples',
1.0, 2.3, 4.5), 'this is yet another string')
```

The marshal module can also handle code objects (it's used to store precompiled
Python modules). Example 4-10 demonstrates.

Example 4-10. Using the marshal Module to Serialize Code

```
File: marshal-example-2.py

import marshal

script = """
print 'hello'
"""

code = compile(script, "<script>", "exec")

data = marshal.dumps(code)

# intermediate format
print type(data), len(data)
```

Example 4-10. Using the marshal Module to Serialize Code (continued)

```
print "-"*50
print repr(data)
print "-"*50

exec marshal.loads(data)
```

<type 'string'> 81
--
'c\000\000\000\000\001\000\000\000s\017\000\000\00
0\177\000\000\177\002\000d\000\000GHd\001\000S(\00
2\000\000\000s\005\000\000\000helloN(\000\000\000
000(\000\000\000\000s\010\000\000\000<script>s\001
\000\000\000?\002\000s\000\000\000\000\000'
--
hello

The pickle Module

The pickle module, shown in Example 4-11, is used to serialize data—that is, convert data to and from character strings, so that they can be stored on file or sent over a network. It's a bit slower than marshal, but it can handle class instances, shared elements, and recursive data structures, among other things.

Example 4-11. Using the pickle Module

```
File: pickle-example-1.py

import pickle

value = (
    "this is a string",
    [1, 2, 3, 4],
    ("more tuples", 1.0, 2.3, 4.5),
    "this is yet another string"
    )

data = pickle.dumps(value)

# intermediate format
print type(data), len(data)

print "-"*50
print data
print "-"*50

print pickle.loads(data)
```

<type 'string'> 121
--
(S'this is a string'

Example 4-11. Using the pickle Module (continued)

```
p0
(lp1
I1
aI2
aI3
aI4
a(S'more tuples'
p2
F1.0
F2.3
F4.5
tp3
S'this is yet another string'
p4
tp5
.
--------------------------------------------------
('this is a string', [1, 2, 3, 4], ('more tuples',
1.0, 2.3, 4.5), 'this is yet another string')
```

On the other hand, `pickle` cannot handle code objects (but see the `copy_reg` module for a way to fix this).

By default, `pickle` uses a text-based format. You can also use a binary format, in which numbers and binary strings are stored in a compact binary format. The binary format usually results in smaller files. This is demonstrated in Example 4-12.

Example 4-12. Using the pickle Module in Binary Mode

```
File: pickle-example-2.py

import pickle
import math

value = (
    "this is a long string" * 100,
    [1.2345678, 2.3456789, 3.4567890] * 100
    )

# text mode
data = pickle.dumps(value)
print type(data), len(data), pickle.loads(data) == value

# binary mode
data = pickle.dumps(value, 1)
print type(data), len(data), pickle.loads(data) == value
```

The cPickle Module

(Optional) The cPickle module shown in Example 4-13 contains a faster reimplementation of the pickle module.

Example 4-13. Using the cPickle Module

```
File: cpickle-example-1.py

try:
    import cPickle
    pickle = cPickle
except ImportError:
    import pickle
```

The copy_reg Module

The copy_reg module provides a registry that you can use to register your own extension types. The pickle and copy modules use this registry to figure out how to process non-standard types.

For example, the standard pickle implementation cannot deal with Python code objects, as shown in the following example:

```
File: copy-reg-example-1.py

import pickle

CODE = """
print 'good evening'
"""

code = compile(CODE, "<string>", "exec")

exec code
exec pickle.loads(pickle.dumps(code))

good evening
Traceback (innermost last):
...
pickle.PicklingError: can't pickle 'code' objects
```

We can work around this by registering a code object handler. Such a handler consists of two parts: a *pickler*, which takes the code object and returns a tuple that can only contain simple datatypes, and an *unpickler*, which takes the contents of such a tuple as its arguments. Example 4-14 demonstrates this.

Example 4-14. Using the copy_reg Module to Enable Pickling of Code Objects

```
File: copy-reg-example-2.py

import copy_reg
import pickle, marshal, types

#
# register a pickle handler for code objects

def code_unpickler(data):
    return marshal.loads(data)

def code_pickler(code):
    return code_unpickler, (marshal.dumps(code),)

copy_reg.pickle(types.CodeType, code_pickler, code_unpickler)

#
# try it out

CODE = """
print "suppose he's got a pointed stick"
"""

code = compile(CODE, "<string>", "exec")

exec code
exec pickle.loads(pickle.dumps(code))

suppose he's got a pointed stick
suppose he's got a pointed stick
```

If you're transferring the pickled data across a network or to another program, the custom unpickler must be available at the receiving end as well.

For the really adventurous, Example 4-15 shows a version that allows you to pickle open file objects.

Example 4-15. Using the copy_reg Module to Enable Pickling of File Objects

```
File: copy-reg-example-3.py

import copy_reg
import pickle, types
import StringIO

#
# register a pickle handler for file objects

def file_unpickler(position, data):
    file = StringIO.StringIO(data)
    file.seek(position)
    return file
```

Example 4-15. Using the copy_reg Module to Enable Pickling of File Objects (continued)

```
def file_pickler(code):
    position = file.tell()
    file.seek(0)
    data = file.read()
    file.seek(position)
    return file_unpickler, (position, data)

copy_reg.pickle(types.FileType, file_pickler, file_unpickler)

#
# try it out

file = open("samples/sample.txt", "rb")

print file.read(120),
print "<here>",
print pickle.loads(pickle.dumps(file)).read()
```

**We will perhaps eventually be writing only small
modules, which are identified by name as they are
used to build larger <here> ones, so that devices like
indentation, rather than delimiters, might become
feasible for expressing local structure in the
source language.
       -- Donald E. Knuth, December 1974**

The pprint Module

The pprint module, shown in Example 4-16, is a "pretty printer" for Python data
structures. It's useful if you have to print non-trivial data structures to the console.

Example 4-16. Using the pprint Module

```
File: pprint-example-1.py

import pprint

data = (
    "this is a string", [1, 2, 3, 4], ("more tuples",
    1.0, 2.3, 4.5), "this is yet another string"
    )

pprint.pprint(data)
```

**('this is a string',
 [1, 2, 3, 4],
 ('more tuples', 1.0, 2.3, 4.5),
 'this is yet another string')**

The repr Module

The repr module provides a version of the built-in repr function, with limits on most sizes (string lengths, recursion, etc). Example 4-17 shows the module in use.

Example 4-17. Using the repr Module

```
File: repr-example-1.py

# note: this overrides the built-in 'repr' function
from repr import repr

# an annoyingly recursive data structure
data = (
    "X" * 100000,
    )
data = [data]
data.append(data)

print repr(data)

[(('XXXXXXXXXXXX...XXXXXXXXXXXX',), [('XXXXXXXXXXXX...XXXXXXXXX
XXX',), [('XXXXXXXXXXXX...XXXXXXXXXXXX',), [('XXXXXXXXXXXX...XX
XXXXXXXXXXX',), [('XXXXXXXXXXXX...XXXXXXXXXXXX',), [(...), [...
]]]]]]]
```

The base64 Module

The base64 encoding scheme is used to convert arbitrary binary data to plain text. To do this, the encoder stores each group of three binary bytes as a group of four characters from the following set:

```
ABCDEFGHIJKLMNOPQRSTUVWXYZ
abcdefghijklmnopqrstuvwxyz
0123456789+/
```

In addition, the = character is used for padding at the end of the data stream.

Example 4-18 shows how the encode and decode functions work on file objects.

Example 4-18. Using the base64 Module to Encode Files

```
File: base64-example-1.py

import base64

MESSAGE = "life of brian"

file = open("out.txt", "w")
file.write(MESSAGE)
file.close()
```

Example 4-18. Using the base64 Module to Encode Files (continued)

```
base64.encode(open("out.txt"), open("out.b64", "w"))
base64.decode(open("out.b64"), open("out.txt", "w"))

print "original:", repr(MESSAGE)
print "encoded message:", repr(open("out.b64").read())
print "decoded message:", repr(open("out.txt").read())
```

original: 'life of brian'
encoded message: 'bGlmZSBvZiBicmlhbg==\012'
decoded message: 'life of brian'

Example 4-19 shows the encodestring and decodestring functions converting
between strings. The functions are currently implemented as wrappers on top of
encode and decode, using StringIO objects for input and output.

Example 4-19. Using the base64 Module to Encode Strings

```
File: base64-example-2.py

import base64

MESSAGE = "life of brian"

data = base64.encodestring(MESSAGE)

original_data = base64.decodestring(data)

print "original:", repr(MESSAGE)
print "encoded data:", repr(data)
print "decoded data:", repr(original_data)
```

original: 'life of brian'
encoded data: 'bGlmZSBvZiBicmlhbg==\012'
decoded data: 'life of brian'

Example 4-20 shows how to convert a username and a password to an HTTP basic
authentication string. (Note that you don't really have to work for the NSA to be
able to decode this format.)

Example 4-20. Using the base64 Module for Basic Authentication

```
File: base64-example-3.py

import base64

def getbasic(user, password):
    # basic authentication (according to HTTP)
    return base64.encodestring(user + ":" + password)

print getbasic("Aladdin", "open sesame")
```

'QWxhZGRpbjpvcGVuIHNlc2FtZQ=='

Finally, Example 4-21 shows a small utility that converts a GIF image to a Python script, for use with the Tkinter library.

Example 4-21. Using the base64 Module to Wrap GIF Images for Tkinter

File: base64-example-4.py

```
import base64, sys

if not sys.argv[1:]:
    print "Usage: gif2tk.py giffile >pyfile"
    sys.exit(1)

data = open(sys.argv[1], "rb").read()

if data[:4] != "GIF8":
    print sys.argv[1], "is not a GIF file"
    sys.exit(1)

print '# generated from', sys.argv[1], 'by gif2tk.py'
print
print 'from Tkinter import PhotoImage'
print
print 'image = PhotoImage(data="""'
print base64.encodestring(data),
print '""")'
```

```
# generated from samples/sample.gif by gif2tk.py

from Tkinter import PhotoImage

image = PhotoImage(data="""
R01GODlhoAB4APcAAAAAAIAAAACAAICAAAAAgIAAgACAgICAgAQEBIwEBIyMBJRU1ISE/LRUBAQE
...
AjmQBFmQBnmQCJmQCrmQDNmQDvmQEBmREnkRAQEAOw==
""")
```

The binhex Module

The binhex module in Example 4-22 converts to and from the Macintosh BinHex format.

Example 4-22. Using the binhex Module

File: binhex-example-1.py

```
import binhex
import sys

infile = "samples/sample.jpg"

binhex.binhex(infile, sys.stdout)
```

Example 4-22. Using the binhex Module (continued)

```
(This file must be converted with BinHex 4.0)

:#R0KEA"XC5jUF'F!2j!)!*!%%TS!N!4RdrrBrq!!%%T'58B!!3%!!!%!!3!!rpX
!3'!)"JB("J8)"'F(#3N)#J'8$3',#''C%K-2&"dD(aiG'K'F)#3Z*b!L,#-F(#J
h+5''-63d0"mR16di-M'Z-c3brpX!3'%*#3N-#''B$3dB-L%F)6+3-[r!!"%)!)!
!J!-")J!#%3%$%3(ra!!I!!!""3'3"J#3#!%#!'3&"JF)#3S,rm3!Y4!!!J%$!')
%!'8&"!3!!!&p!3)$!!34"4)K-8%'%e&K"b*a&$+"ND%))d+a'495dI!N-f*bJJN
```

The quopri Module

The quopri module implements quoted printable encoding, according to the MIME standard.

This encoding can be used to convert text messages that consist mostly of plain U.S. ASCII text, such as messages written in most European languages, to messages that only use U.S. ASCII. This can be quite useful if you're sending stuff via steam-powered mail transports to people using vintage mail agents. Example 4-23 demonstrates.

Example 4-23. Using the quopri Module

```
File: quopri-example-1.py

import quopri
import StringIO

# helpers (the quopri module only supports file-to-file conversion)

def encodestring(instring, tabs=0):
    outfile = StringIO.StringIO()
    quopri.encode(StringIO.StringIO(instring), outfile, tabs)
    return outfile.getvalue()

def decodestring(instring):
    outfile = StringIO.StringIO()
    quopri.decode(StringIO.StringIO(instring), outfile)
    return outfile.getvalue()

#
# try it out

MESSAGE = "å i åa ä e ö!"

encoded_message = encodestring(MESSAGE)
decoded_message = decodestring(encoded_message)

print "original:", MESSAGE
print "encoded message:", repr(encoded_message)
print "decoded message:", decoded_message
```

Example 4-23. Using the quopri Module (continued)

```
original: å i åa ä e ö!
encoded message: '=E5 i =E5a =E4 e =F6!\012'
decoded message: å i åa ä e ö!
```

As Example 4-23 shows, non-U.S. characters are mapped to an equals sign (=) followed by two hexadecimal digits. So it is the equals sign character itself ("=3D"), as well as whitespace at the end of lines ("=20"). Everything else looks just like before. So provided you don't use too many weird characters, the encoded string is nearly as readable as the original.

(Europeans generally hate this encoding and strongly believe that certain U.S. programmers deserve to be slapped in the head with a huge great fish to the jolly music of Edward German . . . .)

The uu Module

The uu encoding scheme is used to convert arbitrary binary data to plain text. This format is quite popular on the Usenet, but is slowly being superseded by base64 encoding.

A uu encoder takes groups of three bytes (24 bits) and converts each group to a sequence of four printable characters (6 bits per character), using characters from chr(32) (space) to chr(95). Including the length marker and line feed characters, uu encoding typically expands data by 40 percent.

An encoded data stream starts with a begin line, which includes the file privileges (the Unix mode field as an octal number) and the filename, and ends with an end line:

```
begin 666 sample.jpg
M_]C_X   02D9)1@ ! 0   0  !   0 #_VP!#  @&!@<&!07'P<'"@,)"0L%#0P
...more lines like this...
end
```

The uu module provides two functions: encode and decode.

The encode(infile, outfile, filename) function, shown in Example 4-24, encodes data from the input file and writes it to the output file. The input and output file arguments can be either filenames or file objects. The third argument is used as filename in the begin field.

Example 4-24. Using the uu Module to Encode a Binary File

File: uu-example-1.py

```
import uu
import os, sys

infile = "samples/sample.jpg"

uu.encode(infile, sys.stdout, os.path.basename(infile))
```

```
begin 666 sample.jpg
M_]C_X  02D9)1@ ! 0  0  0! #_VP!#  @&!@<&!0@'!P<)"0@*#!0-#0P,#!D+
M#!D2$H/\4'1H?'AT:'B8E)P )"()'(L("(#)'I.#"#")H'$F*3(.HM"9RM"C+')I'.
MVP!# 0D'!)@-#1@1$H(1%I(:'AH:'AH:'AH:'AH:'AH:'AH:'AH:'AH:'AH:'AH:'AH:'AH(
M,C(R,C(R,C(R,C(R,C(R,C(R,C(R,C(R,C(R,C(R,C(R,C(R,C(R,C+_P    " #  ( # 2(  A$! Q$!_\0
M'P       04! 0     4$  $%! $(#$            $$         $!$AQ@<("$  0$E)!$@4$  M1    #$$$ P$$ P#%&
```

The decode(infile, outfile) function, shown in Example 4-25, decodes uu-encoded data from the input text file and writes it to the output file. Again, both arguments can be either filenames or file objects.

Example 4-25. Using the uu Module to Decode a uu-Encoded File

File: uu-example-2.py

```
import uu
import StringIO

infile = "samples/sample.uue"
outfile = "samples/sample.jpg"

#
# decode

fi = open(infile)
fo = StringIO.StringIO()

uu.decode(fi, fo)

#
# compare with original data file

data = open(outfile, "rb").read()

if fo.getvalue() == data:
    print len(data), "bytes ok"
```

The binascii Module

The binascii module, shown in Example 4-26, contains support functions for a number of encoding modules, including base64, binhex, and uu.

In 2.0 and newer, it also allows you to convert binary data to and from hexadecimal strings.

Example 4-26. Using the binascii Module

```
File: binascii-example-1.py

import binascii

text = "hello, mrs teal"

data = binascii.b2a_base64(text)
text = binascii.a2b_base64(data)
print text, "<=>", repr(data)

data = binascii.b2a_uu(text)
text = binascii.a2b_uu(data)
print text, "<=>", repr(data)

data = binascii.b2a_hqx(text)
text = binascii.a2b_hqx(data)[0]
print text, "<=>", repr(data)

# 2.0 and newer
data = binascii.b2a_hex(text)
text = binascii.a2b_hex(data)
print text, "<=>", repr(data)

hello, mrs teal <=> 'aGVsbG8sIG1ycyB0ZWFs\012'
hello, mrs teal <=> '/:&5L;&\\L(&UR<R!T96%L\012'
hello, mrs teal <=> 'D\'9XE\'mX)\'ebFb"dC@&X'
hello, mrs teal <=> '68656c6c6f2c206d7273207465616c'
```

5

File Formats

Overview

This chapter describes a number of modules that are used to parse different file formats.

Markup Languages

Python comes with extensive support for the Extensible Markup Language (XML) and Hypertext Markup Language (HTML) file formats. Python also provides basic support for Standard Generalized Markup Language (SGML).

All these formats share the same basic structure because both HTML and XML are derived from SGML. Each document contains a mix of *start tags*, *end tags*, plain text (also called character data), and *entity references*, as shown in the following:

```
<document name="sample.xml">
    <header>This is a header</header>
    <body>This is the body text.  The text can contain
    plain text (&quot;character data&quot;), tags, and
    entities.
    </body>
</document>
```

In the previous example, <document>, <header>, and <body> are start tags. For each start tag, there's a corresponding end tag that looks similar, but has a slash before the tag name. The start tag can also contain one or more *attributes*, like the name attribute in this example.

Everything between a start tag and its matching end tag is called an *element*. In the previous example, the document element contains two other elements: header and body.

Finally, " is a character entity. It is used to represent reserved characters in the text sections. In this case, it's an ampersand (&), which is used to start the entity itself. Other common entities include < for "less than" (<), and > for "greater than" (>).

While XML, HTML, and SGML all share the same building blocks, there are important differences between them. In XML, all elements must have both start tags and end tags, and the tags must be properly nested (if they are, the document is said to be *well-formed*). In addition, XML is case-sensitive, so <document> and <Document> are two different element types.

HTML, in contrast, is much more flexible. The HTML parser can often fill in missing tags; for example, if you open a new paragraph in HTML using the <P> tag without closing the previous paragraph, the parser automatically adds a </P> end tag. HTML is also case-insensitive. On the other hand, XML allows you to define your own elements, while HTML uses a fixed element set, as defined by the HTML specifications.

SGML is even more flexible. In its full incarnation, you can use a custom *declaration* to define how to translate the source text into an element structure, and a *document type description* (DTD) to validate the structure and fill in missing tags. Technically, both HTML and XML are *SGML applications*; they both have their own SGML declaration, and HTML also has a standard DTD.

Python comes with parsers for all markup flavors. While SGML is the most flexible of the formats, Python's sgmllib parser is actually pretty simple. It avoids most of the problems by only understanding enough of the SGML standard to be able to deal with HTML. It doesn't handle DTDs either; instead, you can customize the parser via subclassing.

Python's HTML support is built on the SGML parser. The htmllib parser delegates the actual rendering to a formatter object. The formatter module contains a couple of standard formatters.

Python's XML support is most complex. In Python 1.5.2, the built-in support was limited to the xmllib parser, which is pretty similar to the sgmllib module (with one important difference; xmllib actually tries to support the entire XML standard). Python 2.0 comes with more advanced XML tools, based on the optional expat parser.

Configuration Files

The ConfigParser module reads and writes a simple configuration file format, similar to Windows INI files.

The netrc file reads .netrc configuration files, and the shlex module can be used to read any configuration file using a shell script-like syntax.

Archive Formats

Python's standard library provides support for the popular GZIP and ZIP (2.0 only) formats. The gzip module reads and writes GZIP files, and the zipfile reads and writes ZIP files. Both modules depend on the zlib data compression module.

The xmllib Module

The xmlib module provides a simple XML parser, using regular expressions to pull the XML data apart, as shown in Example 5-1. The parser does basic checks on the document, such as a check to see that there is only one top-level element and a check to see that all tags are balanced.

You feed XML data to this parser piece by piece (as data arrives over a network, for example). The parser calls methods in itself for start tags, data sections, end tags, and entities, among other things.

If you're only interested in a few tags, you can define special start_tag and end_tag methods, where tag is the tag name. The start functions are called with the attributes given as a dictionary.

Example 5-1. Using the xmllib Module to Extract Information from an Element

File: xmllib-example-1.py

```
import xmllib

class Parser(xmllib.XMLParser):
    # get quotation number

    def __init__(self, file=None):
        xmllib.XMLParser.__init__(self)
        if file:
            self.load(file)

    def load(self, file):
        while 1:
            s = file.read(512)
            if not s:
                break
            self.feed(s)
        self.close()

    def start_quotation(self, attrs):
        print "id =>", attrs.get("id")
        raise EOFError
```

Example 5-1. Using the xmllib Module to Extract Information from an Element (continued)

```
try:
    c = Parser()
    c.load(open("samples/sample.xml"))
except EOFError:
    pass
```

id => 031

Example 5-2 contains a simple (and incomplete) rendering engine. The parser maintains an element stack (`__tags`), which it passes to the renderer, together with text fragments. The renderer looks up the current tag hierarchy in a style dictionary, and if it isn't already there, it creates a new style descriptor by combining bits and pieces from the stylesheet.

Example 5-2. Using the xmllib Module

```
File: xmllib-example-2.py

import xmllib
import string, sys

STYLESHEET = {
    # each element can contribute one or more style elements
    "quotation": {"style": "italic"},
    "lang": {"weight": "bold"},
    "name": {"weight": "medium"},
}

class Parser(xmllib.XMLParser):
    # a simple styling engine

    def __init__(self, renderer):
        xmllib.XMLParser.__init__(self)
        self.__data = []
        self.__tags = []
        self.__renderer = renderer

    def load(self, file):
        while 1:
            s = file.read(8192)
            if not s:
                break
            self.feed(s)
        self.close()

    def handle_data(self, data):
        self.__data.append(data)

    def unknown_starttag(self, tag, attrs):
        if self.__data:
            text = string.join(self.__data, "")
```

Example 5-2. Using the xmllib Module (continued)

```
            self.__renderer.text(self.__tags, text)
        self.__tags.append(tag)
        self.__data = []

    def unknown_endtag(self, tag):
        self.__tags.pop()
        if self.__data:
            text = string.join(self.__data, "")
            self.__renderer.text(self.__tags, text)
        self.__data = []

class DumbRenderer:

    def __init__(self):
        self.cache = {}

    def text(self, tags, text):
        # render text in the style given by the tag stack
        tags = tuple(tags)
        style = self.cache.get(tags)
        if style is None:
            # figure out a combined style
            style = {}
            for tag in tags:
                s = STYLESHEET.get(tag)
                if s:
                    style.update(s)
            self.cache[tags] = style # update cache
        # write to standard output
        sys.stdout.write("%s =>\n" % style)
        sys.stdout.write("  " + repr(text) + "\n")

#
# try it out

r = DumbRenderer()
c = Parser(r)
c.load(open("samples/sample.xml"))

{'style': 'italic'} =>
  'I\'ve had a lot of developers come up to me and\012say,
  "I haven\'t had this much fun in a long time. It sure
  beats\012writing '
{'style': 'italic', 'weight': 'bold'} =>
  'Cobol'
{'style': 'italic'} =>
  '" -- '
{'style': 'italic', 'weight': 'medium'} =>
  'James Gosling'
{'style': 'italic'} =>
  ', on\012'
{'weight': 'bold'} =>
```

Example 5-2. Using the xmllib Module (continued)

```
  'Java'
{'style': 'italic'} =>
  '.'
```

The xml.parsers.expat Module

(Optional) The `xml.parsers.expat` module is an interface to James Clark's Expat
XML parser. Example 5-3 demonstrates this full-featured and fast parser, which is
an excellent choice for production use.

Example 5-3. Using the xml.parsers.expat Module

```
File: xml-parsers-expat-example-1.py

from xml.parsers import expat

class Parser:

    def __init__(self):
        self._parser = expat.ParserCreate()
        self._parser.StartElementHandler = self.start
        self._parser.EndElementHandler = self.end
        self._parser.CharacterDataHandler = self.data

    def feed(self, data):
        self._parser.Parse(data, 0)

    def close(self):
        self._parser.Parse("", 1) # end of data
        del self._parser # get rid of circular references

    def start(self, tag, attrs):
        print "START", repr(tag), attrs

    def end(self, tag):
        print "END", repr(tag)

    def data(self, data):
        print "DATA", repr(data)

p = Parser()
p.feed("<tag>data</tag>")
p.close()

START u'tag' {}
DATA u'data'
END u'tag'
```

Note that the parser returns Unicode strings, even if you pass it ordinary text. By
default, the parser interprets the source text as UTF-8 (as per the XML standard).
To use other encodings, make sure the XML file contains an *encoding* directive.

Example 5-4 shows how to read ISO Latin-1 text using xml.parsers.expat.

Example 5-4. Using the xml.parsers.expat Module to Read ISO Latin-1 Text

```
File: xml-parsers-expat-example-2.py

from xml.parsers import expat

class Parser:

    def __init__(self):
        self._parser = expat.ParserCreate()
        self._parser.StartElementHandler = self.start
        self._parser.EndElementHandler = self.end
        self._parser.CharacterDataHandler = self.data

    def feed(self, data):
        self._parser.Parse(data, 0)

    def close(self):
        self._parser.Parse("", 1) # end of data
        del self._parser # get rid of circular references

    def start(self, tag, attrs):
        print "START", repr(tag), attrs

    def end(self, tag):
        print "END", repr(tag)

    def data(self, data):
        print "DATA", repr(data)

p = Parser()
p.feed("""\
<?xml version='1.0' encoding='iso-8859-1'?>
<author>
<name>fredrik lundh</name>
<city>linkÃ¶ping</city>
</author>
"""
)
p.close()

START u'author' {}
DATA u'\012'
START u'name' {}
DATA u'fredrik lundh'
END u'name'
DATA u'\012'
START u'city' {}
DATA u'link\366ping'
END u'city'
DATA u'\012'
END u'author'
```

The sgmllib Module

The `sgmllib` module, shown in Example 5-5, provides a basic SGML parser. It works pretty much the same as the `xmllib` parser, but is less restrictive (and less complete).

Like in `xmllib`, this parser calls methods in itself to deal with things like start tags, data sections, end tags, and entities. If you're only interested in a few tags, you can define special `start` and `end` methods.

Example 5-5. Using the sgmllib Module to Extract the Title Element

```
File: sgmllib-example-1.py

import sgmllib
import string

class FoundTitle(Exception):
    pass

class ExtractTitle(sgmllib.SGMLParser):

    def __init__(self, verbose=0):
        sgmllib.SGMLParser.__init__(self, verbose)
        self.title = self.data = None

    def handle_data(self, data):
        if self.data is not None:
            self.data.append(data)

    def start_title(self, attrs):
        self.data = []

    def end_title(self):
        self.title = string.join(self.data, "")
        raise FoundTitle # abort parsing!

def extract(file):
    # extract title from an HTML/SGML stream
    p = ExtractTitle()
    try:
        while 1:
            # read small chunks
            s = file.read(512)
            if not s:
                break
            p.feed(s)
        p.close()
    except FoundTitle:
        return p.title
    return None

#
```

Example 5-5. Using the sgmllib Module to Extract the Title Element (continued)

```
# try it out

print "html", "=>", extract(open("samples/sample.htm"))
print "sgml", "=>", extract(open("samples/sample.sgm"))
```

html => A Title.
sgml => Quotations

To handle all tags, overload the `unknown_starttag` and `unknown_endtag` methods instead, as Example 5-6 demonstrates.

Example 5-6. Using the sgmllib Module to Format an SGML Document

```
File: sgmllib-example-2.py

import sgmllib
import cgi, sys

class PrettyPrinter(sgmllib.SGMLParser):
    # A simple SGML pretty printer

    def __init__(self):
        # initialize base class
        sgmllib.SGMLParser.__init__(self)
        self.flag = 0

    def newline(self):
        # force newline, if necessary
        if self.flag:
            sys.stdout.write("\n")
        self.flag = 0

    def unknown_starttag(self, tag, attrs):
        # called for each start tag

        # the attrs argument is a list of (attr, value)
        # tuples. convert it to a string.
        text = ""
        for attr, value in attrs:
            text = text + " %s='%s'" % (attr, cgi.escape(value))

        self.newline()
        sys.stdout.write("<%s%s>\n" % (tag, text))

    def handle_data(self, text):
        # called for each text section
        sys.stdout.write(text)
        self.flag = (text[-1:] != "\n")

    def handle_entityref(self, text):
        # called for each entity
        sys.stdout.write("&%s;" % text)
```

Example 5-6. Using the sgmllib Module to Format an SGML Document (continued)

```
    def unknown_endtag(self, tag):
        # called for each end tag
        self.newline()
        sys.stdout.write("<%s>" % tag)

#
# try it out

file = open("samples/sample.sgm")

p = PrettyPrinter()
p.feed(file.read())
p.close()

<chapter>
<title>
Quotations
<title>
<epigraph>
<attribution>
eff-bot, June 1997
<attribution>
<para>
<quote>
Nobody expects the Spanish Inquisition! Amongst
our weaponry are such diverse elements as fear, surprise,
ruthless efficiency, and an almost fanatical devotion to
Guido, and nice red uniforms &mdash; oh, damn!
<quote>
<para>
<epigraph>
<chapter>
```

Example 5-7 checks if an SGML document is "well-formed", in the XML sense. In a well-formed document, all elements are properly nested, with one end tag for each start tag.

To check this, we simply keep a list of open tags, and check that each end tag closes a matching start tag and that there are no open tags when we reach the end of the document.

Example 5-7. Using the sgmllib Module to Check Well-Formedness

```
File: sgmllib-example-3.py

import sgmllib

class WellFormednessChecker(sgmllib.SGMLParser):
    # check that an SGML document is 'well-formed'
    # (in the XML sense).
```

Example 5-7. Using the sgmllib Module to Check Well-Formedness (continued)

```
    def _ _init_ _(self, file=None):
        sgmllib.SGMLParser._ _init_ _(self)
        self.tags = []
        if file:
            self.load(file)

    def load(self, file):
        while 1:
            s = file.read(8192)
            if not s:
                break
            self.feed(s)
        self.close()

    def close(self):
        sgmllib.SGMLParser.close(self)
        if self.tags:
            raise SyntaxError, "start tag %s not closed" % self.tags[-1]

    def unknown_starttag(self, start, attrs):
        self.tags.append(start)

    def unknown_endtag(self, end):
        start = self.tags.pop()
        if end != start:
            raise SyntaxError, "end tag %s does't match start tag %s" %\
                  (end, start)

try:
    c = WellFormednessChecker()
    c.load(open("samples/sample.htm"))
except SyntaxError:
    raise # report error
else:
    print "document is well-formed"
```

Traceback (innermost last):
...
SyntaxError: end tag head does't match start tag meta

Finally, Example 5-8 shows a class that allows you to filter HTML and SGML documents. To use this class, create your own base class, and implement the start and end methods.

Example 5-8. Using the sgmllib Module to Filter SGML Documents

```
File: sgmllib-example-4.py

import sgmllib
import cgi, string, sys

class SGMLFilter(sgmllib.SGMLParser):
```

Example 5-8. Using the sgmllib Module to Filter SGML Documents (continued)

```
    # sgml filter.  override start/end to manipulate
    # document elements

    def __init__(self, outfile=None, infile=None):
        sgmllib.SGMLParser.__init__(self)
        if not outfile:
            outfile = sys.stdout
        self.write = outfile.write
        if infile:
            self.load(infile)

    def load(self, file):
        while 1:
            s = file.read(8192)
            if not s:
                break
            self.feed(s)
        self.close()

    def handle_entityref(self, name):
        self.write("&%s;" % name)

    def handle_data(self, data):
        self.write(cgi.escape(data))

    def unknown_starttag(self, tag, attrs):
        tag, attrs = self.start(tag, attrs)
        if tag:
            if not attrs:
                self.write("<%s>" % tag)
            else:
                self.write("<%s" % tag)
                for k, v in attrs:
                    self.write(" %s=%s" % (k, repr(v)))
                self.write(">")

    def unknown_endtag(self, tag):
        tag = self.end(tag)
        if tag:
            self.write("</%s>" % tag)

    def start(self, tag, attrs):
        return tag, attrs # override

    def end(self, tag):
        return tag # override

class Filter(SGMLFilter):

    def fixtag(self, tag):
        if tag == "em":
            tag = "i"
```

Example 5-8. Using the sgmllib Module to Filter SGML Documents (continued)

```
        if tag == "string":
            tag = "b"
        return string.upper(tag)

    def start(self, tag, attrs):
        return self.fixtag(tag), attrs

    def end(self, tag):
        return self.fixtag(tag)

c = Filter()
c.load(open("samples/sample.htm"))
```

The htmllib Module

The htmllib module contains a tag-driven HTML parser, which sends data to a formatting object. Example 5-9 uses this module. For more examples on how to parse HTML files using this module, see the descriptions of the formatter module.

Example 5-9. Using the htmllib Module

```
File: htmllib-example-1.py

import htmllib
import formatter
import string

class Parser(htmllib.HTMLParser):
    # return a dictionary mapping anchor texts to lists
    # of associated hyperlinks

    def __init__(self, verbose=0):
        self.anchors = {}
        f = formatter.NullFormatter()
        htmllib.HTMLParser.__init__(self, f, verbose)

    def anchor_bgn(self, href, name, type):
        self.save_bgn()
        self.anchor = href

    def anchor_end(self):
        text = string.strip(self.save_end())
        if self.anchor and text:
            self.anchors[text] = self.anchors.get(text, []) + [self.anchor]

file = open("samples/sample.htm")
html = file.read()
file.close()

p = Parser()
p.feed(html)
```

Example 5-9. Using the htmllib Module (continued)

```
p.close()

for k, v in p.anchors.items():
    print k, "=>", v

print
```

link => ['http://www.python.org']

If you're only out to parse an HTML file and not render it to an output device, it's usually easier to use the sgmllib module instead.

The htmlentitydefs Module

The htmlentitydefs module contains a dictionary with many ISO Latin-1 character entities used by HTML. Its use is demonstrated in Example 5-10.

Example 5-10. Using the htmlentitydefs Module

```
File: htmlentitydefs-example-1.py

import htmlentitydefs

entities = htmlentitydefs.entitydefs

for entity in "amp", "quot", "copy", "yen":
    print entity, "=", entities[entity]
```

amp = &
quot = "
copy = \302\251
yen = \302\245

Example 5-11 shows how to combine regular expressions with this dictionary to translate entities in a string (the opposite of cgi.escape).

Example 5-11. Using the htmlentitydefs Module to Translate Entities

```
File: htmlentitydefs-example-2.py

import htmlentitydefs
import re
import cgi

pattern = re.compile("&(\w+?);")

def descape_entity(m, defs=htmlentitydefs.entitydefs):
    # callback: translate one entity to its ISO Latin value
    try:
        return defs[m.group(1)]
    except KeyError:
```

Example 5-11. Using the htmlentitydefs Module to Translate Entities (continued)

```
        return m.group(0) # use as is

def descape(string):
    return pattern.sub(descape_entity, string)

print descape("&lt;spam&amp;eggs&gt;")
print descape(cgi.escape("<spam&eggs>"))
```

<spam&eggs>
<spam&eggs>

Finally, Example 5-12 shows how to use translate reserved XML characters and ISO Latin-1 characters to an XML string. This is similar to cgi.escape, but it also replaces non-ASCII characters.

Example 5-12. Escaping ISO Latin-1 Entities

File: htmlentitydefs-example-3.py

```
import htmlentitydefs
import re, string

# this pattern matches substrings of reserved and non-ASCII characters
pattern = re.compile(r"[&<>\"\x80-\xff]+")

# create character map
entity_map = {}

for i in range(256):
    entity_map[chr(i)] = "&%d;" % i

for entity, char in htmlentitydefs.entitydefs.items():
    if entity_map.has_key(char):
        entity_map[char] = "&%s;" % entity

def escape_entity(m, get=entity_map.get):
    return string.join(map(get, m.group()), "")

def escape(string):
    return pattern.sub(escape_entity, string)

print escape("<spam&eggs>")
print escape("\303\245 i \303\245a \303\244 e \303\266")
```

<spam&eggs>
å i åa ä e ö

The formatter Module

The `formatter` module provides formatter classes that can be used together with the `htmllib` module.

This module provides two class families, *formatters* and *writers*. Formatters convert a stream of tags and data strings from the HTML parser into an event stream suitable for an output device, and writers render that event stream on an output device. Example 5-13 demonstrates.

In most cases, you can use the *AbstractFormatter* class to do the formatting. It calls methods on the writer object, representing different kinds of formatting events. The *AbstractWriter* class simply prints a message for each method call.

Example 5-13. Using the formatter Module to Convert HTML to an Event Stream

```
File: formatter-example-1.py

import formatter
import htmllib

w = formatter.AbstractWriter()
f = formatter.AbstractFormatter(w)

file = open("samples/sample.htm")

p = htmllib.HTMLParser(f)
p.feed(file.read())
p.close()

file.close()

send_paragraph(1)
new_font(('h1', 0, 1, 0))
send_flowing_data('A Chapter.')
send_line_break()
send_paragraph(1)
new_font(None)
send_flowing_data('Some text. Some more text. Some')
send_flowing_data(' ')
new_font((None, 1, None, None))
send_flowing_data('emphasized')
new_font(None)
send_flowing_data(' text. A')
send_flowing_data(' link')
send_flowing_data('[1]')
send_flowing_data('.'
```

In addition to the *AbstractWriter* class, the `formatter` module provides a *NullWriter* class, which ignores all events passed to it, and a *DumbWriter* class that converts the event stream to a plain text document, as shown in Example 5-14.

Example 5-14. Using the formatter Module to Convert HTML to Plain Text

```
File: formatter-example-2.py

import formatter
import htmllib

w = formatter.DumbWriter() # plain text
f = formatter.AbstractFormatter(w)

file = open("samples/sample.htm")

# print html body as plain text
p = htmllib.HTMLParser(f)
p.feed(file.read())
p.close()

file.close()

# print links
print
print
i = 1
for link in p.anchorlist:
    print i, "=>", link
    i = i + 1
```

A Chapter.

Some text. Some more text. Some emphasized text. A link[1].

1 => http://www.python.org

Example 5-15 provides a custom *Writer*, which in this case is subclassed from the *DumbWriter* class. This version keeps track of the current font style and tweaks the output somewhat depending on the font.

Example 5-15. Using the formatter Module with a Custom Writer

```
File: formatter-example-3.py

import formatter
import htmllib, string

class Writer(formatter.DumbWriter):

    def __init__(self):
        formatter.DumbWriter.__init__(self)
        self.tag = ""
        self.bold = self.italic = 0
        self.fonts = []

    def new_font(self, font):
        if font is None:
```

Example 5-15. Using the formatter Module with a Custom Writer (continued)

```
                font = self.fonts.pop()
                self.tag, self.bold, self.italic = font
            else:
                self.fonts.append((self.tag, self.bold, self.italic))
                tag, bold, italic, typewriter = font
                if tag is not None:
                    self.tag = tag
                if bold is not None:
                    self.bold = bold
                if italic is not None:
                    self.italic = italic

    def send_flowing_data(self, data):
        if not data:
            return
        atbreak = self.atbreak or data[0] in string.whitespace
        for word in string.split(data):
            if atbreak:
                self.file.write(" ")
            if self.tag in ("h1", "h2", "h3"):
                word = string.upper(word)
            if self.bold:
                word = "*" + word + "*"
            if self.italic:
                word = "_" + word + "_"
            self.file.write(word)
            atbreak = 1
        self.atbreak = data[-1] in string.whitespace

w = Writer()
f = formatter.AbstractFormatter(w)

file = open("samples/sample.htm")

# print html body as plain text
p = htmllib.HTMLParser(f)
p.feed(file.read())
p.close()
```

_A_ _CHAPTER._

Some text. Some more text. Some *emphasized* text. A link[1].

The ConfigParser Module

The ConfigParser module reads configuration files.

The files should be written in a format similar to Windows INI files. The file contains one or more sections, separated by section names written in brackets. Each section can contain one or more configuration items.

Here's the sample file used in Example 5-16:

```
[book]
title: The Python Standard Library
author: Fredrik Lundh
email: fredrik@pythonware.com
version: 2.0-001115

[ematter]
pages: 250

[hardcopy]
pages: 350
```

Example 5-16 uses the `ConfigParser` module to read the sample configuration file.

Example 5-16. Using the ConfigParser Module

```
File: configparser-example-1.py

import ConfigParser
import string

config = ConfigParser.ConfigParser()

config.read("samples/sample.ini")

# print summary
print
print string.upper(config.get("book", "title"))
print "by", config.get("book", "author"),
print   "(" + config.get("book", "email") + ")"
print
print config.get("ematter", "pages"), "pages"
print

# dump entire config file
for section in config.sections():
    print section
    for option in config.options(section):
        print " ", option, "=", config.get(section, option)

THE PYTHON STANDARD LIBRARY
by Fredrik Lundh (fredrik@pythonware.com)

250 pages

book
  title = The Python Standard Library
  email = fredrik@pythonware.com
  author = Fredrik Lundh
  version = 2.0-001115
  _ _name_ _ = book
ematter
```

Example 5-16. Using the ConfigParser Module (continued)

```
_ _name_ _ = ematter
pages = 250
hardcopy
_ _name_ _ = hardcopy
pages = 350
```

In Python 2.0, the ConfigParser module also allows you to write configuration data to a file, as Example 5-17 shows.

Example 5-17. Using the ConfigParser Module to Write Configuration Data

```
File: configparser-example-2.py

import ConfigParser
import sys

config = ConfigParser.ConfigParser()

# set a number of parameters
config.add_section("book")
config.set("book", "title", "the python standard library")
config.set("book", "author", "fredrik lundh")

config.add_section("ematter")
config.set("ematter", "pages", 250)

# write to screen
config.write(sys.stdout)

[book]
title = the python standard library
author = fredrik lundh

[ematter]
pages = 250
```

The netrc Module

The netrc module parses *.netrc* configuration files, as shown in Example 5-18. Such files are used to store FTP usernames and passwords in a user's home directory (don't forget to configure things so that the file can only be read by the user: "chmod 0600 ~/.netrc," in other words).

Example 5-18. Using the netrc Module

```
File: netrc-example-1.py

import netrc
```

Example 5-18. Using the netrc Module (continued)

```
# default is $HOME/.netrc
info = netrc.netrc("samples/sample.netrc")

login, account, password = info.authenticators("secret.fbi")
print "login", "=>", repr(login)
print "account", "=>", repr(account)
print "password", "=>", repr(password)

login => 'mulder'
account => None
password => 'trustno1'
```

The shlex Module

The shlex module provides a simple lexer (also known as tokenizer) for languages based on the Unix shell syntax. Its use is demonstrated in Example 5-19.

Example 5-19. Using the shlex Module

```
File: shlex-example-1.py

import shlex

lexer = shlex.shlex(open("samples/sample.netrc", "r"))
lexer.wordchars = lexer.wordchars + "._"

while 1:
    token = lexer.get_token()
    if not token:
        break
    print repr(token)

'machine'
'secret.fbi'
'login'
'mulder'
'password'
'trustno1'
'machine'
'non.secret.fbi'
'login'
'scully'
'password'
'noway'
```

The zipfile Module

(New in 2.0) The `zipfile` module allows you to read and write files in the popular ZIP archive format.

Listing the Contents

To list the contents of an existing archive, you can use the `namelist` and `infolist` methods used in Example 5-20. The former returns a list of filenames, and the latter returns a list of *ZipInfo* instances.

Example 5-20. Using the zipfile Module to List Files in a ZIP File

```
File: zipfile-example-1.py

import zipfile

file = zipfile.ZipFile("samples/sample.zip", "r")

# list filenames
for name in file.namelist():
    print name,
print

# list file information
for info in file.infolist():
    print info.filename, info.date_time, info.file_size
```

```
sample.txt sample.jpg
sample.txt (1999, 9, 11, 20, 11, 8) 302
sample.jpg (1999, 9, 18, 16, 9, 44) 4762
```

Reading Data from a ZIP File

To read data from an archive, simply use the `read` method used in Example 5-21. It takes a filename as an argument and returns the data as a string.

Example 5-21. Using the zipfile Module to Read Data from a ZIP File

```
File: zipfile-example-2.py

import zipfile

file = zipfile.ZipFile("samples/sample.zip", "r")

for name in file.namelist():
    data = file.read(name)
    print name, len(data), repr(data[:10])
```

```
sample.txt 302 'We will pe'
sample.jpg 4762 '\377\330\377\340\000\020JFIF'
```

Writing Data to a ZIP File

Adding files to an archive is easy. Just pass the filename, and the name you want that file to have in the archive, to the write method.

The script in Example 5-22 creates a ZIP file containing all files in the samples directory.

Example 5-22. Using the zipfile Module to Store Files in a ZIP File

```
File: zipfile-example-3.py

import zipfile
import glob, os

# open the zip file for writing, and write stuff to it

file = zipfile.ZipFile("test.zip", "w")

for name in glob.glob("samples/*"):
    file.write(name, os.path.basename(name), zipfile.ZIP_DEFLATED)

file.close()

# open the file again, to see what's in it

file = zipfile.ZipFile("test.zip", "r")
for info in file.infolist():
    print info.filename, info.date_time, info.file_size, info.compress_size

sample.wav (1999, 8, 15, 21, 26, 46) 13260 10985
sample.jpg (1999, 9, 18, 16, 9, 44) 4762 4626
sample.au (1999, 7, 18, 20, 57, 34) 1676 1103
...
```

The third, optional argument to the write method controls what compression method to use or, rather, it controls whether data should be compressed at all. The default is zipfile.ZIP_STORED, which stores the data in the archive without any compression at all. If the zlib module is installed, you can also use zipfile.ZIP_DEFLATED, which gives you "deflate" compression.

The zipfile module also allows you to add strings to the archive. However, adding data from a string is a bit tricky; instead of just passing in the archive name and the data, you have to create a *ZipInfo* instance and configure it correctly. Example 5-23 offers a simple solution.

Example 5-23. Using the zipfile Module to Store Strings in a ZIP File

```
File: zipfile-example-4.py

import zipfile
import glob, os, time

file = zipfile.ZipFile("test.zip", "w")

now = time.localtime(time.time())[:6]

for name in ("life", "of", "brian"):
    info = zipfile.ZipInfo(name)
    info.date_time = now
    info.compress_type = zipfile.ZIP_DEFLATED
    file.writestr(info, name*1000)

file.close()

# open the file again, to see what's in it

file = zipfile.ZipFile("test.zip", "r")

for info in file.infolist():
    print info.filename, info.date_time, info.file_size, info.compress_size

life (2000, 12, 1, 0, 12, 1) 4000 26
of (2000, 12, 1, 0, 12, 1) 2000 18
brian (2000, 12, 1, 0, 12, 1) 5000 31
```

The gzip Module

The gzip module allows you to read and write gzip-compressed files as if they
were ordinary files, as shown in Example 5-24.

Example 5-24. Using the gzip Module to Read a Compressed File

```
File: gzip-example-1.py

import gzip

file = gzip.GzipFile("samples/sample.gz")

print file.read()

Well it certainly looks as though we're in for
a splendid afternoon's sport in this the 127th
Upperclass Twit of the Year Show.
```

The standard implementation doesn't support the seek and tell methods. Example
5-25 shows how to add forward seeking.

Example 5-25. Extending the gzip Module to Support seek/tell

File: gzip-example-2.py

```python
import gzip

class gzipFile(gzip.GzipFile):
    # adds seek/tell support to GzipFile

    offset = 0

    def read(self, size=None):
        data = gzip.GzipFile.read(self, size)
        self.offset = self.offset + len(data)
        return data

    def seek(self, offset, whence=0):
        # figure out new position (we can only seek forwards)
        if whence == 0:
            position = offset
        elif whence == 1:
            position = self.offset + offset
        else:
            raise IOError, "Illegal argument"
        if position < self.offset:
            raise IOError, "Cannot seek backwards"

        # skip forward, in 16k blocks
        while position > self.offset:
            if not self.read(min(position - self.offset, 16384)):
                break

    def tell(self):
        return self.offset

#
# try it

file = gzipFile("samples/sample.gz")
file.seek(80)

print file.read()

this the 127th
Upperclass Twit of the Year Show.
```

6

Mail and News Message Processing

Overview

Python comes with a rich set of modules for processing mail and news messages, as well as some common mail archive (mailbox) formats.

The rfc822 Module

The rfc822 module contains a parser for mail and news messages (and any other messages that conform to the RFC 822 standard, such as HTTP headers).

Basically, an RFC 822–style message consists of a number of header fields, followed by at least one blank line, and the message body itself.

For example, here's a short mail message. The first five lines make up the message header, and the actual message (a single line, in this case) follows after an empty line:

```
Message-Id: <20001114144603.00abb310@oreilly.com>
Date: Tue, 14 Nov 2000 14:55:07 -0500
To: "Fredrik Lundh" <fredrik@effbot.org>
From: Frank
Subject: Re: python library book!

Where is it?
```

Example 6-1 shows how the message parser reads the headers and returns a dictionary-like object, with the message headers as keys.

Example 6-1. Using the rfc822 Module

```
File: rfc822-example-1.py

import rfc822

file = open("samples/sample.eml")

message = rfc822.Message(file)

for k, v in message.items():
    print k, "=", v

print len(file.read()), "bytes in body"
```

```
subject = Re: python library book!
from = "Frank" <your@editor>
message-id = <20001114144603.00abb310@oreilly.com>
to = "Fredrik Lundh" <fredrik@effbot.org>
date = Tue, 14 Nov 2000 14:55:07 -0500
25 bytes in body
```

The message object also provides a couple of convenience methods, which parse address fields and dates for you, as shown in Example 6-2.

Example 6-2. Parsing Header Fields Using the rfc822 Module

```
File: rfc822-example-2.py

import rfc822

file = open("samples/sample.eml")

message = rfc822.Message(file)

print message.getdate("date")
print message.getaddr("from")
print message.getaddrlist("to")
```

```
(2000, 11, 14, 14, 55, 7, 0, 0, 0)
('Frank', 'your@editor')
[('Fredrik Lundh', 'fredrik@effbot.org')]
```

The address fields are parsed into (mail, real name) tuples. The date field is parsed into a 9-element time tuple, ready for use with the time module.

The mimetools Module

The *Multipurpose Internet Mail Extensions* (MIME) standard defines how to store non-ASCII text, images, and other data in RFC 822-style messages.

The mimetools module, shown in Example 6-3, contains a number of tools for writing programs that read or write MIME messages. Among other things, it contains a version of the rfc822 module's *Message* class, which knows a bit more about MIME encoded messages.

Example 6-3. Using the mimetools Module

```
File: mimetools-example-1.py

import mimetools

file = open("samples/sample.msg")

msg = mimetools.Message(file)

print "type", "=>", msg.gettype()
print "encoding", "=>", msg.getencoding()
print "plist", "=>", msg.getplist()

print "header", "=>"
for k, v in msg.items():
    print "  ", k, "=", v
```

```
type => text/plain
encoding => 7bit
plist => ['charset="iso-8859-1"']
header =>
   mime-version = 1.0
   content-type = text/plain;
 charset="iso-8859-1"
   to = effbot@spam.egg
   date = Fri, 15 Oct 1999 03:21:15 -0400
   content-transfer-encoding = 7bit
   from = "Fredrik Lundh" <fredrik@pythonware.com>
   subject = By the way...
...
```

The MimeWriter Module

The MimeWriter module (shown in Example 6-4) can be used to write "multipart" messages, as defined by the MIME mail standard.

Example 6-4. Using the MimeWriter Module

```
File: mimewriter-example-1.py

import MimeWriter

# data encoders
import quopri
import base64
import StringIO

import sys

TEXT = """
here comes the image you asked for.  hope
it's what you expected.

</F>"""

FILE = "samples/sample.jpg"

file = sys.stdout

#
# create a mime multipart writer instance

mime = MimeWriter.MimeWriter(file)
mime.addheader("Mime-Version", "1.0")

mime.startmultipartbody("mixed")

# add a text message

part = mime.nextpart()
part.addheader("Content-Transfer-Encoding", "quoted-printable")
part.startbody("text/plain")

quopri.encode(StringIO.StringIO(TEXT), file, 0)

# add an image

part = mime.nextpart()
part.addheader("Content-Transfer-Encoding", "base64")
part.startbody("image/jpeg")

base64.encode(open(FILE, "rb"), file)

mime.lastpart()
```

The output looks something like:

```
Content-Type: multipart/mixed;
    boundary='host.1.-852461.936831373.130.24813'
```

```
--host.1.-852461.936831373.130.24813
Content-Type: text/plain
Context-Transfer-Encoding: quoted-printable

here comes the image you asked for.  hope
it's what you expected.

</F>

--host.1.-852461.936831373.130.24813
Content-Type: image/jpeg
Context-Transfer-Encoding: base64
```

```
/9j/4AAQSkZJRgABAQAAAQABAAD/2wBDAAgGBgcGBQgHBwcJCQgKDBQNDAsLDBkSEw8UHRof
HBwgJC4nICIsIxwcKDcpLDAxNDQ0Hyc5PTgyPC4zNDL/2wBDAQkJCQwLDBgNDRgyIRwhMjIy
...
1e5vLrSYbJnEVpEgjCLx5mPU0qsVK0UaxjdNlS+1U6pfzTR8IzEhj2HrVG6m8m18xc8cIKSC
tCuFyC746j/Cq2pTia4WztfmKjGBXTCmo6IUpt==
```

```
--host.1.-852461.936831373.130.24813--
```

Example 6-5, which is a bit larger, uses a helper class that stores each subpart in the most suitable way.

Example 6-5. A Helper Class for the MimeWriter Module

```
File: mimewriter-example-2.py

import MimeWriter
import string, StringIO, sys
import re, quopri, base64

# check if string contains non-ascii characters
must_quote = re.compile("[\177-\377]").search


#
# encoders

def encode_quoted_printable(infile, outfile):
    quopri.encode(infile, outfile, 0)

class Writer:

    def __init__(self, file=None, blurb=None):
        if file is None:
            file = sys.stdout
        self.file = file
        self.mime = MimeWriter.MimeWriter(file)
        self.mime.addheader("Mime-Version", "1.0")

        file = self.mime.startmultipartbody("mixed")
        if blurb:
            file.write(blurb)
```

Example 6-5. A Helper Class for the MimeWriter Module (continued)

```python
    def close(self):
        "End of message"
        self.mime.lastpart()
        self.mime = self.file = None

    def write(self, data, mimetype="text/plain"):
        "Write data from string or file to message"

        # data is either an opened file or a string
        if type(data) is type(""):
            file = StringIO.StringIO(data)
        else:
            file = data
            data = None

        part = self.mime.nextpart()

        typ, subtyp = string.split(mimetype, "/", 1)

        if typ == "text":

            # text data
            encoding = "quoted-printable"
            encoder = lambda i, o: quopri.encode(i, o, 0)

            if data and not must_quote(data):
                # copy, don't encode
                encoding = "7bit"
                encoder = None

        else:

            # binary data (image, audio, application, ...)
            encoding = "base64"
            encoder = base64.encode

        #
        # write part headers

        if encoding:
            part.addheader("Content-Transfer-Encoding", encoding)

        part.startbody(mimetype)

        #
        # write part body

        if encoder:
            encoder(file, self.file)
        elif data:
            self.file.write(data)
        else:
```

Example 6-5. A Helper Class for the MimeWriter Module (continued)

```
            while 1:
                data = infile.read(16384)
                if not data:
                    break
                outfile.write(data)

#
# try it out

BLURB = "if you can read this, your mailer is not MIME-aware\n"

mime = Writer(sys.stdout, BLURB)

# add a text message
mime.write("""\
here comes the image you asked for.  hope
it's what you expected.
""", "text/plain")

# add an image
mime.write(open("samples/sample.jpg", "rb"), "image/jpeg")

mime.close()
```

The mailbox Module

The mailbox module contains code that deals with a number of different mailbox formats (mostly Unix formats), as shown in Example 6-6. Most mailbox formats simply store plain RFC 822–style messages in a long text file, using some kind of separator line to tell one message from another.

Example 6-6. Using the mailbox Module

```
File: mailbox-example-1.py

import mailbox

mb = mailbox.UnixMailbox(open("/var/spool/mail/effbot"))

while 1:
    msg = mb.next()
    if not msg:
        break
    for k, v in msg.items():
        print k, "=", v
    body = msg.fp.read()
    print len(body), "bytes in body"

subject = for he's a ...
message-id = <199910150027.CAA03202@spam.egg>
```

Example 6-6. Using the mailbox Module (continued)

```
received = (from fredrik@pythonware.com)
 by spam.egg (8.8.7/8.8.5) id CAA03202
 for effbot; Fri, 15 Oct 1999 02:27:36 +0200
from = Fredrik Lundh <fredrik@pythonware.com>
date = Fri, 15 Oct 1999 12:35:36 +0200
to = effbot@spam.egg
1295 bytes in body
```

The mailcap Module

The mailcap module in Example 6-7 contains code that deals with *mailcap* files, which contain information on how to handle different document formats (on Unix platforms).

Example 6-7. Using the mailcap Module to Get a Capability Dictionary

```
File: mailcap-example-1.py

import mailcap

caps = mailcap.getcaps()

for k, v in caps.items():
    print k, "=", v
```

```
image/* = [{'view': 'pilview'}]
application/postscript = [{'view': 'ghostview'}]
```

In Example 6-7, the system uses pilview for all kinds of images, and ghostscript viewer for PostScript documents. Example 6-8 shows how to find a viewer using mailcap.

Example 6-8. Using the mailcap Module to Find a Viewer

```
File: mailcap-example-2.py

import mailcap

caps = mailcap.getcaps()

command, info = mailcap.findmatch(
    caps, "image/jpeg", "view", "samples/sample.jpg"
    )

print command
```

```
pilview samples/sample.jpg
```

The mimetypes Module

The mimetypes module contains support for determining the MIME type for a given uniform resource locator. This is based on a built-in table, plus Apache and Netscape configuration files, if they are found. This module is demonstrated in Example 6-9.

Example 6-9. Using the mimetypes Module

```
File: mimetypes-example-1.py

import mimetypes
import glob, urllib

for file in glob.glob("samples/*"):
    url = urllib.pathname2url(file)
    print file, mimetypes.guess_type(url)

samples\sample.au ('audio/basic', None)
samples\sample.ini (None, None)
samples\sample.jpg ('image/jpeg', None)
samples\sample.msg (None, None)
samples\sample.tar ('application/x-tar', None)
samples\sample.tgz ('application/x-tar', 'gzip')
samples\sample.txt ('text/plain', None)
samples\sample.wav ('audio/x-wav', None)
samples\sample.zip ('application/zip', None)
```

The packmail Module

(Obsolete) The packmail module contains tools to create Unix *shell archives*. If you have the right tools installed (if you have a Unix box, they are installed), you can unpack such an archive simply by executing it. Example 6-10 shows how to pack a single file using packmail, while Example 6-11 shows how the module can pack an entire directory tree.

Example 6-10. Using the packmail Module to Pack a Single File

```
File: packmail-example-1.py

import packmail
import sys

packmail.pack(sys.stdout, "samples/sample.txt", "sample.txt")

echo sample.txt
sed "s/^X//" >sample.txt <<"!"
XWe will perhaps eventually be writing only small
Xmodules, which are identified by name as they are
Xused to build larger ones, so that devices like
Xindentation, rather than delimiters, might become
```

Example 6-10. Using the packmail Module to Pack a Single File (continued)

```
Xfeasible for expressing local structure in the
Xsource language.
X     -- Donald E. Knuth, December 1974
!
```

Example 6-11. Using the packmail Module to Pack an Entire Directory Tree

```
File: packmail-example-2.py

import packmail
import sys

packmail.packtree(sys.stdout, "samples")
```

Note that this module cannot handle binary files, such as sound snippets and images.

The mimify Module

The mimify module converts MIME-encoded text messages from encoded formats to plain text (typically ISO Latin 1), and back. It can be used as a command-line tool and as a conversion filter for certain mail agents:

```
$ mimify.py -e raw-message mime-message
$ mimify.py -d mime-message raw-message
```

It can also be used as a module, as shown in Example 6-12.

Example 6-12. Using the mimify Module to Decode a Message

```
File: mimify-example-1.py

import mimify
import sys

mimify.unmimify("samples/sample.msg", sys.stdout, 1)
```

Here's a MIME message containing two parts, one encoded as quoted-printable and the other as base64. The third argument to unmimify controls whether base64-encoded parts should be decoded or not:

```
MIME-Version: 1.0
Content-Type: multipart/mixed; boundary='boundary'

this is a multipart sample file.  the two
parts both contain ISO Latin 1 text, with
different encoding techniques.

--boundary
Content-Type: text/plain
Content-Transfer-Encoding: quoted-printable
```

```
sillmj=F6lke! blindstyre! medisterkorv!

--boundary
Content-Type: text/plain
Content-Transfer-Encoding: base64

a29tIG5lciBiYXJhLCBvbSBkdSB09nJzIQ==

--boundary--
```

Here's the decoded result (much more readable, at least if you know the language):

```
MIME-Version: 1.0
Content-Type: multipart/mixed; boundary= 'boundary'

this is a multipart sample file.  the two
parts both contain ISO Latin 1 text, with
different encoding techniques.

--boundary
Content-Type: text/plain

sillmjölke! blindstyre! medisterkorv!

--boundary
Content-Type: text/plain

kom ner bara, om du törs!
```

Example 6-13 demonstrates that encoding messages is just as easy.

Example 6-13. Using the mimify Module to Encode a Message

```
File: mimify-example-2.py

import mimify
import StringIO, sys

#
# decode message into a string buffer

file = StringIO.StringIO()

mimify.unmimify("samples/sample.msg", file, 1)

#
# encode message from string buffer

file.seek(0) # rewind

mimify.mimify(file, sys.stdout)
```

The multifile Module

The multifile module is a support module that allows you to treat each part of a multipart MIME message as an individual file, as shown in Example 6-14.

Example 6-14. Using the multifile Module

```
File: multifile-example-1.py

import multifile
import cgi, rfc822

infile = open("samples/sample.msg")

message = rfc822.Message(infile)

# print parsed header
for k, v in message.items():
    print k, "=", v

# use cgi support function to parse content-type header
type, params = cgi.parse_header(message["content-type"])

if type[:10] == "multipart/":

    # multipart message
    boundary = params["boundary"]

    file = multifile.MultiFile(infile)

    file.push(boundary)

    while file.next():

        submessage = rfc822.Message(file)

        # print submessage
        print "-" * 68
        for k, v in submessage.items():
            print k, "=", v
        print
        print file.read()

    file.pop()

else:

    # plain message
    print infile.read()
```

7

Network Protocols

*"Increasingly, people seem to misinterpret complexity as
sophistication, which is baffling—the incomprehensible should
cause suspicion rather than admiration. Possibly this trend results
from a mistaken belief that using a somewhat mysterious device confers
an aura of power on the user."*
—Niklaus Wirth

Overview

This chapter describes Python's socket protocol support and the networking modules built on top of the socket module. These include client handlers for most popular Internet protocols, as well as several frameworks that can be used to implement Internet servers.

For the low-level examples in this chapter, I'll use two protocols for illustration: the Internet Time Protocol and the Hypertext Transfer Protocol.

Internet Time Protocol

The Internet Time Protocol (RFC 868, Postel and Harrenstien, 1983) is a simple protocol that allows a network client to get the current time from a server.

Since this protocol is relatively lightweight, many (but far from all) Unix systems provide this service. It's also about as easy to implement as a network protocol can possibly be. The server simply waits for a connection request and immediately returns the current time as a 4-byte integer containing the number of seconds since January 1, 1900.

In fact, the protocol is so simple that I can include the entire specification:

```
File: rfc868.txt

Network Working Group                                    J. Postel - ISI
Request for Comments: 868                            K. Harrenstien - SRI
                                                               May 1983


                               Time Protocol


This RFC specifies a standard for the ARPA Internet community.  Hosts on
the ARPA Internet that choose to implement a Time Protocol are expected
to adopt and implement this standard.

This protocol provides a site-independent, machine readable date and
time.  The Time service sends back to the originating source the time in
seconds since midnight on January first 1900.

One motivation arises from the fact that not all systems have a
date/time clock, and all are subject to occasional human or machine
error.  The use of time-servers makes it possible to quickly confirm or
correct a system's idea of the time, by making a brief poll of several
independent sites on the network.

This protocol may be used either above the Transmission Control Protocol
(TCP) or above the User Datagram Protocol (UDP).

When used via TCP the time service works as follows:

    S: Listen on port 37 (45 octal).
    U: Connect to port 37.
    S: Send the time as a 32 bit binary number.
    U: Receive the time.
    U: Close the connection.
    S: Close the connection.

The server listens for a connection on port 37.  When the connection
is established, the server returns a 32-bit time value and closes the
connection.  If the server is unable to determine the time at its
site, it should either refuse the connection or close it without
sending anything.

When used via UDP the time service works as follows:

    S: Listen on port 37 (45 octal).
    U: Send an empty datagram to port 37.
    S: Receive the empty datagram.
    S: Send a datagram containing the time as a 32 bit binary number.
    U: Receive the time datagram.

The server listens for a datagram on port 37.  When a datagram
arrives, the server returns a datagram containing the 32-bit time
value.  If the server is unable to determine the time at its site, it
should discard the arriving datagram and make no reply.
```

The Time

The time is the number of seconds since 00:00 (midnight) 1 January 1900
GMT, such that the time 1 is 12:00:01 am on 1 January 1900 GMT; this
base will serve until the year 2036.

For example:

```
the time  2,208,988,800 corresponds to 00:00  1 Jan 1970 GMT,
          2,398,291,200 corresponds to 00:00  1 Jan 1976 GMT,
          2,524,521,600 corresponds to 00:00  1 Jan 1980 GMT,
          2,629,584,000 corresponds to 00:00  1 May 1983 GMT,
   and -1,297,728,000 corresponds to 00:00 17 Nov 1858 GMT.
```

Hypertext Transfer Protocol

The Hypertext Transfer Protocol (HTTP, RFC 2616, Fielding et al.) is something
completely different. The most recent specification (Version 1.1) is over 100 pages.

In its simplest form, this protocol is very straightforward. To fetch a document, the
client connects to the server and sends a request such as the following:

```
GET /hello.txt HTTP/1.0
Host: hostname
User-Agent: name

[optional request body]
```

In return, the server returns a response like this:

```
HTTP/1.0 200 OK
Content-Type: text/plain
Content-Length: 7

Hello
```

Both the request and response headers usually contain more fields, but the Host
field in the request header is the only one that must always be present.

The header lines are separated by "\r\n", and the header must be followed by an
empty line, even if there is no body (this applies to both the request and the
response).

The rest of the HTTP specification deals with stuff like content negotiation, cache
mechanics, persistent connections, and much more. For the full story, see *Hypertext TransferProtocol—HTTP/1.1* (*http://www.w3.org/Protocols*).

The socket Module

The socket module implements an interface to the socket communication layer. You can create both client and server sockets using this module.

Let's start with a client example. The client in Example 7-1 connects to a time protocol server, reads the 4-byte response, and converts it to a time value.

Example 7-1. Using the socket Module to Implement a Time Client

```
File: socket-example-1.py

import socket
import struct, time

# server
HOST = "www.python.org"
PORT = 37

# reference time (in seconds since 1900-01-01 00:00:00)
TIME1970 = 2208988800L # 1970-01-01 00:00:00

# connect to server
s = socket.socket(socket.AF_INET, socket.SOCK_STREAM)
s.connect((HOST, PORT))

# read 4 bytes, and convert to time value
t = s.recv(4)
t = struct.unpack("!I", t)[0]
t = int(t - TIME1970)

s.close()

# print results
print "server time is", time.ctime(t)
print "local clock is", int(time.time()) - t, "seconds off"

server time is Sat Oct 09 16:42:36 1999
local clock is 8 seconds off
```

The socket factory function creates a new socket of the given type (in this case, an Internet stream socket, also known as a TCP socket). The connect method attempts to connect this socket to the given server. Once that has succeeded, the recv method is used to read data.

Creating a server socket is done in a similar fashion. But instead of connecting to a server, you bind the socket to a port on the local machine, tell it to listen for incoming connection requests, and process each request as fast as possible.

Example 7-2 creates a time server, bound to port 8037 on the local machine (port numbers up to 1024 are reserved for system services, and you have to have root privileges to use them to implement services on a Unix system).

Example 7-2. Using the socket Module to Implement a Time Server

```
File: socket-example-2.py

import socket
import struct, time

# user-accessible port
PORT = 8037

# reference time
TIME1970 = 2208988800L

# establish server
service = socket.socket(socket.AF_INET, socket.SOCK_STREAM)
service.bind(("", PORT))
service.listen(1)

print "listening on port", PORT

while 1:
    # serve forever
    channel, info = service.accept()
    print "connection from", info
    t = int(time.time()) + TIME1970
    t = struct.pack("!I", t)
    channel.send(t) # send timestamp
    channel.close() # disconnect
```

listening on port 8037
connection from ('127.0.0.1', 1469)
connection from ('127.0.0.1', 1470)
...

The listen call tells the socket that we're willing to accept incoming connections. The argument gives the size of the connection queue (which holds connection requests that our program hasn't gotten around to processing yet). Finally, the accept loop returns the current time to any client bold enough to connect.

Note that the accept function returns a new socket object, which is directly connected to the client. The original socket is only used to establish the connection; all further traffic goes via the new socket.

To test this server, we can use Example 7-3, a generalized version of Example 7-1.

Example 7-3. A Time Protocol Client

```
File: timeclient.py

import socket
import struct, sys, time

# default server
```

Example 7-3. A Time Protocol Client (continued)

```
host = "localhost"
port = 8037

# reference time (in seconds since 1900-01-01 00:00:00)
TIME1970 = 2208988800L # 1970-01-01 00:00:00

def gettime(host, port):
    # fetch time buffer from stream server
    s = socket.socket(socket.AF_INET, socket.SOCK_STREAM)
    s.connect((host, port))
    t = s.recv(4)
    s.close()
    t = struct.unpack("!I", t)[0]
    return int(t - TIME1970)

if __name__ == "__main__":
    # command-line utility
    if sys.argv[1:]:
        host = sys.argv[1]
        if sys.argv[2:]:
            port = int(sys.argv[2])
        else:
            port = 37 # default for public servers

    t = gettime(host, port)
    print "server time is", time.ctime(t)
    print "local clock is", int(time.time()) - t, "seconds off"
```

```
server time is Sat Oct 09 16:58:50 1999
local clock is 0 seconds off
```

The sample script in Example 7-3 can also be used as a module; to get the current time from a server, import the timeclient module, then call the gettime function.

Thus far, we've used stream (or TCP) sockets. The time protocol specification also mentions UDP sockets, or datagrams. Stream sockets work pretty much like a phone line; you'll know if someone at the remote end picks up the receiver, and you'll notice when she hangs up. In contrast, sending datagrams is more like shouting into a dark room. There might be someone there, but you won't know unless she replies.

Example 7-4 shows that you don't need to connect to send data over a datagram socket. Instead, you use the sendto method, which takes both the data and the address of the receiver. To read incoming datagrams, use the recvfrom method.

Example 7-4. Using the socket Module to Implement a Datagram Time Client

```
File: socket-example-4.py

import socket
import struct, time

# server
HOST = "localhost"
PORT = 8037

# reference time (in seconds since 1900-01-01 00:00:00)
TIME1970 = 2208988800L # 1970-01-01 00:00:00

# connect to server
s = socket.socket(socket.AF_INET, socket.SOCK_DGRAM)

# send empty packet
s.sendto("", (HOST, PORT))

# read 4 bytes from server, and convert to time value
t, server = s.recvfrom(4)
t = struct.unpack("!I", t)[0]
t = int(t - TIME1970)

s.close()

print "server time is", time.ctime(t)
print "local clock is", int(time.time()) - t, "seconds off"

server time is Sat Oct 09 16:42:36 1999
local clock is 8 seconds off
```

Note that recvfrom returns two values: the actual data and the address of the
sender. Use the latter if you need to reply.

Example 7-5 shows the corresponding server.

Example 7-5. Using the socket Module to Implement a Datagram Time Server

```
File: socket-example-5.py

import socket
import struct, time

# user-accessible port
PORT = 8037

# reference time
TIME1970 = 2208988800L

# establish server
service = socket.socket(socket.AF_INET, socket.SOCK_DGRAM)
service.bind(("", PORT))
```

Example 7-5. Using the socket Module to Implement a Datagram Time Server (continued)

```
print "listening on port", PORT

while 1:
    # serve forever
    data, client = service.recvfrom(0)
    print "connection from", client
    t = int(time.time()) + TIME1970
    t = struct.pack("!I", t)
    service.sendto(t, client) # send timestamp

listening on port 8037
connection from ('127.0.0.1', 1469)
connection from ('127.0.0.1', 1470)
...
```

The main difference is that the server uses bind to assign a known port number to the socket and sends data back to the client address returned by recvfrom.

The select Module

This select module, shown in Example 7-6, allows you to check for incoming data on one or more sockets, pipes, or other compatible stream objects.

You can pass one or more sockets to the select function to wait for them to become readable, writable, or signal an error:

- A socket becomes *ready for reading* when someone connects after a call to listen (which means that accept won't block) when data arrives from the remote end, or when the socket is closed or reset (in this case, recv will return an empty string).

- A socket becomes *ready for writing* when the connection is established after a non-blocking call to connect or when data can be written to the socket.

- A socket signals an *error condition* when the connection fails after a non-blocking call to connect.

Example 7-6. Using the select Module to Wait for Data Arriving Over Sockets

```
File: select-example-1.py

import select
import socket
import time

PORT = 8037

TIME1970 = 2208988800L

service = socket.socket(socket.AF_INET, socket.SOCK_STREAM)
```

Example 7-6. Using the select Module to Wait for Data Arriving Over Sockets (continued)

```
service.bind(("", PORT))
service.listen(1)

print "listening on port", PORT

while 1:
    is_readable = [service]
    is_writable = []
    is_error = []
    r, w, e = select.select(is_readable, is_writable, is_error, 1.0)
    if r:
        channel, info = service.accept()
        print "connection from", info
        t = int(time.time()) + TIME1970
        t = chr(t>>24&255) + chr(t>>16&255) + chr(t>>8&255) + chr(t&255)
        channel.send(t) # send timestamp
        channel.close() # disconnect
    else:
        print "still waiting"
```

```
listening on port 8037
still waiting
still waiting
connection from ('127.0.0.1', 1469)
still waiting
connection from ('127.0.0.1', 1470)
...
```

In Example 7-6, we wait for the listening socket to become readable, which indicates that a connection request has arrived. We treat the channel socket as usual, since it's not very likely that writing the four bytes will fill the network buffers. If you need to send larger amounts of data to the client, you should add the data to the is_writable list at the top of the loop and write only when told to by select.

If you set the socket in *non-blocking mode* (by calling the setblocking method), you can use select to wait for a socket to become connected, but the asyncore module (see the next section) provides a powerful framework that handles all this for you, so I won't go into further detail here.

The asyncore Module

The asyncore module provides a "reactive" socket implementation. Instead of creating socket objects and calling methods on them to do things, this module allows you to write code that is called when something can be done. To implement an asynchronous socket handler, subclass the *dispatcher* class, and override one or more of the following methods:

- `handle_connect` is called when a connection is successfully established.

- `handle_expt` is called when a connection fails.

- `handle_accept` is called when a connection request is made to a listening socket. The callback should call the `accept` method to get the client socket.

- `handle_read` is called when there is data waiting to be read from the socket. The callback should call the `recv` method to get the data.

- `handle_write` is called when data can be written to the socket. Use the `send` method to write data.

- `handle_close` is called when the socket is closed or reset.

- `handle_error(type, value, traceback)` is called if a Python error occurs in any of the other callbacks. The default implementation prints an abbreviated traceback to `sys.stdout`.

Example 7-7 shows a time client, similar to the one for the `socket` module.

Example 7-7. Using the asyncore Module to Get the Time from a Time Server

```
File: asyncore-example-1.py

import asyncore
import socket, time

# reference time (in seconds since 1900-01-01 00:00:00)
TIME1970 = 2208988800L # 1970-01-01 00:00:00

class TimeRequest(asyncore.dispatcher):
    # time requestor (as defined in RFC 868)

    def __init__(self, host, port=37):
        asyncore.dispatcher.__init__(self)
        self.create_socket(socket.AF_INET, socket.SOCK_STREAM)
        self.connect((host, port))

    def writable(self):
        return 0 # don't have anything to write

    def handle_connect(self):
        pass # connection succeeded

    def handle_expt(self):
        self.close() # connection failed, shutdown

    def handle_read(self):
        # get local time
        here = int(time.time()) + TIME1970
```

Example 7-7. Using the asyncore Module to Get the Time from a Time Server (continued)

```
        # get and unpack server time
        s = self.recv(4)
        there = ord(s[3]) + (ord(s[2])<<8) + (ord(s[1])<<16) + (ord(s[0])<<24L)

        self.adjust_time(int(here - there))

        self.handle_close() # we don't expect more data

    def handle_close(self):
        self.close()

    def adjust_time(self, delta):
        # override this method!
        print "time difference is", delta

#
# try it out

request = TimeRequest("www.python.org")

asyncore.loop()
```

log: adding channel <TimeRequest   at 8cbe90>
time difference is 28
log: closing channel 192:<TimeRequest connected at 8cbe90>

If you don't want the log messages, override the log method in your *dispatcher* subclass.

Example 7-8 shows the corresponding time server. Note that it uses two *dispatcher* subclasses, one for the listening socket, and one for the client channel.

Example 7-8. Using the asyncore Module to Implement a Time Server

```
File: asyncore-example-2.py

import asyncore
import socket, time

# reference time
TIME1970 = 2208988800L

class TimeChannel(asyncore.dispatcher):

    def handle_write(self):
        t = int(time.time()) + TIME1970
        t = chr(t>>24&255) + chr(t>>16&255) + chr(t>>8&255) + chr(t&255)
        self.send(t)
        self.close()

class TimeServer(asyncore.dispatcher):
```

Example 7-8. Using the asyncore Module to Implement a Time Server (continued)

```
def __init__(self, port=37):
    self.port = port
    self.create_socket(socket.AF_INET, socket.SOCK_STREAM)
    self.bind(("", port))
    self.listen(5)
    print "listening on port", self.port

def handle_accept(self):
    channel, addr = self.accept()
    TimeChannel(channel)

server = TimeServer(8037)
asyncore.loop()
```

log: adding channel <TimeServer at 8cb940>
listening on port 8037
log: adding channel <TimeChannel at 8b2fd0>
log: closing channel 52:<TimeChannel connected at 8b2fd0>

In addition to the plain *dispatcher*, this module also includes a *dispatcher_with_send* class. This class allows you send larger amounts of data, without clogging up the network transport buffers.

The module in Example 7-9 defines an *AsyncHTTP* class based on the *dispatcher_with_send* class. When you create an instance of this class, it issues an HTTP GET request and sends the incoming data to a "consumer" target object.

Example 7-9. Using the asyncore Module to Do HTTP Requests

```
File: SimpleAsyncHTTP.py

import asyncore
import string, socket
import StringIO
import mimetools, urlparse

class AsyncHTTP(asyncore.dispatcher_with_send):
    # HTTP requester

    def __init__(self, uri, consumer):
        asyncore.dispatcher_with_send.__init__(self)

        self.uri = uri
        self.consumer = consumer

        # turn the uri into a valid request
        scheme, host, path, params, query, fragment = urlparse.urlparse(uri)
        assert scheme == "http", "only supports HTTP requests"
        try:
            host, port = string.split(host, ":", 1)
            port = int(port)
```

Example 7-9. Using the asyncore Module to Do HTTP Requests (continued)

```
        except (TypeError, ValueError):
            port = 80 # default port
        if not path:
            path = "/"
        if params:
            path = path + ";" + params
        if query:
            path = path + "?" + query

        self.request = "GET %s HTTP/1.0\r\nHost: %s\r\n\r\n" % (path, host)

        self.host = host
        self.port = port

        self.status = None
        self.header = None

        self.data = ""

        # get things going!
        self.create_socket(socket.AF_INET, socket.SOCK_STREAM)
        self.connect((host, port))

    def handle_connect(self):
        # connection succeeded
        self.send(self.request)

    def handle_expt(self):
        # connection failed; notify consumer (status is None)
        self.close()
        try:
            http_header = self.consumer.http_header
        except AttributeError:
            pass
        else:
            http_header(self)

    def handle_read(self):
        data = self.recv(2048)
        if not self.header:
            self.data = self.data + data
            try:
                i = string.index(self.data, "\r\n\r\n")
            except ValueError:
                return # continue
            else:
                # parse header
                fp = StringIO.StringIO(self.data[:i+4])
                # status line is "HTTP/version status message"
                status = fp.readline()
                self.status = string.split(status, " ", 2)
                # followed by a rfc822-style message header
```

Example 7-9. Using the asyncore Module to Do HTTP Requests (continued)

```
            self.header = mimetools.Message(fp)
            # followed by a newline, and the payload (if any)
            data = self.data[i+4:]
            self.data = ""
            # notify consumer (status is non-zero)
            try:
                http_header = self.consumer.http_header
            except AttributeError:
                pass
            else:
                http_header(self)
            if not self.connected:
                return # channel was closed by consumer

    self.consumer.feed(data)

def handle_close(self):
    self.consumer.close()
    self.close()
```

Example 7-10 shows a simple script that uses that class.

Example 7-10. Using the SimpleAsyncHTTP Class

```
File: asyncore-example-3.py

import SimpleAsyncHTTP
import asyncore

class DummyConsumer:
    size = 0

    def http_header(self, request):
        # handle header
        if request.status is None:
            print "connection failed"
        else:
            print "status", "=>", request.status
            for key, value in request.header.items():
                print key, "=", value

    def feed(self, data):
        # handle incoming data
        self.size = self.size + len(data)

    def close(self):
        # end of data
        print self.size, "bytes in body"

#
# try it out

consumer = DummyConsumer()
```

Example 7-10. Using the SimpleAsyncHTTP Class (continued)

```
request = SimpleAsyncHTTP.AsyncHTTP(
    "http://www.pythonware.com",
    consumer
    )

asyncore.loop()
```

```
log: adding channel <AsyncHTTP  at 8e2850>
status => ['HTTP/1.1', '200', 'OK\015\012']
server = Apache/Unix (Unix)
content-type = text/html
content-length = 3730
...
3730 bytes in body
log: closing channel 156:<AsyncHTTP connected at 8e2850>
```

Note that the consumer interface is designed to be compatible with the htmllib
and xmllib parsers, allowing you to parse HTML or XML data on the fly. Note that
the http_header method is optional; if it isn't defined, it's simply ignored.

A problem with Example 7-10 is that it doesn't work for redirected resources.
Example 7-11 adds an extra consumer layer, which handles the redirection.

Example 7-11. Using the SimpleAsyncHTTP Class with Redirection

```
File: asyncore-example-4.py

import SimpleAsyncHTTP
import asyncore

class DummyConsumer:
    size = 0

    def http_header(self, request):
        # handle header
        if request.status is None:
            print "connection failed"
        else:
            print "status", "=>", request.status
            for key, value in request.header.items():
                print key, "=", value

    def feed(self, data):
        # handle incoming data
        self.size = self.size + len(data)

    def close(self):
        # end of data
        print self.size, "bytes in body"

class RedirectingConsumer:
```

Example 7-11. Using the SimpleAsyncHTTP Class with Redirection (continued)

```
    def _ _init_ _(self, consumer):
        self.consumer = consumer

    def http_header(self, request):
        # handle header
        if request.status is None or\
            request.status[1] not in ("301", "302"):
            try:
                http_header = self.consumer.http_header
            except AttributeError:
                pass
            else:
                return http_header(request)
        else:
            # redirect!
            uri = request.header["location"]
            print "redirecting to", uri, "..."
            request.close()
            SimpleAsyncHTTP.AsyncHTTP(uri, self)

    def feed(self, data):
        self.consumer.feed(data)

    def close(self):
        self.consumer.close()

#
# try it out

consumer = RedirectingConsumer(DummyConsumer())

request = SimpleAsyncHTTP.AsyncHTTP(
    "http://www.pythonware.com/library",
    consumer
    )

asyncore.loop()

log: adding channel <AsyncHTTP  at 8e64b0>
redirecting to http://www.pythonware.com/library/ ...
log: closing channel 48:<AsyncHTTP connected at 8e64b0>
log: adding channel <AsyncHTTP  at 8ea790>
status => ['HTTP/1.1', '200', 'OK\015\012']
server = Apache/Unix (Unix)
content-type = text/html
content-length = 387
...
387 bytes in body
log: closing channel 236:<AsyncHTTP connected at 8ea790>
```

If the server returns status 301 (permanent redirection) or 302 (temporary redirection), the redirecting consumer closes the current request and then issues a new one for the new address. All other calls to the consumer are delegated to the original consumer.

The asynchat Module

The asynchat module is an extension to asyncore. It provides additional support for line-oriented protocols. It also provides improved buffering support, via the push methods and the "producer" mechanism.

Example 7-12 implements a very minimal HTTP responder. It simply returns an HTML document containing information from an HTTP request (the output appears in the browser window).

Example 7-12. Using the asynchat Module to Implement a Minimal HTTP Server

```
File: asynchat-example-1.py

import asyncore, asynchat
import os, socket, string

PORT = 8000

class HTTPChannel(asynchat.async_chat):

    def __init__(self, server, sock, addr):
        asynchat.async_chat.__init__(self, sock)
        self.set_terminator("\r\n")
        self.request = None
        self.data = ""
        self.shutdown = 0

    def collect_incoming_data(self, data):
        self.data = self.data + data

    def found_terminator(self):
        if not self.request:
            # got the request line
            self.request = string.split(self.data, None, 2)
            if len(self.request) != 3:
                self.shutdown = 1
            else:
                self.push("HTTP/1.0 200 OK\r\n")
                self.push("Content-type: text/html\r\n")
                self.push("\r\n")
            self.data = self.data + "\r\n"
            self.set_terminator("\r\n\r\n") # look for end of headers
        else:
            # return payload.
            self.push("<html><body><pre>\r\n")
            self.push(self.data)
            self.push("</pre></body></html>\r\n")
            self.close_when_done()
```

Example 7-12. Using the asynchat Module to Implement a Minimal HTTP Server (continued)

```
class HTTPServer(asyncore.dispatcher):

    def __init__(self, port):
        self.create_socket(socket.AF_INET, socket.SOCK_STREAM)
        self.bind(("", port))
        self.listen(5)

    def handle_accept(self):
        conn, addr = self.accept()
        HTTPChannel(self, conn, addr)

#
# try it out

s = HTTPServer(PORT)
print "serving at port", PORT, "..."
asyncore.loop()
```

```
GET / HTTP/1.1
Accept: */*
Accept-Language: en, sv
Accept-Encoding: gzip, deflate
User-Agent: Mozilla/4.0 (compatible; Bruce/1.0)
Host: localhost:8000
Connection: Keep-Alive
```

The producer interface allows you to "push" objects that are too large to store in memory. asyncore calls the producer's more method whenever it needs more data. To signal end of file, just return an empty string.

Example 7-13 implements a very simple file-based HTTP server, using a simple *FileProducer* class that reads data from a file, a few kilobytes at the time.

Example 7-13. Using the asynchat Module to Implement a Simple HTTP Server

```
File: asynchat-example-2.py

import asyncore, asynchat
import os, socket, string, sys
import StringIO, mimetools

ROOT = "."

PORT = 8000

class HTTPChannel(asynchat.async_chat):

    def __init__(self, server, sock, addr):
        asynchat.async_chat.__init__(self, sock)
        self.server = server
        self.set_terminator("\r\n\r\n")
        self.header = None
```

```python
        self.data = ""
        self.shutdown = 0

    def collect_incoming_data(self, data):
        self.data = self.data + data
        if len(self.data) > 16384:
            # limit the header size to prevent attacks
            self.shutdown = 1

    def found_terminator(self):
        if not self.header:
            # parse http header
            fp = StringIO.StringIO(self.data)
            request = string.split(fp.readline(), None, 2)
            if len(request) != 3:
                # badly formed request; just shut down
                self.shutdown = 1
            else:
                # parse message header
                self.header = mimetools.Message(fp)
                self.set_terminator("\r\n")
                self.server.handle_request(
                    self, request[0], request[1], self.header
                    )
                self.close_when_done()
            self.data = ""
        else:
            pass # ignore body data, for now

    def pushstatus(self, status, explanation="OK"):
        self.push("HTTP/1.0 %d %s\r\n" % (status, explanation))


class FileProducer:
    # a producer that reads data from a file object

    def __init__(self, file):
        self.file = file

    def more(self):
        if self.file:
            data = self.file.read(2048)
            if data:
                return data
            self.file = None
        return ""


class HTTPServer(asyncore.dispatcher):

    def __init__(self, port=None, request=None):
        if not port:
```

Example 7-13. Using the asynchat Module to Implement a Simple HTTP Server (continued)

```
                port = 80
        self.port = port
        if request:
            self.handle_request = request # external request handler
        self.create_socket(socket.AF_INET, socket.SOCK_STREAM)
        self.bind(("", port))
        self.listen(5)

    def handle_accept(self):
        conn, addr = self.accept()
        HTTPChannel(self, conn, addr)

    def handle_request(self, channel, method, path, header):
        try:
            # this is not safe!
            while path[:1] == "/":
                path = path[1:]
            filename = os.path.join(ROOT, path)
            print path, "=>", filename
            file = open(filename, "r")
        except IOError:
            channel.pushstatus(404, "Not found")
            channel.push("Content-type: text/html\r\n")
            channel.push("\r\n")
            channel.push("<html><body>File not found.</body></html>\r\n")
        else:
            channel.pushstatus(200, "OK")
            channel.push("Content-type: text/html\r\n")
            channel.push("\r\n")
            channel.push_with_producer(FileProducer(file))

#
# try it out

s = HTTPServer(PORT)
print "serving at port", PORT
asyncore.loop()

serving at port 8000
log: adding channel <HTTPServer  at 8e54d0>
log: adding channel <HTTPChannel  at 8e64a0>
samples/sample.htm => .\samples/sample.htm
log: closing channel 96:<HTTPChannel connected at 8e64a0>
```

The urllib Module

The urlib module provides a unified client interface for HTTP, FTP, and gopher. It automatically picks the right protocol handler based on the uniform resource locator (URL) passed to the library.

Fetching data from a URL is extremely easy. Just call the urlopen method, and read from the returned stream object, as shown in Example 7-14.

Example 7-14. Using the urllib Module to Fetch a Remote Resource

```
File: urllib-example-1.py

import urllib

fp = urllib.urlopen("http://www.python.org")

op = open("out.html", "wb")

n = 0

while 1:
    s = fp.read(8192)
    if not s:
        break
    op.write(s)
    n = n + len(s)

fp.close()
op.close()

for k, v in fp.headers.items():
    print k, "=", v

print "copied", n, "bytes from", fp.url
```

```
server = Apache/1.3.6 (Unix)
content-type = text/html
accept-ranges = bytes
date = Mon, 11 Oct 1999 20:11:40 GMT
connection = close
etag = "741e9-7870-37f356bf"
content-length = 30832
last-modified = Thu, 30 Sep 1999 12:25:35 GMT
copied 30832 bytes from http://www.python.org
```

Note that stream object provides some non-standard attributes. headers is a *Message* object (as defined by the mimetools module), and url contains the actual URL. The latter is updated if the server redirects the client to a new URL.

The urlopen function is actually a helper function, which creates an instance of the *FancyURLopener* class and calls its open method. To get special behavior, you can subclass that class. For instance, the class in Example 7-15 automatically logs in to the server when necessary.

Example 7-15. Using the urllib Module with Automatic Authentication

```
File: urllib-example-3.py

import urllib

class myURLOpener(urllib.FancyURLopener):
    # read an URL, with automatic HTTP authentication

    def setpasswd(self, user, passwd):
        self.__user = user
        self.__passwd = passwd

    def prompt_user_passwd(self, host, realm):
        return self.__user, self.__passwd

urlopener = myURLOpener()
urlopener.setpasswd("mulder", "trustno1")

fp = urlopener.open("http://www.secretlabs.com")
print fp.read()
```

The urlparse Module

The urlparse module contains functions to process URLs, and to convert between URLs and platform-specific filenames. Example 7-16 demonstrates.

Example 7-16. Using the urlparse Module

```
File: urlparse-example-1.py

import urlparse

print urlparse.urlparse("http://host/path;params?query#fragment")
```

('http', 'host', '/path', 'params', 'query', 'fragment')

A common use is to split an HTTP URL into host and path components (an HTTP request involves asking the host to return data identified by the path), as shown in Example 7-17.

Example 7-17. Using the urlparse Module to Parse HTTP Locators

```
File: urlparse-example-2.py

import urlparse

scheme, host, path, params, query, fragment =\
        urlparse.urlparse("http://host/path;params?query#fragment")

if scheme == "http":
    print "host", "=>", host
    if params:
```

Example 7-17. Using the urlparse Module to Parse HTTP Locators (continued)

```
        path = path + ";" + params
    if query:
        path = path + "?" + query
    print "path", "=>", path
```

host => host
path => /path;params?query

Alternatively, Example 7-18 shows how you can use the `urlunparse` function to put the URL back together again.

Example 7-18. Using the urlparse Module to Parse HTTP Locators

```
File: urlparse-example-3.py

import urlparse

scheme, host, path, params, query, fragment =\
        urlparse.urlparse("http://host/path;params?query#fragment")

if scheme == "http":
    print "host", "=>", host
    print "path", "=>", urlparse.urlunparse(
    (None, None, path, params, query, None)
    )
```

host => host
path => /path;params?query

Example 7-19 uses the `urljoin` function to combine an absolute URL with a second, possibly relative URL.

Example 7-19. Using the urlparse Module to Combine Relative Locators

```
File: urlparse-example-4.py

import urlparse

base = "http://spam.egg/my/little/pony"

for path in "/index", "goldfish", "../black/cat":
    print path, "=>", urlparse.urljoin(base, path)
```

/index => http://spam.egg/index
goldfish => http://spam.egg/my/little/goldfish
../black/cat => http://spam.egg/my/black/cat

The cookie Module

(New in 2.0) This module provides basic cookie support for HTTP clients and servers. Example 7-20 shows its use.

Example 7-20. Using the cookie Module

```
File: cookie-example-1.py

import Cookie
import os, time

cookie = Cookie.SimpleCookie()
cookie["user"] = "Mimi"
cookie["timestamp"] = time.time()

print cookie

# simulate CGI roundtrip
os.environ["HTTP_COOKIE"] = str(cookie)

print

cookie = Cookie.SmartCookie()
cookie.load(os.environ["HTTP_COOKIE"])

for key, item in cookie.items():
    # dictionary items are "Morsel" instances
    # use value attribute to get actual value
    print key, repr(item.value)

Set-Cookie: timestamp=736513200;
Set-Cookie: user=Mimi;

user 'Mimi'
timestamp '736513200'
```

The robotparser Module

(New in 2.0) The robotparser module reads robots.txt files, which are used to implement the *Robot Exclusion Protocol* (*http://info.webcrawler.com/mak/pro-jects/robots/robots.html*).

If you're implementing an HTTP robot that will visit arbitrary sites on the Net (not just your own sites), it's a good idea to use this module to check that you really are welcome. Example 7-21 demonstrates the robotparser module.

Example 7-21. Using the robotparser Module

```
File: robotparser-example-1.py

import robotparser

r = robotparser.RobotFileParser()
r.set_url("http://www.python.org/robots.txt")
r.read()

if r.can_fetch("*", "/index.html"):
    print "may fetch the home page"

if r.can_fetch("*", "/tim_one/index.html"):
    print "may fetch the tim peters archive"

may fetch the home page
```

The ftplib Module

The ftplib module contains a *File Transfer Protocol* (FTP) client implementation.

Example 7-22 demonstrates how to log in and get a directory listing of the login directory. Note that the format of the directory listing is server dependent (it's usually the same as the format used by the directory listing utility on the server host platform).

Example 7-22. Using the ftplib Module to Get a Directory Listing

```
File: ftplib-example-1.py

import ftplib

ftp = ftplib.FTP("www.python.org")
ftp.login("anonymous", "ftplib-example-1")

print ftp.dir()

ftp.quit()

total 34
drwxrwxr-x  11 root     4127         512 Sep 14 14:18 .
drwxrwxr-x  11 root     4127         512 Sep 14 14:18 ..
drwxrwxr-x   2 root     4127         512 Sep 13 15:18 RCS
lrwxrwxrwx   1 root     bin           11 Jun 29 14:34 README -> welcome.msg
drwxr-xr-x   3 root     wheel        512 May 19  1998 bin
drwxr-sr-x   3 root     1400         512 Jun  9  1997 dev
drwxrwxr--   2 root     4127         512 Feb  8  1998 dup
drwxr-xr-x   3 root     wheel        512 May 19  1998 etc
...
```

Downloading files is easy; just use the appropriate retr function. Note that when you download a text file, you have to add line endings yourself. The function in

Example 7-23 uses a `lambda` expression to do that on the fly.

Example 7-23. Using the ftplib Module to Retrieve Files

```
File: ftplib-example-2.py

import ftplib
import sys

def gettext(ftp, filename, outfile=None):
    # fetch a text file
    if outfile is None:
        outfile = sys.stdout
    # use a lambda to add newlines to the lines read from the server
    ftp.retrlines("RETR " + filename, lambda s, w=outfile.write: w(s+"\n"))

def getbinary(ftp, filename, outfile=None):
    # fetch a binary file
    if outfile is None:
        outfile = sys.stdout
    ftp.retrbinary("RETR " + filename, outfile.write)

ftp = ftplib.FTP("www.python.org")
ftp.login("anonymous", "ftplib-example-2")

gettext(ftp, "README")
getbinary(ftp, "welcome.msg")
```

WELCOME to python.org, the Python programming language home site.

You are number %N of %M allowed users. Ni!

Python Web site: http://www.python.org/

CONFUSED FTP CLIENT? Try begining your login password with '-' dash.
This turns off continuation messages that may be confusing your client.
...

Finally, Example 7-24 is a simple one that copies files to the FTP server. This script uses the file extension to figure out if the file is a text file or a binary file.

Example 7-24. Using the ftplib Module to Store Files

```
File: ftplib-example-3.py

import ftplib
import os

def upload(ftp, file):
    ext = os.path.splitext(file)[1]
    if ext in (".txt", ".htm", ".html"):
        ftp.storlines("STOR " + file, open(file))
    else:
        ftp.storbinary("STOR " + file, open(file, "rb"), 1024)
```

Example 7-24. Using the ftplib Module to Store Files (continued)

```
ftp = ftplib.FTP("ftp.fbi.gov")
ftp.login("mulder", "trustno1")

upload(ftp, "trixie.zip")
upload(ftp, "file.txt")
upload(ftp, "sightings.jpg")
```

The gopherlib Module

The gopherlib module contains a gopher client implementation, shown in Example 7-25.

Example 7-25. Using the gopherlib Module

```
File: gopherlib-example-1.py

import gopherlib

host = "gopher.spam.egg"

f = gopherlib.send_selector("1/", host)
for item in gopherlib.get_directory(f):
    print item

['0', "About Spam.Egg's Gopher Server", "0/About's Spam.Egg's
Gopher Server", 'gopher.spam.egg', '70', '+']
['1', 'About Spam.Egg', '1/Spam.Egg', 'gopher.spam.egg', '70', '+']
['1', 'Misc', '1/Misc', 'gopher.spam.egg', '70', '+']
...
```

The httplib Module

The httplib module, shown in Example 7-26, provides an HTTP client interface.

Example 7-26. Using the httplib Module

```
File: httplib-example-1.py

import httplib

USER_AGENT = "httplib-example-1.py"

class Error:
    # indicates an HTTP error
    def __init__(self, url, errcode, errmsg, headers):
        self.url = url
        self.errcode = errcode
        self.errmsg = errmsg
        self.headers = headers
    def __repr__(self):
```

Example 7-26. Using the httplib Module (continued)

```
        return (
            "<Error for %s: %s %s>" %
            (self.url, self.errcode, self.errmsg)
            )

class Server:

    def _ _init_ _(self, host):
        self.host = host

    def fetch(self, path):
        http = httplib.HTTP(self.host)

        # write header
        http.putrequest("GET", path)
        http.putheader("User-Agent", USER_AGENT)
        http.putheader("Host", self.host)
        http.putheader("Accept", "*/*")
        http.endheaders()

        # get response
        errcode, errmsg, headers = http.getreply()

        if errcode != 200:
            raise Error(errcode, errmsg, headers)

        file = http.getfile()
        return file.read()

if _ _name_ _ == "_ _main_ _":

    server = Server("www.pythonware.com")
    print server.fetch("/index.htm")
```

Note that the HTTP client provided httplib blocks while waiting for the server to respond. For an asynchronous solution, which among other things allows you to issue multiple requests in parallel, see the examples for the asyncore module.

Posting Data to an HTTP Server

The httplib module also allows you to send other HTTP commands, such as POST, as shown in Example 7-27.

Example 7-27. Using the httplib Module to Post Data

```
File: httplib-example-2.py

import httplib

USER_AGENT = "httplib-example-2.py"
```

Example 7-27. Using the httplib Module to Post Data (continued)

```
def post(host, path, data, type=None):

    http = httplib.HTTP(host)

    # write header
    http.putrequest("PUT", path)
    http.putheader("User-Agent", USER_AGENT)
    http.putheader("Host", host)
    if type:
        http.putheader("Content-Type", type)
    http.putheader("Content-Length", str(len(size)))
    http.endheaders()

    # write body
    http.send(data)

    # get response
    errcode, errmsg, headers = http.getreply()

    if errcode != 200:
        raise Error(errcode, errmsg, headers)

    file = http.getfile()
    return file.read()

if __name__ == "__main__":

    post("www.spam.egg", "/bacon.htm", "a piece of data", "text/plain")
```

The poplib Module

The poplib module (shown in Example 7-28) provides a *Post Office Protocol* (POP3) client implementation. This protocol is used to "pop" (copy) messages from a central mail server to your local computer.

Example 7-28. Using the poplib Module

```
File: poplib-example-1.py

import poplib
import string, random
import StringIO, rfc822

SERVER = "pop.spam.egg"

USER  = "mulder"
PASSWORD = "trustno1"

# connect to server
server = poplib.POP3(SERVER)
```

Example 7-28. Using the poplib Module (continued)

```
# login
server.user(USER)
server.pass_(PASSWORD)

# list items on server
resp, items, octets = server.list()

# download a random message
id, size = string.split(random.choice(items))
resp, text, octets = server.retr(id)

text = string.join(text, "\n")
file = StringIO.StringIO(text)

message = rfc822.Message(file)

for k, v in message.items():
    print k, "=", v

print message.fp.read()

subject = ANN: (the eff-bot guide to) The Standard Python Library
message-id = <199910120808.KAA09206@spam.egg>
received = (from fredrik@spam.egg)
 by spam.egg (8.8.7/8.8.5) id KAA09206
 for mulder; Tue, 12 Oct 1999 10:08:47 +0200
from = Fredrik Lundh <fredrik@spam.egg>
date = Tue, 12 Oct 1999 10:08:47 +0200
to = mulder@spam.egg

...
```

The imaplib Module

The imaplib module, shown in Example 7-29, provides an *Internet Message Access Protocol* (IMAP) client implementation. This protocol lets you access mail folders stored on a central mail server as if they were local.

Example 7-29. Using the imaplib Module

```
File: imaplib-example-1.py

import imaplib
import string, random
import StringIO, rfc822

SERVER = "imap.spam.egg"

USER  = "mulder"
PASSWORD = "trustno1"
```

Example 7-29. Using the imaplib Module (continued)

```
# connect to server
server = imaplib.IMAP4(SERVER)

# login
server.login(USER, PASSWORD)
server.select()

# list items on server
resp, items = server.search(None, "ALL")
items = string.split(items[0])

# fetch a random item
id = random.choice(items)
resp, data = server.fetch(id, "(RFC822)")
text = data[0][1]

file = StringIO.StringIO(text)

message = rfc822.Message(file)

for k, v in message.items():
    print k, "=", v

print message.fp.read()

server.logout()
```

```
subject = ANN: (the eff-bot guide to) The Standard Python Library
message-id = <199910120816.KAA12177@larch.spam.egg>
to = mulder@spam.egg
date = Tue, 12 Oct 1999 10:16:19 +0200 (MET DST)
from = <effbot@spam.egg>
received = (effbot@spam.egg) by imap.algonet.se (8.8.8+Sun/8.6.12)
id KAA12177 for effbot@spam.egg; Tue, 12 Oct 1999 10:16:19 +0200
(MET DST)

body text for test 5
```

The smtplib Module

The smtplib module (shown in Example 7-30) provides a *Simple Mail Transfer Protocol* (SMTP) client implementation. This protocol is used to send mail through Unix mail servers.

To read mail, use the poplib or imaplib modules.

Example 7-30. Using the smtplib Module

```
File: smtplib-example-1.py

import smtplib
import string, sys

HOST = "localhost"

FROM = "effbot@spam.egg"
TO = "fredrik@spam.egg"

SUBJECT = "for your information!"

BODY = "next week: how to fling an otter"

body = string.join((
    "From: %s" % FROM,
    "To: %s" % TO,
    "Subject: %s" % SUBJECT,
    "",
    BODY), "\r\n")

print body

server = smtplib.SMTP(HOST)
server.sendmail(FROM, [TO], body)
server.quit()
```

```
From: effbot@spam.egg
To: fredrik@spam.egg
Subject: for your information!

next week: how to fling an otter
```

The telnetlib Module

The `telnetlib` module provides a telnet client implementation.

Example 7-31 connects to a Unix computer, logs in, and then retrieves a directory listing.

Example 7-31. Using the telnetlib Module to Log In to a Remote Server

```
File: telnetlib-example-1.py

import telnetlib
import sys

HOST = "spam.egg"

USER = "mulder"
PASSWORD = "trustno1"
```

Example 7-31. Using the telnetlib Module to Log In to a Remote Server (continued)

```
telnet = telnetlib.Telnet(HOST)

telnet.read_until("login: ")
telnet.write(USER + "\n")

telnet.read_until("Password: ")
telnet.write(PASSWORD + "\n")

telnet.write("ls librarybook\n")
telnet.write("exit\n")

print telnet.read_all()

[spam.egg mulder]$ ls
README                          os-path-isabs-example-1.py
SimpleAsyncHTTP.py              os-path-isdir-example-1.py
aifc-example-1.py               os-path-isfile-example-1.py
anydbm-example-1.py             os-path-islink-example-1.py
array-example-1.py              os-path-ismount-example-1.py
...
```

The nntplib Module

The nntplib module provides a *Network News Transfer Protocol* (NNTP) client implementation.

Listing messages

Prior to reading messages from a news server, you have to connect to the server and then select a newsgroup. The script in Example 7-32 also downloads a complete list of all messages on the server and extracts some more or less interesting statistics from that list.

Example 7-32. Using the nntplib Module to List Messages

```
File: nntplib-example-1.py

import nntplib
import string

SERVER = "news.spam.egg"
GROUP  = "comp.lang.python"
AUTHOR = "fredrik@pythonware.com" # eff-bots human alias

# connect to server
server = nntplib.NNTP(SERVER)

# choose a newsgroup
resp, count, first, last, name = server.group(GROUP)
print "count", "=>", count
```

Example 7-32. Using the nntplib Module to List Messages (continued)

```
print "range", "=>", first, last

# list all items on the server
resp, items = server.xover(first, last)

# extract some statistics
authors = {}
subjects = {}
for id, subject, author, date, message_id, references, size, lines in items:
    authors[author] = None
    if subject[:4] == "Re: ":
        subject = subject[4:]
    subjects[subject] = None
    if string.find(author, AUTHOR) >= 0:
        print id, subject

print "authors", "=>", len(authors)
print "subjects", "=>", len(subjects)
```

```
count => 607
range => 57179 57971
57474 Three decades of Python!
...
57477 More Python books coming...
authors => 257
subjects => 200
```

Downloading Messages

Downloading a message is easy. Just call the `article` method, as shown in Example 7-33.

Example 7-33. Using the nntplib Module to Download Messages

```
File: nntplib-example-2.py

import nntplib
import string

SERVER = "news.spam.egg"
GROUP  = "comp.lang.python"
KEYWORD = "tkinter"

# connect to server
server = nntplib.NNTP(SERVER)

resp, count, first, last, name = server.group(GROUP)
resp, items = server.xover(first, last)
for id, subject, author, date, message_id, references, size, lines in items:
    if string.find(string.lower(subject), KEYWORD) >= 0:
        resp, id, message_id, text = server.article(id)
```

Example 7-33. Using the nntplib Module to Download Messages (continued)

```
        print author
        print subject
        print len(text), "lines in article"
```

"Fredrik Lundh" <fredrik@pythonware.com>
Re: Programming Tkinter (In Python)
110 lines in article
...

Example 7-34 shows how you can further manipulate the messages by wrapping it
up in a *Message* object (using the rfc822 module).

Example 7-34. Using the nntplib and rfc822 Modules to Process Messages

```
File: nntplib-example-3.py

import nntplib
import string, random
import StringIO, rfc822

SERVER = "news.spam.egg"
GROUP  = "comp.lang.python"

# connect to server
server = nntplib.NNTP(SERVER)

resp, count, first, last, name = server.group(GROUP)
for i in range(10):
    try:
        id = random.randint(int(first), int(last))
        resp, id, message_id, text = server.article(str(id))
    except (nntplib.error_temp, nntplib.error_perm):
        pass # no such message (maybe it was deleted?)
    else:
        break # found a message!
else:
    raise SystemExit

text = string.join(text, "\n")
file = StringIO.StringIO(text)

message = rfc822.Message(file)

for k, v in message.items():
    print k, "=", v

print message.fp.read()
```

mime-version = 1.0
content-type = text/plain; charset="iso-8859-1"
message-id = <008501bf1417$1cf90b70$f29b12c2@sausage.spam.egg>
lines = 22

Example 7-34. Using the nntplib and rfc822 Modules to Process Messages (continued)

```
...
from = "Fredrik Lundh" <fredrik@pythonware.com>
nntp-posting-host = parrot.python.org
subject = ANN: (the eff-bot guide to) The Standard Python Library
...
</F>
```

Once you've gotten this far, you can use modules like `htmllib`, `uu`, and `base64` to further process the messages.

The SocketServer Module

The `SocketServer` module provides a framework for various kinds of socket-based servers. The module provides a number of classes that can be mixed and matched to create servers for different purposes.

Example 7-35 implements an Internet Time Protocol server using this module. Use the `timeclient` script to try it out.

Example 7-35. Using the SocketServer Module

```
File: socketserver-example-1.py

import SocketServer
import time

# user-accessible port
PORT = 8037

# reference time
TIME1970 = 2208988800L

class TimeRequestHandler(SocketServer.StreamRequestHandler):
    def handle(self):
        print "connection from", self.client_address
        t = int(time.time()) + TIME1970
        b = chr(t>>24&255) + chr(t>>16&255) + chr(t>>8&255) + chr(t&255)
        self.wfile.write(b)

server = SocketServer.TCPServer(("", PORT), TimeRequestHandler)
print "listening on port", PORT
server.serve_forever()

connection from ('127.0.0.1', 1488)
connection from ('127.0.0.1', 1489)
...
```

The BaseHTTPServer Module

This is a basic framework for HTTP servers, built on top of the SocketServer framework.

Example 7-36 generates a random message each time you reload the page. The path variable contains the current URL, which you can use to generate different contents for different URLs (as it stands, the script returns an error page for anything but the root path).

Example 7-36. Using the BaseHTTPServer Module

```
File: basehttpserver-example-1.py

import BaseHTTPServer
import cgi, random, sys

MESSAGES = [
    "That's as maybe, it's still a frog.",
    "Albatross! Albatross! Albatross!",
    "It's Wolfgang Amadeus Mozart.",
    "A pink form from Reading.",
    "Hello people, and welcome to 'It's a Tree.'"
    "I simply stare at the brick and it goes to sleep.",
]

class Handler(BaseHTTPServer.BaseHTTPRequestHandler):

    def do_GET(self):
        if self.path != "/":
            self.send_error(404, "File not found")
            return
        self.send_response(200)
        self.send_header("Content-type", "text/html")
        self.end_headers()
        try:
            # redirect stdout to client
            stdout = sys.stdout
            sys.stdout = self.wfile
            self.makepage()
        finally:
            sys.stdout = stdout # restore

    def makepage(self):
        # generate a random message
        tagline = random.choice(MESSAGES)
        print "<html>"
        print "<body>"
        print "<p>Today's quote: "
        print "<i>%s</i>" % cgi.escape(tagline)
        print "</body>"
        print "</html>"
```

Example 7-36. Using the BaseHTTPServer Module (continued)

```
PORT = 8000

httpd = BaseHTTPServer.HTTPServer(("", PORT), Handler)
print "serving at port", PORT
httpd.serve_forever()
```

See the SimpleHTTPServer and CGIHTTPServer modules for more extensive HTTP frameworks.

The SimpleHTTPServer Module

The SimpleHTTPServer module is a simple HTTP server that provides standard GET and HEAD request handlers. The pathname given by the client is interpreted as a relative filename (relative to the current directory when the server was started, that is). The module's use is demonstrated in Example 7-37.

Example 7-37. Using the SimpleHTTPServer Module

```
File: simplehttpserver-example-1.py

import SimpleHTTPServer
import SocketServer

# minimal web server.  serves files relative to the
# current directory.

PORT = 8000

Handler = SimpleHTTPServer.SimpleHTTPRequestHandler

httpd = SocketServer.TCPServer(("", PORT), Handler)

print "serving at port", PORT
httpd.serve_forever()
```

```
serving at port 8000
localhost - - [11/Oct/1999 15:07:44] code 403, message Directory listing not sup
ported
localhost - - [11/Oct/1999 15:07:44] "GET / HTTP/1.1" 403 -
localhost - - [11/Oct/1999 15:07:56] "GET /samples/sample.htm HTTP/1.1" 200 -
```

The server ignores drive letters and relative pathnames (such as '..'). However, it does not implement any other access control mechanisms, so be careful.

Example 7-38 implements a truly minimal web proxy. When sent to a proxy, the HTTP requests should include the full URI for the target server. This server uses urllib to fetch data from the target.

Example 7-38. Using the SimpleHTTPServer Module as a Proxy

```
File: simplehttpserver-example-2.py

# a truly minimal HTTP proxy

import SocketServer
import SimpleHTTPServer
import urllib

PORT = 1234

class Proxy(SimpleHTTPServer.SimpleHTTPRequestHandler):
    def do_GET(self):
        self.copyfile(urllib.urlopen(self.path), self.wfile)

httpd = SocketServer.ForkingTCPServer(('', PORT), Proxy)
print "serving at port", PORT
httpd.serve_forever()
```

The CGIHTTPServer Module

The CGIHTTPServer module shown in Example 7-39 is a simple HTTP server that can call external scripts through the common gateway interface (CGI).

Example 7-39. Using the CGIHTTPServer Module

```
File: cgihttpserver-example-1.py

import CGIHTTPServer
import BaseHTTPServer

class Handler(CGIHTTPServer.CGIHTTPRequestHandler):
    cgi_directories = ["/cgi"]

PORT = 8000

httpd = BaseHTTPServer.HTTPServer(("", PORT), Handler)
print "serving at port", PORT
httpd.serve_forever()
```

The cgi Module

The cgi module provides a number of support functions and classes for CGI scripts. Among other things, it can parse CGI form data.

Example 7-40 shows a simple CGI script that returns a list of a files in a given directory (relative to the root directory specified in the script).

Example 7-40. Using the cgi Module

File: cgi-example-1.py

```python
import cgi
import os, urllib

ROOT = "samples"

# header
print "text/html"
print

query = os.environ.get("QUERY_STRING")
if not query:
    query = "."

script = os.environ.get("SCRIPT_NAME", "")
if not script:
    script = "cgi-example-1.py"

print "<html>"
print "<head>"
print "<title>file listing</title>"
print "</head>"
print "</html>"

print "<body>"

try:
    files = os.listdir(os.path.join(ROOT, query))
except os.error:
    files = []

for file in files:
    link = cgi.escape(file)
    if os.path.isdir(os.path.join(ROOT, query, file)):
        href = script + "?" + os.path.join(query, file)
        print "<p><a href= '%s'>%s</a>" % (href, cgi.escape(link))
    else:
        print "<p>%s" % link

print "</body>"
print "</html>"
```

```
text/html

<html>
<head>
<title>file listing</title>
</head>
</html>
<body>
<p>sample.gif
```

Example 7-40. Using the cgi Module (continued)

```
<p>sample.gz
<p>sample.netrc
...
<p>sample.txt
<p>sample.xml
<p>sample~
<p><a href='cgi-example-1.py?web'>web</a>
</body>
</html>
```

The webbrowser Module

(New in 2.0) The webbrowser module provides a basic interface to the system's standard web browser. It provides an open function, which takes a filename or a URL, and displays it in the browser. If you call open again, it attempts to display the new page in the same browser window. Example 7-41 demonstrates the webbrowser module.

Example 7-41. Using the webbrowser Module

```
File: webbrowser-example-1.py

import webbrowser
import time

webbrowser.open("http://www.pythonware.com")

# wait a while, and then go to another page
time.sleep(5)
webbrowser.open(
    "http://www.pythonware.com/people/fredrik/librarybook.htm"
    )
```

On Unix, this module supports lynx, Netscape, Mosaic, Konquerer, and Grail. On Windows and Macintosh, it uses the standard browser (as defined in the registry or the Internet configuration panel).

8

Internationalization

The locale Module

The locale module, as shown in Example 8-1, provides an interface to C's localization functions. It also provides functions to convert between numbers and strings based on the current locale. (Functions like int and float, as well as the numeric conversion functions in string, are not affected by the current locale.)

Example 8-1. Using the locale Module for Data Formatting

```
File: locale-example-1.py

import locale

print "locale", "=>", locale.setlocale(locale.LC_ALL, "")

# integer formatting
value = 4711
print locale.format("%d", value, 1), "==",
print locale.atoi(locale.format("%d", value, 1))

# floating point
value = 47.11
print locale.format("%f", value, 1), "==",
print locale.atof(locale.format("%f", value, 1))

info = locale.localeconv()
print info["int_curr_symbol"]

locale => Swedish_Sweden.1252
4 711 == 4711
47,110000 == 47.11
SEK
```

Example 8-2 shows how you can use the locale module to get the platform locale.

Example 8-2. Using the locale Module to Get the Platform Locale

```
File: locale-example-2.py

import locale

language, encoding = locale.getdefaultlocale()

print "language", language
print "encoding", encoding

language sv_SE
encoding cp1252
```

The unicodedata Module

(New in 2.0) The unicodedata module contains Unicode character properties, such
as character categories, decomposition data, and numerical values. Its use is
shown in Example 8-3.

Example 8-3. Using the unicodedata Module

```
File: unicodedata-example-1.py

import unicodedata

for char in [u"A", u"-", u"1", u"\N{LATIN CAPITAL LETTER O WITH DIAERESIS}"]:
    print repr(char),
    print unicodedata.category(char),
    print repr(unicodedata.decomposition(char)),


    print unicodedata.decimal(char, None),
    print unicodedata.numeric(char, None)

u'A' Lu '' None None
u'-' Pd '' None None
u'1' Nd '' 1 1.0
u'\303\226' Lu '004F 0308' None None
```

Note that in Python 2.0, properties for CJK ideographs and Hangul syllables are
missing. This affects characters in the range 0x3400-0x4DB5, 0x4E00-0x9FA5, and
0xAC00-D7A3. The first character in each range has correct properties, so you can
work around this problem by simply mapping each character to the beginning:

```
    def remap(char):
        # fix for broken unicode property database in Python 2.0
        c = ord(char)
        if 0x3400 <= c <= 0x4DB5:
            return unichr(0x3400)
        if 0x4E00 <= c <= 0x9FA5:
            return unichr(0x4E00)
```

```
    if 0xAC00 <= c <= 0xD7A3:
        return unichr(0xAC00)
    return char
```

This bug has been fixed in Python 2.1.

The ucnhash Module

(Implementation, 2.0 only) The ucnhash module is an implementation module, which provides a name to character code mapping for Unicode string literals. If this module is present, you can use \N{} escapes to map Unicode character names to codes, as shown in Example 8-4.

Example 8-4. Using the ucnhash Module

```
File: ucnhash-example-1.py

# Python imports this module automatically, when it sees
# the first \N{} escape
# import ucnhash

print repr(u"\N{FROWN}")
print repr(u"\N{SMILE}")
print repr(u"\N{SKULL AND CROSSBONES}")

u'\u2322'
u'\u2323'
u'\u2620'
```

9

Multimedia Modules

"Wot? No quote?"
—Guido van Rossum

Overview

Python comes with a small set of modules for dealing with image files and audio files.

See the *Pythonware Image Library* (PIL, *http://www.pythonware.com/products/pil/*) and *PythonWare Sound Toolkit* (PST, *http://www.pythonware.com/products/pst/*) for more alternatives.

The imghdr Module

The imghdr module identifies different image file formats. The current version identifies bmp, gif, jpeg, pbm, pgm, png, ppm, rast (Sun raster), rgb (SGI), tiff, and xbm images. Example 9-1 demonstrates.

Example 9-1. Using the imghdr Module

```
File: imghdr-example-1.py

import imghdr

result = imghdr.what("samples/sample.jpg")

if result:
    print "file format:", result
else:
    print "cannot identify file"
```

file format: jpeg

Example 9-1. Using the imghdr Module (continued)

```
import Image

im = Image.open("samples/sample.jpg")
print im.format, im.mode, im.size
```

The sndhdr module

This sndhdr module, shown in Example 9-2, can be used to identify different audio file formats and extract basic information about a file's contents.

If successful, the what function returns a 5-tuple, containing the filetype, the sampling rate, the number of channels, the number of frames in the file (–1 means unknown), and the number of bits per sample.

Example 9-2. Using the sndhdr Module

```
File: sndhdr-example-1.py

import sndhdr

result = sndhdr.what("samples/sample.wav")

if result:
    print "file format:", result
else:
    print "cannot identify file"
```

file format: ('wav', 44100, 1, -1, 16)

The whatsound Module

(Obsolete) The whatsound module is an alias for sndhdr. It is used in Example 9-3.

Example 9-3. Using the whatsound Module

```
File: whatsound-example-1.py

import whatsound # same as sndhdr

result = whatsound.what("samples/sample.wav")

if result:
    print "file format:", result
else:
    print "cannot identify file"
```

file format: ('wav', 44100, 1, -1, 16)

The aifc Module

The `aifc` module reads and writes AIFF and AIFC audio files (as used on SGI and
Macintosh computers). Example 9-4 shows how it's used.

Example 9-4. Using the aifc Module

```
File: SimpleAsyncHTTP.py

import asyncore
import string, socket
import StringIO
import mimetools, urlparse

class AsyncHTTP(asyncore.dispatcher_with_send):
    # HTTP requestor

    def __init__(self, uri, consumer):
        asyncore.dispatcher_with_send.__init__(self)

        self.uri = uri
        self.consumer = consumer

        # turn the uri into a valid request
        scheme, host, path, params, query, fragment = urlparse.urlparse(uri)
        assert scheme == "http", "only supports HTTP requests"
        try:
            host, port = string.split(host, ":", 1)
            port = int(port)
        except (TypeError, ValueError):
            port = 80 # default port
        if not path:
            path = "/"
        if params:
            path = path + ";" + params
        if query:
            path = path + "?" + query

        self.request = "GET %s HTTP/1.0\r\nHost: %s\r\n\r\n" % (path, host)

        self.host = host
        self.port = port

        self.status = None
        self.header = None

        self.data = ""

        # get things going!
        self.create_socket(socket.AF_INET, socket.SOCK_STREAM)
        self.connect((host, port))

    def handle_connect(self):
```

Example 9-4. Using the aifc Module (continued)

```
        # connection succeeded
        self.send(self.request)

    def handle_expt(self):
        # connection failed; notify consumer (status is None)
        self.close()
        try:
            http_header = self.consumer.http_header
        except AttributeError:
            pass
        else:
            http_header(self)

    def handle_read(self):
        data = self.recv(2048)
        if not self.header:
            self.data = self.data + data
            try:
                i = string.index(self.data, "\r\n\r\n")
            except ValueError:
                return # continue
            else:
                # parse header
                fp = StringIO.StringIO(self.data[:i+4])
                # status line is "HTTP/version status message"
                status = fp.readline()
                self.status = string.split(status, " ", 2)
                # followed by a rfc822-style message header
                self.header = mimetools.Message(fp)
                # followed by a newline, and the payload (if any)
                data = self.data[i+4:]
                self.data = ""
                # notify consumer (status is non-zero)
                try:
                    http_header = self.consumer.http_header
                except AttributeError:
                    pass
                else:
                    http_header(self)
                if not self.connected:
                    return # channel was closed by consumer

        self.consumer.feed(data)

    def handle_close(self):
        self.consumer.close()
        self.close()
```

The sunau Module

The sunau module in Example 9-5 reads and writes Sun AU audio files.

Example 9-5. Using the sunau Module

```
File: sunau-example-1.py

import sunau

w = sunau.open("samples/sample.au", "r")

if w.getnchannels() == 1:
    print "mono,",
else:
    print "stereo,",

print w.getsampwidth()*8, "bits,",
print w.getframerate(), "Hz sampling rate"
```

mono, 16 bits, 8012 Hz sampling rate

The sunaudio Module

The sunaudio module, shown in Example 9-6, identifies Sun AU audio files and extracts basic information about the file contents. The sunau module provides more complete support for Sun AU files.

Example 9-6. Using the sunaudio Module

```
File: sunaudio-example-1.py

import sunaudio

file = "samples/sample.au"

print sunaudio.gethdr(open(file, "rb"))
```

(6761, 1, 8012, 1, 'sample.au')

The wave Module

The wave module reads and writes Microsoft WAV audio files, as Example 9-7 shows.

Example 9-7. Using the wave Module

```
File: wave-example-1.py

import wave
```

Example 9-7. Using the wave Module (continued)

```
w = wave.open("samples/sample.wav", "r")

if w.getnchannels() == 1:
    print "mono,",
else:
    print "stereo,",

print w.getsampwidth()*8, "bits,",
print w.getframerate(), "Hz sampling rate"

mono, 16 bits, 44100 Hz sampling rate
```

The audiodev Module

(Unix only) The audiodev module provides sound playing support for Sun and SGI computers. Example 9-8 demonstrates this module.

Example 9-8. Using the audiodev Module

```
File: audiodev-example-1.py

import audiodev
import aifc

sound = aifc.open("samples/sample.aiff", "r")

player = audiodev.AudioDev()

player.setoutrate(sound.getframerate())
player.setsampwidth(sound.getsampwidth())
player.setnchannels(sound.getnchannels())

bytes_per_frame = sound.getsampwidth() * sound.getnchannels()
bytes_per_second = sound.getframerate() * bytes_per_frame

while 1:
    data = sound.readframes(bytes_per_second)
    if not data:
        break
    player.writeframes(data)

player.wait()
```

The winsound Module

(Windows only) The winsound module allows you to play Wave sound files on a Windows machine. Example 9-9 shows how winsound is used.

Example 9-9. Using the winsound Module

```
File: winsound-example-1.py

import winsound

file = "samples/sample.wav"

winsound.PlaySound(
    file,
    winsound.SND_FILENAME|winsound.SND_NOWAIT,
    )
```

The colorsys Module

The colorsys module (shown in Example 9-10) contains functions to convert between RGB, YIQ (video), HLS, and HSV color values.

Example 9-10. Using the colorsys Module

```
File: colorsys-example-1.py

import colorsys

# gold
r, g, b = 1.00, 0.84, 0.00

print "RGB", (r, g, b)

y, i, q = colorsys.rgb_to_yiq(r, g, b)
print "YIQ", (y, i, q), "=>", colorsys.yiq_to_rgb(y, i, q)

h, l, s = colorsys.rgb_to_hls(r, g, b)
print "HLS", (h, l, s), "=>", colorsys.hls_to_rgb(h, l, s)

h, s, v = colorsys.rgb_to_hsv(r, g, b)
print "HSV", (h, s, v), "=>", colorsys.hsv_to_rgb(h, s, v)

RGB (1.0, 0.84, 0.0)
YIQ (0.7956, 0.3648, -0.2268) => (0.9999998292, 0.8400000312, 0.0)
HLS (0.14, 0.5, 1.0) => (1.0, 0.84, 0.0)
HSV (0.14, 1.0, 1.0) => (1.0, 0.84, 0.0)
```

10

Data Storage

"Unlike mainstream component programming, scripts usually do not introduce new components but simply 'wire' existing ones. Scripts can be seen as introducing behavior but no new state ... Of course, there is nothing to stop a 'scripting' language from introducing persistent state — it then simply turns into a normal programming language."
—Clemens Szyperski, in *Component Software*

Overview

Python comes with drivers for a number of very similar database managers, all modeled after Unix's dbm library. These databases behave like ordinary dictionaries, except that you can only use strings for keys and values (the shelve module can handle any kind of value).

The anydbm Module

The anydbm module provides a unified interface to the simple database drivers supported by Python.

The first time it is imported, the anydbm module looks for a suitable database driver, testing for dbhash, gdbm, dbm, or dumbdbm, in that order. If no such module is found, it raises an ImportError exception.

In Example 10-1, the open function is used to open or create a database, using the chosen database handler.

Example 10-1. Using the anydbm Module

```
File: anydbm-example-1.py

import anydbm

db = anydbm.open("database", "c")
db["1"] = "one"
db["2"] = "two"
db["3"] = "three"
db.close()

db = anydbm.open("database", "r")
for key in db.keys():
    print repr(key), repr(db[key])

'2' 'two'
'3' 'three'
'1' 'one'
```

The whichdb Module

The whichdb module can be used to figure out which database handler was used for a given database file, as shown in Example 10-2.

Example 10-2. Using the whichdb Module

```
File: whichdb-example-1.py

import whichdb

filename = "database"

result = whichdb.whichdb(filename)

if result:
    print "file created by", result
    handler = _ _import_ _(result)
    db = handler.open(filename, "r")
    print db.keys()
else:
    # cannot identify data base
    if result is None:
        print "cannot read database file", filename
    else:
        print "cannot identify database file", filename
    db = None
```

Example 10-2 uses the _ _import_ _ function to import a module with the given name.

The shelve Module

The shelve module, shown in Example 10-3, uses the database handlers to implement persistent dictionaries. A shelve object uses string keys, but the value can be of any datatype, as long as it can be handled by the pickle module.

Example 10-3. Using the shelve Module

```
File: shelve-example-1.py

import shelve

db = shelve.open("database", "c")
db["one"] = 1
db["two"] = 2
db["three"] = 3
db.close()

db = shelve.open("database", "r")
for key in db.keys():
    print repr(key), repr(db[key])
```

```
'one' 1
'three' 3
'two' 2
```

Example 10-4 shows how to use the shelve module with a given database driver.

Example 10-4. Using the shelve Module with a Given Database

```
File: shelve-example-3.py

import shelve
import gdbm

def gdbm_shelve(filename, flag="c"):
    return shelve.Shelf(gdbm.open(filename, flag))

db = gdbm_shelve("dbfile")
```

The dbhash Module

(Optional) The dbhash module provides a dbm-compatible interface to the bsddb database handler. Example 10-5 uses this module.

Example 10-5. Using the dbhash Module

```
File: dbhash-example-1.py

import dbhash

db = dbhash.open("dbhash", "c")
```

Example 10-5. Using the dbhash Module (continued)

```
db["one"] = "the foot"
db["two"] = "the shoulder"
db["three"] = "the other foot"
db["four"] = "the bridge of the nose"
db["five"] = "the naughty bits"
db["six"] = "just above the elbow"
db["seven"] = "two inches to the right of a very naughty bit indeed"
db["eight"] = "the kneecap"
db.close()

db = dbhash.open("dbhash", "r")
for key in db.keys():
    print repr(key), repr(db[key])
```

The dbm Module

(Optional) The dbm module provides an interface to the dbm database handler
(available on many Unix platforms). This is shown in Example 10-6.

Example 10-6. Using the dbm Module

```
File: dbm-example-1.py

import dbm

db = dbm.open("dbm", "c")
db["first"] = "bruce"
db["second"] = "bruce"
db["third"] = "bruce"
db["fourth"] = "bruce"
db["fifth"] = "michael"
db["fifth"] = "bruce" # overwrite
db.close()

db = dbm.open("dbm", "r")
for key in db.keys():
    print repr(key), repr(db[key])

'first' 'bruce'
'second' 'bruce'
'fourth' 'bruce'
'third' 'bruce'
'fifth' 'bruce'
```

The dumbdbm Module

The dumbdbm module, shown in Example 10-7, is a very simple database implementation, similar to dbm and friends, but written in pure Python. It uses two files: a binary file (*.dat*), which contain the data, and a text file (*.dir*), which contains data descriptors.

Example 10-7. Using the dumbdbm Module

```
File: dumbdbm-example-1.py

import dumbdbm

db = dumbdbm.open("dumbdbm", "c")
db["first"] = "fear"
db["second"] = "surprise"
db["third"] = "ruthless efficiency"
db["fourth"] = "an almost fanatical devotion to the Pope"
db["fifth"] = "nice red uniforms"
db.close()

db = dumbdbm.open("dumbdbm", "r")
for key in db.keys():
    print repr(key), repr(db[key])

'first' 'fear'
'third' 'ruthless efficiency'
'fifth' 'nice red uniforms'
'second' 'surprise'
'fourth' 'an almost fanatical devotion to the Pope'
```

The gdbm Module

(Optional) The gdbm module provides an interface to the GNU dbm database handler, as Example 10-8 shows.

Example 10-8. Using the gdbm Module

```
File: gdbm-example-1.py

import gdbm

db = gdbm.open("gdbm", "c")
db["1"] = "call"
db["2"] = "the"
db["3"] = "next"
db["4"] = "defendant"
db.close()
```

Example 10-8. Using the gdbm Module (continued)

```
db = gdbm.open("gdbm", "r")

keys = db.keys()
keys.sort()
for key in keys:
    print db[key],
```

call the next defendant

11

Tools and Utilities

The standard library comes with a number of modules that can be used both as modules and as command-line utilities.

The dis Module

The dis module is the Python disassembler. It converts byte codes to a format that is slightly more appropriate for human consumption.

You can run the disassembler from the command line. It compiles the given script and prints the disassembled byte codes to the terminal:

```
$ dis.py hello.py

            0 SET_LINENO          0

            3 SET_LINENO          1
            6 LOAD_CONST          0 ('hello again, and welcome to the show')
            9 PRINT_ITEM
           10 PRINT_NEWLINE
           11 LOAD_CONST          1 (None)
           14 RETURN_VALUE
```

You can also use dis as a module. The dis function takes a class, method, function, or code object as its single argument. Example 11-1 uses the module.

Example 11-1. Using the dis Module

```
File: dis-example-1.py

import dis

def procedure():
    print 'hello'
```

Example 11-1. Using the dis Module (continued)

```
dis.dis(procedure)

        0 SET_LINENO          3

        3 SET_LINENO          4
        6 LOAD_CONST          1 ('hello')
        9 PRINT_ITEM
       10 PRINT_NEWLINE
       11 LOAD_CONST          0 (None)
       14 RETURN_VALUE
```

The pdb Module

The pdb module is the standard Python debugger. It is based on the bdb debugger framework.

You can run the debugger from the command line (type n [or next] to go to the next line and help to get a list of available commands):

```
$ pdb.py hello.py
> hello.py(0)?()
(Pdb) n
> hello.py()
(Pdb) n
hello again, and welcome to the show
--Return--
> hello.py(1)?()->None
(Pdb)
```

Example 11-2 shows how to start the debugger from inside a program.

Example 11-2. Using the pdb Module

```
File: pdb-example-1.py

import pdb

def test(n):
    j = 0
    for i in range(n):
        j = j + i
    return n

db = pdb.Pdb()
db.runcall(test, 1)

> pdb-example-1.py(3)test()
-> def test(n):
(Pdb) s
> pdb-example-1.py(4)test()
-> j = 0
```

Example 11-2. Using the pdb Module (continued)

```
(Pdb) s
> pdb-example-1.py(5)test()
-> for i in range(n):
...
```

The bdb Module

The bdb module provides a framework for debuggers. You can use this to create your own custom debuggers, as Example 11-3 shows.

To implement custom behavior, subclass the *Bdb* class, and override the user methods (which are called whenever the debugger stops). To control the debugger, use the various set methods.

Example 11-3. Using the bdb Mdule

```
File: bdb-example-1.py

import bdb
import time

def spam(n):
    j = 0
    for i in range(n):
        j = j + i
    return n

def egg(n):
    spam(n)
    spam(n)
    spam(n)
    spam(n)

def test(n):
    egg(n)

class myDebugger(bdb.Bdb):

    run = 0

    def user_call(self, frame, args):
        name = frame.f_code.co_name or "<unknown>"
        print "call", name, args
        self.set_continue() # continue

    def user_line(self, frame):
        if self.run:
            self.run = 0
            self.set_trace() # start tracing
        else:
            # arrived at breakpoint
```

Example 11-3. Using the bdb Mdule (continued)

```
                name = frame.f_code.co_name or "<unknown>"
                filename = self.canonic(frame.f_code.co_filename)
                print "break at", filename, frame.f_lineno, "in", name
            print "continue..."
            self.set_continue() # continue to next breakpoint

    def user_return(self, frame, value):
        name = frame.f_code.co_name or "<unknown>"
        print "return from", name, value
        print "continue..."
        self.set_continue() # continue

    def user_exception(self, frame, exception):
        name = frame.f_code.co_name or "<unknown>"
        print "exception in", name, exception
        print "continue..."
        self.set_continue() # continue

db = myDebugger()
db.run = 1
db.set_break("bdb-example-1.py", 7)
db.runcall(test, 1)

continue...
call egg None
call spam None
break at C:\ematter\librarybook\bdb-example-1.py 7 in spam
continue...
call spam None
break at C:\ematter\librarybook\bdb-example-1.py 7 in spam
continue...
call spam None
break at C:\ematter\librarybook\bdb-example-1.py 7 in spam
continue...
call spam None
break at C:\ematter\librarybook\bdb-example-1.py 7 in spam
continue...
```

The profile Module

The profile module is the standard Python profiler.

Like the disassembler and the debugger, you can run the profiler from the command line:

```
$ profile.py hello.py

hello again, and welcome to the show

        3 function calls in 0.785 CPU seconds
```

```
Ordered by: standard name

ncalls  tottime  percall  cumtime  percall filename:lineno(function)
     1    0.001    0.001    0.002    0.002 <string>:1(?)
     1    0.001    0.001    0.001    0.001 hello.py:1(?)
     1    0.783    0.783    0.785    0.785 profile:0(execfile('hello.py'))
     0    0.000             0.000          profile:0(profiler)
```

It can also be used to profile part of a program, as Example 11-4 shows.

Example 11-4. Using the profile Module

```
File: profile-example-1.py

import profile

def func1():
    for i in range(1000):
        pass

def func2():
    for i in range(1000):
        func1()

profile.run("func2()")
```

```
       1003 function calls in 2.380 CPU seconds

   Ordered by: standard name

ncalls  tottime  percall  cumtime  percall filename:lineno(function)
     1    0.000    0.000    2.040    2.040 <string>:1(?)
  1000    1.950    0.002    1.950    0.002 profile-example-1.py:3(func1)
     1    0.090    0.090    2.040    2.040 profile-example-1.py:7(func2)
     1    0.340    0.340    2.380    2.380 profile:0(func2())
     0    0.000             0.000          profile:0(profiler)
```

You can modify the report to suit your needs, via the pstats module.

The pstats Module

The pstats module is a tool that analyzes data collected by the Python profiler, as Example 11-5 shows.

Example 11-5. Using the pstats Module

```
File: pstats-example-1.py

import pstats
import profile

def func1():
    for i in range(1000):
```

Example 11-5. Using the pstats Module (continued)

```
        pass

def func2():
    for i in range(1000):
        func1()

p = profile.Profile()
p.run("func2()")

s = pstats.Stats(p)
s.sort_stats("time", "name").print_stats()

         1003 function calls in 1.574 CPU seconds

   Ordered by: internal time, function name

   ncalls  tottime  percall  cumtime  percall filename:lineno(function)
     1000    1.522    0.002    1.522    0.002 pstats-example-1.py:4(func1)
        1    0.051    0.051    1.573    1.573 pstats-example-1.py:8(func2)
        1    0.001    0.001    1.574    1.574 profile:0(func2())
        1    0.000    0.000    1.573    1.573 <string>:1(?)
        0    0.000             0.000          profile:0(profiler)
```

The tabnanny Module

(New in 2.0) The tabnanny module checks Python source files for ambigous indentation. If a file mixes tabs and spaces in a way that throws off indentation, no matter what tab size you're using, the nanny complains.

In the badtabs.py file used in the following examples, the first line after the if
statement uses four spaces followed by a tab. The second uses spaces only.

```
$ tabnanny.py -v samples/badtabs.py
';samples/badtabs.py': *** Line 3: trouble in tab city! ***
offending line:      print "world"

indent not equal e.g. at tab sizes 1, 2, 3, 5, 6, 7, 9
```

Since the Python interpreter reads a tab as eight spaces, the script will run correctly. It will also display correctly in any editor that assumes that a tab is either
eight or four spaces. That's not enough to fool the tab nanny, of course.

Example 11-6 shows how you can also use tabnanny from your own programs.

Example 11-6. Using the tabnanny Module

```
File: tabnanny-example-1.py

import tabnanny
```

Example 11-6. Using the tabnanny Module (continued)

```
FILE = "samples/badtabs.py"

file = open(FILE)
for line in file.readlines():
    print repr(line)

# let tabnanny look at it
tabnanny.check(FILE)
```

```
'if 1:\012'
'    \011print "hello"\012'
'        print "world"\012'
samples/badtabs.py 3 '        print "world"'\012'
```

To capture the output, you can redirect sys.stdout to a StringIO object.

12

Platform-Specific Modules

Overview

This chapter describes some platform-specific modules. I've emphasized modules that are available on entire families of platforms (such as Unix or the Windows family).

The fcntl Module

(Unix only) The fcntl module provides an interface to the ioctl and fcntl functions on Unix. They are used for "out of band" operations on file handles and I/O device handles. This includes things like reading extended attributes, controlling blocking, modifying terminal behavior, and so on.

Exactly how to use these functions is highly platform dependent. For more information on what you can do on your platform, check the corresponding Unix man-pages.

This module also provides an interface to Unix's file locking mechanisms. Example 12-1 uses the flock function to place an *advisory lock* on the file, while it is being updated.

The output shown later was obtained by running three instances of the program in parallel, like this (all on one command line):

```
python fcntl-example-1.py& python fcntl-example-1.py&
   python fcntl-example-1.py&
```

If you comment out the call to flock, the counter will not be updated properly.

Example 12-1. Using the fcntl Module

```
File: fcntl-example-1.py

import fcntl, FCNTL
import os, time

FILE = "counter.txt"

if not os.path.exists(FILE):
    # create the counter file if it doesn't exist
    file = open(FILE, "w")
    file.write("0")
    file.close()

for i in range(20):
    # increment the counter
    file = open(FILE, "r+")
    fcntl.flock(file.fileno(), FCNTL.LOCK_EX)
    counter = int(file.readline()) + 1
    file.seek(0)
    file.write(str(counter))
    file.close() # unlocks the file
    print os.getpid(), "=>", counter
    time.sleep(0.1)

30940 => 1
30942 => 2
30941 => 3
30940 => 4
30941 => 5
30942 => 6
```

The pwd Module

(Unix only) The pwd module provides an interface to the Unix password "database" (*/etc/passwd* and friends). This database (usually a plain-text file) contains information about the user accounts on the local machine. Example 12-2 demonstrates pwd.

Example 12-2. Using the pwd Module

```
File: pwd-example-1.py

import pwd
import os

print pwd.getpwuid(os.getgid())
print pwd.getpwnam("root")

('effbot', 'dsWjk8', 4711, 4711, 'eff-bot', '/home/effbot', '/bin/bosh')
('root', 'hs2giiw', 0, 0, 'root', '/root', '/bin/bash')
```

The getpwall function returns a list of database entries for all available users. This can be useful if you want to search for a user.

If you have to look up many names, you can use getpwall to preload a dictionary, as shown in Example 12-3.

Example 12-3. Using the pwd Module

```
File: pwd-example-2.py

import pwd
import os

# preload password dictionary
_pwd = {}
for info in pwd.getpwall():
    _pwd[info[0]] = _pwd[info[2]] = info

def userinfo(uid):
    # name or uid integer
    return _pwd[uid]

print userinfo(os.getuid())
print userinfo("root")

('effbot', 'dsWjk8', 4711, 4711, 'eff-bot', '/home/effbot', '/bin/bosh')
('root', 'hs2giiw', 0, 0, 'root', '/root', '/bin/bash')
```

The grp Module

(Unix only) The grp module provides an interface to the Unix group database (*/etc/group*). The getgrgid function returns data for a given group identity (see Example 12-4), and getgrnam returns data for a group name.

Example 12-4. Using the grp Module

```
File: grp-example-1.py

import grp
import os

print grp.getgrgid(os.getgid())
print grp.getgrnam("wheel")

('effbot', '', 4711, ['effbot'])
('wheel', '', 10, ['root', 'effbot', 'gorbot', 'timbot'])
```

The getgrall function returns a list of database entries for all available groups.

If you're going to do a lot of group queries, you can save some time by using get-grall to copy all the (current) groups into a dictionary. The groupinfo function in Example 12-5 returns the information for either a group identifier (an integer) or a group name (a string).

Example 12-5. Using the grp Module to Cache Group Information

```
File: grp-example-2.py

import grp
import os

# preload password dictionary
_grp = {}
for info in grp.getgrall():
    _grp[info[0]] = _grp[info[2]] = info

def groupinfo(gid):
    # name or gid integer
    return _grp[gid]

print groupinfo(os.getgid())
print groupinfo("wheel")
```

```
('effbot', '', 4711, ['effbot'])
('wheel', '', 10, ['root', 'effbot', 'gorbot', 'timbot'])
```

The nis Module

(Unix only, Optional) The nis module provides an interface to the NIS (yellow pages) services, as Example 12-6 shows. It can be used to fetch values from a NIS database, if available.

Example 12-6. Using the nis Module

```
File: nis-example-1.py

import nis
import string

print nis.cat("ypservers")
print string.split(nis.match("bacon", "hosts.byname"))
```

```
{'bacon.spam.egg': 'bacon.spam.egg'}
['194.18.155.250', 'bacon.spam.egg', 'bacon', 'spam-010']
```

The curses Module

(Unix only, Optional) The curses module gives you better control of the text terminal window, in a terminal-independent way. Example 12-7 shows its use.

Example 12-7. Using the curses Module

```
File: curses-example-1.py

import curses

text = [
    "a very simple curses demo",
    "",
    "(press any key to exit)"
]

# connect to the screen
screen = curses.initscr()

# setup keyboard
curses.noecho() # no keyboard echo
curses.cbreak() # don't wait for newline

# screen size
rows, columns = screen.getmaxyx()

# draw a border around the screen
screen.border()

# display centered text
y = (rows - len(text)) / 2

for line in text:
    screen.addstr(y, (columns-len(line))/2, line)
    y = y + 1

screen.getch()

curses.endwin()
```

The termios Module

(Unix only, Optional) The termios module provides an interface to the Unix terminal control facilities. It can be used to control most aspects of the terminal communication ports.

In Example 12-8, this module is used to temporarily disable keyboard echo (which is controlled by the ECHO flag in the third flag field).

Example 12-8. Using the termios Module

File: termios-example-1.py

```
import termios, TERMIOS
import sys

fileno = sys.stdin.fileno()

attr = termios.tcgetattr(fileno)
orig = attr[:]

print "attr =>", attr[:4] # flags

# disable echo flag
attr[3] = attr[3] & ~TERMIOS.ECHO

try:
    termios.tcsetattr(fileno, TERMIOS.TCSADRAIN, attr)
    message = raw_input("enter secret message: ")
    print
finally:
    # restore terminal settings
    termios.tcsetattr(fileno, TERMIOS.TCSADRAIN, orig)

print "secret =>", repr(message)
```

```
attr => [1280, 5, 189, 35387]
enter secret message:
secret => 'and now for something completely different'
```

The tty Module

(Unix only) The tty module contains some utility functions for dealing with tty devices. Example 12-9 shows how to switch the terminal window over to "raw" mode, and back again.

Example 12-9. Using the tty Module

File: tty-example-1.py

```
import tty
import os, sys

fileno = sys.stdin.fileno()

tty.setraw(fileno)
print raw_input("raw input: ")

tty.setcbreak(fileno)
print raw_input("cbreak input: ")

os.system("stty sane") # ...
```

Example 12-9. Using the tty Module (continued)

```
raw input: this is raw input
cbreak input: this is cbreak input
```

The resource Module

(Unix only, Optional) The resource module is used to query or modify the system resource current settings limits. Example 12-10 shows how to use the module to query, and Example 12-11 shows how to modify resource limits.

Example 12-10. Using the resource Module to Query Current Settings

```
File: resource-example-1.py

import resource

print "usage stats", "=>", resource.getrusage(resource.RUSAGE_SELF)
print "max cpu", "=>", resource.getrlimit(resource.RLIMIT_CPU)
print "max data", "=>", resource.getrlimit(resource.RLIMIT_DATA)
print "max processes", "=>", resource.getrlimit(resource.RLIMIT_NPROC)
print "page size", "=>", resource.getpagesize()
```

```
usage stats => (0.03, 0.02, 0, 0, 0, 0, 75, 168, 0, 0, 0, 0, 0, 0, 0, 0)
max cpu => (2147483647, 2147483647)
max data => (2147483647, 2147483647)
max processes => (256, 256)
page size => 4096
```

Example 12-11. Using the resource Module to Limit Resources

```
File: resource-example-2.py

import resource

resource.setrlimit(resource.RLIMIT_CPU, (0, 1))

# pretend we're busy
for i in range(1000):
    for j in range(1000):
        for k in range(1000):
            pass
```

```
CPU time limit exceeded
```

The syslog Module

(Unix only, Optional) The syslog module sends messages to the system logger facility (syslogd). Exactly what happens to these messages is system-dependent, but they usually end up in a log file named */var/log/messages, /var/adm/syslog,* or some variation thereof. (If you cannot find it, check with your system administrator.) Example 12-12 demonstrates.

Example 12-12. Using the syslog Module

```
File: syslog-example-1.py

import syslog
import sys

syslog.openlog(sys.argv[0])

syslog.syslog(syslog.LOG_NOTICE, "a log notice")
syslog.syslog(syslog.LOG_NOTICE, "another log notice: %s" % "watch out!")

syslog.closelog()
```

The msvcrt Module

(Windows/DOS only) The msvcrt module gives you access to a number of functions in the Microsoft Visual C/C++ Runtime Library (MSVCRT).

Example 12-13 demonstrates the getch function reading a single keypress from the console.

Example 12-13. Using the msvcrt Module to Get Key Presses

```
File: msvcrt-example-1.py

import msvcrt

print "press 'escape' to quit..."

while 1:
    char = msvcrt.getch()
    if char == chr(27):
        break
    print char,
    if char == chr(13):
        print
```

```
press 'escape' to quit...
h e l l o
```

The kbhit function returns true if a key has been pressed (which means that getch won't block), as shown in Example 12-14.

Example 12-14. Using the msvcrt Module to Poll the Keyboard

```
File: msvcrt-example-2.py

import msvcrt
import time

print "press SPACE to enter the serial number"

while not msvcrt.kbhit() or msvcrt.getch() != " ":
    # do something else
    print ".",
    time.sleep(0.1)

print

# clear the keyboard buffer
while msvcrt.kbhit():
    msvcrt.getch()

serial = raw_input("enter your serial number: ")

print "serial number is", serial
```

press SPACE to enter the serial number
. . . . .
enter your serial number: 10
serial number is 10

The `locking` function in Example 12-15 can be used to implement cross-process file locking under Windows.

Example 12-15. Using the msvcrt Module for File Locking

```
File: msvcrt-example-3.py

import msvcrt
import os

LK_UNLCK = 0 # unlock the file region
LK_LOCK = 1 # lock the file region
LK_NBLCK = 2 # non-blocking lock
LK_RLCK = 3 # lock for writing
LK_NBRLCK = 4 # non-blocking lock for writing

FILE = "counter.txt"

if not os.path.exists(FILE):
    file = open(FILE, "w")
    file.write("0")
    file.close()

for i in range(20):
    file = open(FILE, "r+")
```

Example 12-15. Using the msvcrt Module for File Locking (continued)

```
    # look from current position (0) to end of file
    msvcrt.locking(file.fileno(), LK_LOCK, os.path.getsize(FILE))
    counter = int(file.readline()) + 1
    file.seek(0)
    file.write(str(counter))
    file.close() # unlocks the file
    print os.getpid(), "=>", counter
    time.sleep(0.1)
```

```
208 => 21
208 => 22
208 => 23
208 => 24
208 => 25
208 => 26
```

The nt Module

(Implementation, Windows only) The nt module is an implementation module used by the os module on Windows platforms. There's hardly any reason to use this module directly; use os instead. Example 12-16 shows its use.

Example 12-16. Using the nt Module

```
File: nt-example-1.py

import nt

# in real life, use os.listdir and os.stat instead!
for file in nt.listdir("."):
    print file, nt.stat(file)[6]
```

```
aifc-example-1.py 314
anydbm-example-1.py 259
array-example-1.py 48
```

The _winreg Module

(Windows only, New in 2.0) The _winreg module provides a basic interface to the Windows registry database. Example 12-17 demonstrates the module.

Example 12-17. Using the _winreg Module

```
File: winreg-example-1.py

import _winreg

explorer = _winreg.OpenKey(
    _winreg.HKEY_CURRENT_USER,
    "Software\\Microsoft\\Windows\CurrentVersion\\Explorer"
```

Example 12-17. Using the _winreg Module (continued)

```
    )

#list values owned by this registry key
try:
    i = 0
    while 1:
      name, value, type= _winreg.EnumValue(explorer, i)
      print repr(name),
      i += 1
except WindowsError:
    print

value, type = _winreg.QueryValueEx(explorer, "Logon User Name")

print
print "user is", repr(value)
```

'Logon User Name' 'CleanShutdown' 'ShellState' 'Shutdown Setting'
'Reason Setting' 'FaultCount' 'FaultTime' 'IconUnderline'...

user is u'Effbot'

The posix Module

(Implementation, Unix/POSIX only) The `posix` module is an implementation module used by the `os` module on Unix and other POSIX systems. While everything in here can be (and should be) accessed via the `os` module, you may wish to explicitly refer to this module in situations where you want to make it clear that you expect POSIX behavior. Example 12-18 demonstrates.

Example 12-18. Using the posix Module

File: posix-example-1.py

```
import posix

for file in posix.listdir("."):
    print file, posix.stat(file)[6]
```

aifc-example-1.py 314
anydbm-example-1.py 259
array-example-1.py 48

13

Implementation Support Modules

The dospath Module

The dospath module, shown in Example 13-1, provides os.path functionality on DOS platforms. You can also use it to handle DOS paths on other platforms.

Example 13-1. Using the dospath Module

```
File: dospath-example-1.py

import dospath

file = "/my/little/pony"

print "isabs", "=>", dospath.isabs(file)
print "dirname", "=>", dospath.dirname(file)
print "basename", "=>", dospath.basename(file)
print "normpath", "=>", dospath.normpath(file)
print "split", "=>", dospath.split(file)
print "join", "=>", dospath.join(file, "zorba")

isabs => 1
dirname => /my/little
basename => pony
normpath => \my\little\pony
split => ('/my/little', 'pony')
join => /my/little/pony\zorba
```

Note that Python's DOS support can use both forward (/) and backward slashes (\) as directory separators.

The macpath Module

The macpath module (see Example 13-2) provides os.path functionality on Macintosh platforms. You can also use it to handle Macintosh paths on other platforms.

Example 13-2. Using the macpath Module

```
File: macpath-example-1.py

import macpath

file = "my:little:pony"

print "isabs", "=>", macpath.isabs(file)
print "dirname", "=>", macpath.dirname(file)
print "basename", "=>", macpath.basename(file)
print "normpath", "=>", macpath.normpath(file)
print "split", "=>", macpath.split(file)
print "join", "=>", macpath.join(file, "zorba")

isabs => 1
dirname => my:little
basename => pony
normpath => my:little:pony
split => ('my:little', 'pony')
join => my:little:pony:zorba
```

The ntpath Module

The ntpath module (see Example 13-3) provides os.path functionality on Windows platforms. You can also use it to handle Windows paths on other platforms.

Example 13-3. Using the ntpath Module

```
File: ntpath-example-1.py

import ntpath

file = "/my/little/pony"

print "isabs", "=>", ntpath.isabs(file)
print "dirname", "=>", ntpath.dirname(file)
print "basename", "=>", ntpath.basename(file)
print "normpath", "=>", ntpath.normpath(file)
print "split", "=>", ntpath.split(file)
print "join", "=>", ntpath.join(file, "zorba")

isabs => 1
dirname => /my/little
basename => pony
```

Example 13-3. Using the ntpath Module (continued)

```
normpath => \my\little\pony
split => ('/my/little', 'pony')
join => /my/little/pony\zorba
```

Note that this module treats both forward slashes (/) and backward slashes (\) as directory separators.

The posixpath Module

The posixpath module, shown in Example 13-4, provides os.path functionality on Unix and other POSIX-compatible platforms. You can also use it to handle POSIX paths on other platforms. In addition, it can be used to process URLs.

Example 13-4. Using the posixpath Module

```
File: posixpath-example-1.py

import posixpath

file = "/my/little/pony"

print "isabs", "=>", posixpath.isabs(file)
print "dirname", "=>", posixpath.dirname(file)
print "basename", "=>", posixpath.basename(file)
print "normpath", "=>", posixpath.normpath(file)
print "split", "=>", posixpath.split(file)
print "join", "=>", posixpath.join(file, "zorba")

isabs => 1
dirname => /my/little
basename => pony
normpath => /my/little/pony
split => ('/my/little', 'pony')
join => /my/little/pony/zorba
```

The strop Module

(Obsolete) The strop is a low-level module that provides fast C implementations of most functions in the string module. It is automatically included by string, so there's seldom any need to access it directly.

However, one reason to use this module is if you need to tweak the path *before* you start loading Python modules. Example 13-5 demonstrates the module.

Example 13-5. Using the strop Module

```
File: strop-example-1.py

import strop
import sys

# assuming we have an executable named ".../executable", add a
# directory named ".../executable-extra" to the path

if strop.lower(sys.executable)[-4:] == ".exe":
    extra = sys.executable[:-4] # windows
else:
    extra = sys.executable

sys.path.insert(0, extra + "-extra")

import mymodule
```

In Python 2.0 and later, you should use string methods instead of `strop`. In Example 13-5, replace "`strop.lower(sys.executable)`" with "`sys.executable.lower()`."

The imp Module

The `imp` module contains functions that can be used to implement your own `import` behavior. Example 13-6 overloads the import statement with a version that logs from where it gets the modules.

Example 13-6. Using the imp Module

```
File: imp-example-1.py

import imp
import sys

def my_import(name, globals=None, locals=None, fromlist=None):
    try:
        module = sys.modules[name] # already imported?
    except KeyError:
        file, pathname, description = imp.find_module(name)
        print "import", name, "from", pathname, description
        module = imp.load_module(name, file, pathname, description)
    return module

import __builtin__
__builtin__.__import__ = my_import

import xmllib

import xmllib from /python/lib/xmllib.py ('.py', 'r', 1)
import re from /python/lib/re.py ('.py', 'r', 1)
```

Example 13-6. Using the imp Module (continued)

```
import sre from /python/lib/sre.py ('.py', 'r', 1)
import sre_compile from /python/lib/sre_compile.py ('.py', 'r', 1)
import _sre from /python/_sre.pyd ('.pyd', 'rb', 3)
```

Note that the alternative version shown here doesn't support packages. For a more extensive example, see the sources for the knee module.

The new Module

(Optional in 1.5.2) The new modules is a low-level module that allows you to create various kinds of internal objects, such as class objects, function objects, and other kinds that are usually created by the Python runtime system. Example 13-7 demonstrates this module.

Note that if you're using 1.5.2, you may have to rebuild Python to use this module; it isn't enabled by the default on all platforms. In 2.0 and later, however, it's always available.

Example 13-7. Using the new Module

```
File: new-example-1.py

import new

class Sample:

    a = "default"

    def __init__(self):
        self.a = "initialised"

    def __repr__(self):
        return self.a

#
# create instances

a = Sample()
print "normal", "=>", a

b = new.instance(Sample, {})
print "new.instance", "=>", b

b.__init__()
print "after __init__", "=>", b

c = new.instance(Sample, {"a": "assigned"})
print "new.instance w. dictionary", "=>", c

normal => initialised
```

Example 13-7. Using the new Module (continued)

```
new.instance => default
after _ _init_ _ => initialised
new.instance w. dictionary => assigned
```

The pre Module

(Implementation) The pre module, used in Example 13-8, is a low-level implementation module for the 1.5.2 re module. There's usually no need to use this module directly (and code using it may stop working in future releases).

Example 13-8. Using the pre Module

```
File: pre-example-1.py

import pre

p = pre.compile("[Python]+")

print p.findall("Python is not that bad")

['Python', 'not', 'th', 't']
```

The sre Module

(Implementation) The sre module, used in Example 13-9, is a low-level implementation module for the 2.0 re module. There's usually no need to use this module directly (and code using it may stop working in future releases).

Example 13-9. Using the sre Module

```
File: sre-example-1.py

import sre

text = "The Bookshop Sketch"

# a single character
m = sre.match(".", text)
if m: print repr("."), "=>", repr(m.group(0))

# and so on, for all 're' examples...

'.' => 'T'
```

The py_compile Module

The py_compile module, shown in Example 13-10, allows you to explicitly compile Python modules to bytecode. It behaves like Python's import statement, but takes a filename, not a module name.

Example 13-10. Using the py_compile Module

```
File: py-compile-example-1.py

import py_compile

# explicitly compile this module
py_compile.compile("py-compile-example-1.py")
```

The compileall module can be used to compile all Python files in an entire directory tree.

The compileall Module

The compileall module (see Example 13-11) contains functions to compile all Python scripts in a given directory (or along the Python path) to byte code. It can also be used as a script (on Unix platforms, it's automatically run when Python is installed).

Example 13-11. Using the compileall Module to Compile All Scripts in a Directory

```
File: compileall-example-1.py

import compileall

print "This may take a while!"

compileall.compile_dir(".", force=1)

This may take a while!
Listing . ...
Compiling .\SimpleAsyncHTTP.py ...
Compiling .\aifc-example-1.py ...
Compiling .\anydbm-example-1.py ...
...
```

The ihooks Module

The ihooks module, shown in Example 13-12, provides a framework for import replacements. The idea is to allow several alternate import mechanisms to coexist.

Example 13-12. Using the ihooks Module

```
File: ihooks-example-1.py

import ihooks, imp, os

def import_from(filename):
    "Import module from a named file"

    loader = ihooks.BasicModuleLoader()
    path, file = os.path.split(filename)
    name, ext  = os.path.splitext(file)
    m = loader.find_module_in_dir(name, path)
    if not m:
        raise ImportError, name
    m = loader.load_module(name, m)
    return m

colorsys = import_from("/python/lib/colorsys.py")

print colorsys
```

<module 'colorsys' from '/python/lib/colorsys.py'>

The linecache Module

The linecache module in Example 13-13 is used to read lines from module source code. It caches recently visited modules (the entire source file, actually).

Example 13-13. Using the linecache module

```
File: linecache-example-1.py

import linecache

print linecache.getline("linecache-example-1.py", 5)
```

print linecache.getline("linecache-example-1.py", 5)

This module is used by the traceback module.

The macurl2path Module

(Implementation) The macurl2path module, shown in Example 13-14, contains code to map between URLs and Macintosh filenames. It should not be used directly; use the mechanisms in urllib instead.

Example 13-14. Using the macurl2path Module

File: macurl2path-example-1.py

```
import macurl2path

file = ":my:little:pony"

print macurl2path.pathname2url(file)
print macurl2path.url2pathname(macurl2path.pathname2url(file))
```

my/little/pony
:my:little:pony

The nturl2path module

(Implementation) The nturl2path module, shown in Example 13-15, contains code
to map between URLs and Windows filenames.

Example 13-15. Using the nturl2path Module

File: nturl2path-example-1.py

```
import nturl2path

file = r"c:\my\little\pony"

print nturl2path.pathname2url(file)
print nturl2path.url2pathname(nturl2path.pathname2url(file))
```

///C|/my/little/pony
C:\my\little\pony

This module should not be used directly; for portability, access these functions via
the urllib module instead, as shown in Example 13-16.

Example 13-16. Using the nturl2path Module via the urllib Module

File: nturl2path-example-2.py

```
import urllib

file = r"c:\my\little\pony"

print urllib.pathname2url(file)
print urllib.url2pathname(urllib.pathname2url(file))
```

///C|/my/little/pony
C:\my\little\pony

The tokenize Module

s The `tokenize` module splits a Python source file into individual tokens. It can be used for syntax highlighting or for various kinds of code-analysis tools.

In Example 13-17, we simply print the tokens.

Example 13-17. Using the tokenize Module

```
File: tokenize-example-1.py

import tokenize

file = open("tokenize-example-1.py")

def handle_token(type, token, (srow, scol), (erow, ecol), line):
    print "%d,%d-%d,%d:\t%s\t%s" % \
        (srow, scol, erow, ecol, tokenize.tok_name[type], repr(token))

tokenize.tokenize(
    file.readline,
    handle_token
    )

1,0-1,6:     NAME      'import'
1,7-1,15:    NAME      'tokenize'
1,15-1,16:   NEWLINE   '
'
2,0-2,1:     NL        '
'
3,0-3,4:     NAME      'file'
3,5-3,6:     OP        '='
3,7-3,11:    NAME      'open'
3,11-3,12:   OP        '('
3,12-3,35:   STRING    '"tokenize-example-1.py"'
3,35-3,36:   OP        ')'
3,36-3,37:   NEWLINE   '
'
...
```

Note that the `tokenize` function takes two callable objects: the first argument is called repeatedly to fetch new code lines, and the second argument is called for each token.

The keyword Module

The `keyword` module (see Example 13-18) contains a list of the keywords used in the current version of Python. It also provides a dictionary with the keywords as keys, and a predicate function that can be used to check if a given word is a Python keyword.

Example 13-18. Using the keyword Module

```
File: keyword-example-1.py

import keyword

name = raw_input("Enter module name: ")

if keyword.iskeyword(name):
    print name, "is a reserved word."
    print "here's a complete list of reserved words:"
    print keyword.kwlist
```

Enter module name: assert
assert is a reserved word.
here's a complete list of reserved words:
['and', 'assert', 'break', 'class', 'continue', 'def', 'del',
'elif', 'else', 'except', 'exec', 'finally', 'for', 'from',
'global', 'if', 'import', 'in', 'is', 'lambda', 'not', 'or',
'pass', 'print', 'raise', 'return', 'try', 'while']

The parser Module

(Optional) The parser module provides an interface to Python's built-in parser and compiler.

Example 13-19 compiles a simple expression into an *abstract syntax tree* (AST), turns the AST into a nested list, dumps the contents of the tree (where each node contains either a grammar symbol or a token), increments all numbers by one, and, finally, turns the list back into a code object. At least that's what I think it does.

Example 13-19. Using the parser Module

```
File: parser-example-1.py

import parser
import symbol, token

def dump_and_modify(node):
    name = symbol.sym_name.get(node[0])
    if name is None:
        name = token.tok_name.get(node[0])
    print name,
    for i in range(1, len(node)):
        item = node[i]
        if type(item) is type([]):
            dump_and_modify(item)
        else:
            print repr(item)
            if name == "NUMBER":
                # increment all numbers!
```

Example 13-19. Using the parser Module (continued)

```
                node[i] = repr(int(item)+1)

ast = parser.expr("1 + 3")

list = ast.tolist()

dump_and_modify(list)

ast = parser.sequence2ast(list)

print eval(parser.compileast(ast))

eval_input testlist test and_test not_test comparison
expr xor_expr and_expr shift_expr arith_expr term factor
power atom NUMBER '1'
PLUS '+'
term factor power atom NUMBER '3'
NEWLINE ''
ENDMARKER ''
6
```

The symbol Module

The symbol module, used in Example 13-20, contains a listing of non-terminal symbols from the Python grammar. It's probably only useful if you're dabbling with the parser module.

Example 13-20. Using the symbol Module

```
File: symbol-example-1.py

import symbol

print "print", symbol.print_stmt
print "return", symbol.return_stmt

print 268
return 274
```

The token Module

The token module, shown in Example 13-21, contains a list of all tokens used by the standard Python tokenizer.

Example 13-21. Using the token Module

```
File: token-example-1.py

import token
```

Example 13-21. Using the token Module (continued)

```
print "NUMBER", token.NUMBER
print "PLUS", token.STAR
print "STRING", token.STRING
```

NUMBER 2
PLUS 16
STRING 3

14

Other Modules

Overview

This chapter describes a number of less-common modules. Some are useful, others are quite obscure, and some are just plain obsolete.

The pyclbr Module

The pyclbr module, shown in Example 14-1, contains a basic Python class parser.

In 1.5.2, the module exports a single function, readmodule, which parses a given module, and returns a list of all classes defined at the module's top level.

Example 14-1. Using the pyclbr Module

```
File: pyclbr-example-1.py

import pyclbr

mod = pyclbr.readmodule("cgi")

for k, v in mod.items():
    print k, v
```

```
MiniFieldStorage <pyclbr.Class instance at 7873b0>
InterpFormContentDict <pyclbr.Class instance at 79bd00>
FieldStorage <pyclbr.Class instance at 790e20>
SvFormContentDict <pyclbr.Class instance at 79b5e0>
StringIO <pyclbr.Class instance at 77dd90>
FormContent <pyclbr.Class instance at 79bd60>
FormContentDict <pyclbr.Class instance at 79a9c0>
```

In 2.0 and later, there's also an alternative interface, readmodule_ex, which returns global functions as well. This is shown in Example 14-2.

Example 14-2. Using the pyclbr Module to Read Classes and Functions

```
File: pyclbr-example-3.py

import pyclbr

# 2.0 and later
mod = pyclbr.readmodule_ex("cgi")

for k, v in mod.items():
    print k, v
```

```
MiniFieldStorage <pyclbr.Class instance at 00905D2C>
parse_header <pyclbr.Function instance at 00905BD4>
test <pyclbr.Function instance at 00906FBC>
print_environ_usage <pyclbr.Function instance at 00907C94>
parse_multipart <pyclbr.Function instance at 00905294>
FormContentDict <pyclbr.Class instance at 008D3494>
initlog <pyclbr.Function instance at 00904AAC>
parse <pyclbr.Function instance at 00904EFC>
StringIO <pyclbr.Class instance at 00903EAC>
SvFormContentDict <pyclbr.Class instance at 00906824>
...
```

To get more information about each class, use the various attributes in the *Class* instances, as Example 14-3 shows.

Example 14-3. Using the pyclbr Module

```
File: pyclbr-example-2.py

import pyclbr
import string

mod = pyclbr.readmodule("cgi")

def dump(c):
    # print class header
    s = "class " + c.name
    if c.super:
        s = s +  "(" + string.join(map(lambda v: v.name, c.super), ", ") + ")"
    print s + ":"
    # print method names, sorted by line number
    methods = c.methods.items()
    methods.sort(lambda a, b: cmp(a[1], b[1]))
    for method, lineno in methods:
        print "  def " + method
    print

for k, v in mod.items():
    dump(v)
```

```
class MiniFieldStorage:
  def __init__
```

Example 14-3. Using the pyclbr Module (continued)

```
def _ _repr_ _

class InterpFormContentDict(SvFormContentDict):
  def _ _getitem_ _
  def values
  def items
```

. . .

The filecmp Module

(New in 2.0) The `filecmp` module, shown in Example 14-4, contains functions to compare files and directories.

Example 14-4. Using the filecmp Module

```
File: filecmp-example-1.py

import filecmp

if filecmp.cmp("samples/sample.au", "samples/sample.wav"):
    print "files are identical"
else:
    print "files differ!"

# files differ!
```

In 1.5.2 and earlier, you can use the `cmp` and `dircmp` modules instead.

The cmd Module

The `cmd` module (see Example 14-5) provides a simple framework for command-line interfaces (CLI). This is used by the `pdb` debugger module, but you can also use it for your own programs.

To implement your own command-line interface, subclass the *Cmd* class, and define `do` and `help` methods. The base class automatically turns all `do` methods into commands and uses the `help` methods to show help information.

Example 14-5. Using the cmd Module

```
File: cmd-example-1.py

import cmd
import string, sys

class CLI(cmd.Cmd):

    def _ _init_ _(self):
```

Example 14-5. Using the cmd Module (continued)

```
        cmd.Cmd.__init__(self)
        self.prompt = '> '

    def do_hello(self, arg):
        print "hello again", arg, "!"

    def help_hello(self):
        print "syntax: hello [message]",
        print "-- prints a hello message"

    def do_quit(self, arg):
        sys.exit(1)

    def help_quit(self):
        print "syntax: quit",
        print "-- terminates the application"

    # shortcuts
    do_q = do_quit

#
# try it out

cli = CLI()
cli.cmdloop()

> help

Documented commands (type help <topic>):
========================================
hello           quit

Undocumented commands:
======================
help            q

> hello world
hello again world !
> q
```

The rexec Module

The rexec module, shown in Example 14-6, provides versions of exec, eval, and import, which execute code in a restricted execution environment. In this environment, functions that can damage resources on the local machine are no longer available.

Example 14-6. Using the rexec Module

```
File: rexec-example-1.py

import rexec

r = rexec.RExec()
print r.r_eval("1+2+3")
print r.r_eval("__import__('os').remove('file')")
```

```
6
Traceback (innermost last):
  File "rexec-example-1.py", line 5, in ?
    print r.r_eval("__import__('os').remove('file')")
  File "/usr/local/lib/python1.5/rexec.py", line 257, in r_eval
    return eval(code, m.__dict__)
  File "<string>", line 0, in ?
AttributeError: remove
```

The Bastion Module

The Bastion module, shown in Example 14-7, allows you to control how a given object is used. It can be used to pass objects from unrestricted parts of your application to code running in restricted mode.

To create a restricted instance, simply call the Bastion wrapper. By default, all instance variables are hidden, as well as all methods that start with an underscore.

Example 14-7. Using the Bastion Module

```
File: bastion-example-1.py

import Bastion

class Sample:
    value = 0

    def _set(self, value):
        self.value = value

    def setvalue(self, value):
        if 10 < value <= 20:
            self._set(value)
        else:
            raise ValueError, "illegal value"

    def getvalue(self):
        return self.value

#
# try it

s = Sample()
```

Example 14-7. Using the Bastion Module (continued)

```
s._set(100) # cheat
print s.getvalue()

s = Bastion.Bastion(Sample())
s._set(100) # attempt to cheat
print s.getvalue()

100
Traceback (innermost last):
...
AttributeError: _set
```

You can control which functions to publish. In Example 14-8, the internal method can be called from outside, but the getvalue no longer works.

Example 14-8. Using the Bastion Module with a Non-Standard Filter

```
File: bastion-example-2.py

import Bastion

class Sample:
    value = 0

    def _set(self, value):
        self.value = value

    def setvalue(self, value):
        if 10 < value <= 20:
            self._set(value)
        else:
            raise ValueError, "illegal value"

    def getvalue(self):
        return self.value

#
# try it

def is_public(name):
    return name[:3] != "get"

s = Bastion.Bastion(Sample(), is_public)
s._set(100) # this works
print s.getvalue() # but not this

100
Traceback (innermost last):
...
AttributeError: getvalue
```

The readline Module

(Optional) The `readline` module, shown in Example 14-9, activates input editing on Unix, using the GNU readline library (or compatible).

Once imported, this module provides improved command-line editing, as well as command history. It also enhances the `input` and `raw_input` functions.

Example 14-9. Using the readline Module

```
File: readline-example-1.py

import readline # activate readline editing
```

The rlcompleter Module

(Optional, Unix only) The `rlcompleter` module provides word completion for the `readline` module.

To enable word completion, just import this module. By default, the completion function is bound to the Esc key. Press Esc twice to finish the current word. To change the key, you can use something like:

```
import readline
readline.parse_and_bind("tab: complete")
```

The script in Example 14-10 shows how to use the completion functions from within a program.

Example 14-10. Using the rlcompleter Module to Expand Names

```
File: rlcompleter-example-1.py

import rlcompleter
import sys

completer = rlcompleter.Completer()

for phrase in "co", "sys.p", "is":
    print phrase, "=>",
    # emulate readline completion handler
    try:
        for index in xrange(sys.maxint):
            term = completer.complete(phrase, index)
            if term is None:
                break
            print term,
    except:
        pass
    print
```

Example 14-10. Using the rlcompleter Module to Expand Names (continued)

```
co => continue compile complex coerce completer
sys.p => sys.path sys.platform sys.prefix
is => is isinstance issubclass
```

The statvfs Module

The statvfs module, used in Example 14-11, contains a number of constants and test functions that can be used with the optional os.statvfs function, which returns information about a filesystem.

Example 14-11. Using the statvfs Module

```
File: statvfs-example-1.py

import statvfs
import os

st = os.statvfs(".")

print "preferred block size", "=>", st[statvfs.F_BSIZE]
print "fundamental block size", "=>", st[statvfs.F_FRSIZE]
print "total blocks", "=>", st[statvfs.F_BLOCKS]
print "total free blocks", "=>", st[statvfs.F_BFREE]
print "available blocks", "=>", st[statvfs.F_BAVAIL]
print "total file nodes", "=>", st[statvfs.F_FILES]
print "total free nodes", "=>", st[statvfs.F_FFREE]
print "available nodes", "=>", st[statvfs.F_FAVAIL]
print "max file name length", "=>", st[statvfs.F_NAMEMAX]

preferred block size => 8192
fundamental block size => 1024
total blocks => 749443
total free blocks => 110442
available blocks => 35497
total file nodes => 92158
total free nodes => 68164
available nodes => 68164
max file name length => 255
```

The calendar Module

The calendar module is a Python reimplementation of the Unix *cal* command. It simply prints the calendar for any given month or year to standard output.

In Example 14-12, `prmonth(year, month)` prints the calendar for a given month.

Example 14-12. Using the calendar Module

File: `calendar-example-1.py`

```
import calendar
calendar.prmonth(1999, 12)
```

```
     December 1999
 Mo Tu We Th Fr Sa Su
        1  2  3  4  5
  6  7  8  9 10 11 12
 13 14 15 16 17 18 19
 20 21 22 23 24 25 26
 27 28 29 30 31
```

In Example 14-13, `prcal(year)` prints the calendar for a given year.

Example 14-13. Using the calendar Module

File: `calendar-example-2.py`

```
import calendar
calendar.prcal(2000)
```

```
                                  2000

       January                 February                   March
 Mo Tu We Th Fr Sa Su    Mo Tu We Th Fr Sa Su    Mo Tu We Th Fr Sa Su
                 1  2           1  2  3  4  5  6           1  2  3  4  5
  3  4  5  6  7  8  9     7  8  9 10 11 12 13     6  7  8  9 10 11 12
 10 11 12 13 14 15 16    14 15 16 17 18 19 20    13 14 15 16 17 18 19
 17 18 19 20 21 22 23    21 22 23 24 25 26 27    20 21 22 23 24 25 26
 24 25 26 27 28 29 30    28 29                   27 28 29 30 31
 31

        April                     May                      June
 Mo Tu We Th Fr Sa Su    Mo Tu We Th Fr Sa Su    Mo Tu We Th Fr Sa Su
                 1  2     1  2  3  4  5  6  7              1  2  3  4
  3  4  5  6  7  8  9     8  9 10 11 12 13 14     5  6  7  8  9 10 11
 10 11 12 13 14 15 16    15 16 17 18 19 20 21    12 13 14 15 16 17 18
 17 18 19 20 21 22 23    22 23 24 25 26 27 28    19 20 21 22 23 24 25
 24 25 26 27 28 29 30    29 30 31                26 27 28 29 30

        July                    August                   September
 Mo Tu We Th Fr Sa Su    Mo Tu We Th Fr Sa Su    Mo Tu We Th Fr Sa Su
                 1  2           1  2  3  4  5  6                 1  2  3
  3  4  5  6  7  8  9     7  8  9 10 11 12 13     4  5  6  7  8  9 10
 10 11 12 13 14 15 16    14 15 16 17 18 19 20    11 12 13 14 15 16 17
 17 18 19 20 21 22 23    21 22 23 24 25 26 27    18 19 20 21 22 23 24
 24 25 26 27 28 29 30    28 29 30 31             25 26 27 28 29 30
 31
```

Example 14-13. Using the calendar Module (continued)

```
          October                    November                    December
Mo Tu We Th Fr Sa Su        Mo Tu We Th Fr Sa Su        Mo Tu We Th Fr Sa Su
                   1                 1  2  3  4  5                    1  2  3
 2  3  4  5  6  7  8          6  7  8  9 10 11 12          4  5  6  7  8  9 10
 9 10 11 12 13 14 15         13 14 15 16 17 18 19         11 12 13 14 15 16 17
16 17 18 19 20 21 22         20 21 22 23 24 25 26         18 19 20 21 22 23 24
23 24 25 26 27 28 29         27 28 29 30                 25 26 27 28 29 30 31
30 31
```

Note that the calendars are printed using European conventions; in other words, Monday is the first day of the week.

This module contains a number of support functions that can be useful if you want to output calendars in other formats. It's probably easiest to copy the entire file, and tweak it to suit your needs.

The sched Module

The sched module is a simple event scheduler for non-threaded environments. Example 14-14 demonstrates.

Example 14-14. Using the sched Module

```
File: sched-example-1.py

import sched
import time, sys

scheduler = sched.scheduler(time.time, time.sleep)

# add a few operations to the queue
scheduler.enter(0.5, 100, sys.stdout.write, ("one\n",))
scheduler.enter(1.0, 300, sys.stdout.write, ("three\n",))
scheduler.enter(1.0, 200, sys.stdout.write, ("two\n",))

scheduler.run()

one
two
three
```

The statcache Module

The statcache module, shown in Example 14-15, contains a function that returns information about files. It's an extension of the os.stat function in that it keeps a cache with recently collected information.

Example 14-15. Using the statcache Module

File: statcache-example-1.py

```
import statcache
import os, stat, time

now = time.time()
for i in range(1000):
    st = os.stat("samples/sample.txt")
print "os.stat", "=>", time.time() - now

now = time.time()
for i in range(1000):
    st = statcache.stat("samples/sample.txt")
print "statcache.stat", "=>", time.time() - now

print "mode", "=>", oct(stat.S_IMODE(st[stat.ST_MODE]))
print "size", "=>", st[stat.ST_SIZE]
print "last modified", "=>", time.ctime(st[stat.ST_MTIME])
```

```
os.stat => 0.371000051498
statcache.stat => 0.0199999809265
mode => 0666
size => 305
last modified => Sun Oct 10 18:39:37 1999
```

The grep Module

The grep module provides different ways to search for text in text files, as Example 14-16 shows.

Example 14-16. Using the grep Module

File: grep-example-1.py

```
import grep
import glob

grep.grep("\<rather\>", glob.glob("samples/*.txt"))

# 4: indentation, rather than delimiters, might become
```

The dircache Module

(Obsolete) The dircache module contains a function to get a list of files in a directory. It's an extension of the os.listdir function in that it keeps a cache to avoid rereading a directory that hasn't been modified. Example 14-17 demonstrates this.

Example 14-17. Using the dircache Module

```
File: dircache-example-1.py

import dircache

import os, time

#
# test cached version

t0 = time.clock()

for i in range(100):
    dircache.listdir(os.sep)

print "cached", time.clock() - t0

#
# test standard version

t0 = time.clock()

for i in range(100):
    os.listdir(os.sep)

print "standard", time.clock() - t0

cached 0.0664509964968
standard 0.5560845807
```

The dircmp Module

(Obsolete, Only in 1.5.2) The dircmp module provides a class that can be used to
compare the contents of two disk directories, as Example 14-18 shows.

Example 14-18. Using the dircmp Module

```
File: dircmp-example-1.py

import dircmp

d = dircmp.dircmp()
d.new("samples", "oldsamples")
d.run()
d.report()

diff samples oldsamples
Only in samples : ['sample.aiff', 'sample.au', 'sample.wav']
Identical files : ['sample.gif', 'sample.gz', 'sample.jpg', ...]
```

In Python 2.0 and later, this module has been replaced by filecmp.

The cmp Module

(Obsolete, Only in 1.5.2) The cmp module contains a function to compare two files, as Example 14-19 demonstrates.

Example 14-19. Using the cmp Module

```
File: cmp-example-1.py

import cmp

if cmp.cmp("samples/sample.au", "samples/sample.wav"):
    print "files are identical"
else:
    print "files differ!"
```

files differ!

In Python 2.0 and later, this module has been replaced by the filecmp module.

The cmpcache Module

(Obsolete, Only in 1.5.2) The cmpcache module contains a function that compares two files. It's an extension of the cmp module in that it keeps a cache over recently made comparisons. Example 14-20 shows the module's use.

Example 14-20. Using the cmpcache Module

```
File: cmpcache-example-1.py

import cmpcache

if cmpcache.cmp("samples/sample.au", "samples/sample.wav"):
    print "files are identical"
else:
    print "files differ!"
```

files differ!

In Python 2.0 and later, this module has been replaced by the filecmp module.

The util Module

(Obsolete, Only in 1.5.2) The util module is included for backward-compatibility only. New code should use the replacement constructs shown in Examples 14-21 through 14-23.

Example 14-21 shows how remove(sequence, item) removes the given item, if found in the sequence.

Example 14-21. Emulating the util Module's remove Function

File: util-example-1.py

```
def remove(sequence, item):
    if item in sequence:
        sequence.remove(item)
```

Example 14-22 shows how `readfile(filename)` ⇒ `string` reads the contents of a text file as a single string.

Example 14-22. Emulating the util Module's readfile Function

File: util-example-2.py

```
def readfile(filename):
    file = open(filename, "r")
    return file.read()
```

Example 14-23 shows how `readopenfile(file)` ⇒ `string` returns the contents of an open file (or other file object).

Example 14-23. Emulating the util Module's readopenfile Function

File: util-example-3.py

```
def readopenfile(file):
    return file.read()
```

The soundex Module

(Optional, Only 1.5.2) The `soundex` module implements a simple hash algorithm, which converts words to 6-character strings based on their English pronunciation.

As of Version 2.0, this module is no longer included.

`get_soundex(word)` returns the `soundex` string for the given word. Words that sound similar should give the same `soundex` string. `sound_similar(word1, word2)` returns true if the two words have the same `soundex`. Example 14-24 uses both functions.

Example 14-24. Using the soundex Module

File: soundex-example-1.py

```
import soundex

a = "fredrik"
b = "friedrich"

print soundex.get_soundex(a), soundex.get_soundex(b)
```

Example 14-24. Using the soundex Module (continued)

```
print soundex.sound_similar(a, b)
```

F63620 F63620
1

The timing Module

(Obsolete, Unix only) The `timing` module can be used to time the execution of a
Python program. Example 14-25 demonstrates.

Example 14-25. Using the timing Module

```
File: timing-example-1.py

import timing
import time

def procedure():
    time.sleep(1.234)

timing.start()
procedure()
timing.finish()

print "seconds:", timing.seconds()
print "milliseconds:", timing.milli()
print "microseconds:", timing.micro()
```

seconds: 1
milliseconds: 1239
microseconds: 1239999

The script in Example 14-26 shows how you can emulate this module using functions in the standard `time` module.

Example 14-26. Emulating the timing Module

```
File: timing-example-2.py

import time

t0 = t1 = 0

def start():
    global t0
    t0 = time.time()
```

Example 14-26. Emulating the timing Module (continued)

```
def finish():
    global t1
    t1 = time.time()

def seconds():
    return int(t1 - t0)

def milli():
    return int((t1 - t0) * 1000)

def micro():
    return int((t1 - t0) * 1000000)
```

You can use `time.clock()` instead of `time.time()` to get CPU time, where supported.

The posixfile Module

(Obsolete, Unix only) The `posixfile` module provides a file-like object with support for file locking, as Example 14-27 shows. New programs should use the `fcntl` module instead.

Example 14-27. Using the posixfile Module

```
File: posixfile-example-1.py

import posixfile
import string

filename = "counter.txt"

try:
    # open for update
    file = posixfile.open(filename, "r+")
    counter = int(file.read(6)) + 1
except IOError:
    # create it
    file = posixfile.open(filename, "w")
    counter = 0

file.lock("w|", 6)

file.seek(0) # rewind
file.write("%06d" % counter)

file.close() # releases lock
```

The bisect Module

The bisect module provides functions to insert items in sorted sequences.

insort(sequence, item) inserts an item into the sequence, keeping it sorted. The sequence can be any mutable sequence object that implements _ _getitem_ _ and insert; Example 14-28 demonstrates.

Example 14-28. Using the bisect Module to Insert Items in an Ordered List

```
File: bisect-example-1.py

import bisect

list = [10, 20, 30]

bisect.insort(list, 25)
bisect.insort(list, 15)

print list
```

[10, 15, 20, 25, 30]

In Example 14-29, bisect(sequence, item) ⇒ index returns the index where the item should be inserted. The sequence is not modified.

Example 14-29. Using the bisect Module to Find Insertion Points

```
File: bisect-example-2.py

import bisect

list = [10, 20, 30]

print list
print bisect.bisect(list, 25)
print bisect.bisect(list, 15)
```

[10, 20, 30]
2
1

The knee Module

The knee module is a Python reimplementation of the package import mechanism that was introduced in Python 1.5. Since this is already supported by the standard interpreter, this module is mainly provided to show how things are done in there. It does work, though. Just import the module to enable it, as Example 14-30 shows.

Example 14-30. Using the knee Module

```
File: knee-example-1.py

import knee

# that's all, folks!
```

The tzparse Module

(Obsolete) The (highly incomplete) tzparse module contains a parser for time zone specifications. When you import this module, it parses the content of the TZ environment variable; Example 14-31 demonstrates.

Example 14-31. Using the tzparse Module

```
File: tzparse-example-1.py

import os
if not os.environ.has_key("TZ"):
    # set it to something...
    os.environ["TZ"] = "EST+5EDT;100/2,300/2"

# importing this module will parse the TZ variable
import tzparse

print "tzparams", "=>", tzparse.tzparams
print "timezone", "=>", tzparse.timezone
print "altzone", "=>", tzparse.altzone
print "daylight", "=>", tzparse.daylight
print "tzname", "=>", tzparse.tzname

tzparams => ('EST', 5, 'EDT', 100, 2, 300, 2)
timezone => 18000
altzone => 14400
daylight => 1
tzname => ('EST', 'EDT')
```

In addition to the variables shown in Example 14-31, this module contains a number of time manipulation functions that use the defined time zone.

The regex Module

(Obsolete) The regex module, shown in Example 14-32, is the old (pre-1.5) regular expression machinery. New code should use re where possible.

Note that regex is faster than the re module used in Python 1.5.2, but slower than the new version used in 1.6 and later.

Example 14-32. Using the regex Module

```
File: regex-example-1.py

import regex

text = "Man's crisis of identity in the latter half of the 20th century"

p = regex.compile("latter") # literal
print p.match(text)
print p.search(text), repr(p.group(0))

p = regex.compile("[0-9]+") # number
print p.search(text), repr(p.group(0))

p = regex.compile("\<\w\w\>") # two-letter word
print p.search(text), repr(p.group(0))

p = regex.compile("\w+$") # word at the end
print p.search(text), repr(p.group(0))

-1
32 'latter'
51 '20'
13 'of'
56 'century'
```

The regsub Module

(Obsolete) The `regsub` module, shown in Example 14-33, provides string replacements, based on regular expressions. New code should use the `re` module's `replace` function instead.

Example 14-33. Using the regsub Module

```
File: regsub-example-1.py

import regsub

text = "Well, there's spam, egg, sausage, and spam."

print regsub.sub("spam", "ham", text) # just the first
print regsub.gsub("spam", "bacon", text) # all of them

Well, there's ham, egg, sausage, and spam.
Well, there's bacon, egg, sausage, and bacon.
```

The reconvert Module

(Obsolete) The `reconvert` module, shown in Example 14-34, converts old-style regular expressions as used by the `regex` module to the new style used by the `re` module. It can also be used as a command-line tool.

Example 14-34. Using the reconvert Module

```
File: reconvert-example-1.py

import reconvert

for pattern in "abcd", "a\(b*c\)d", "\<\w+\>":
    print pattern, "=>", reconvert.convert(pattern)

abcd => abcd
a\(b*c\)d => a(b*c)d
\<\w+\> => \b\w+\b
```

The regex_syntax Module

(Obsolete) The `regex_syntax` module, shown in Example 14-35, contains a bunch of flags that can be used to change the behavior of the `regex` regular expression module.

Example 14-35. Using the regex_syntax Module

```
File: regex-syntax-example-1.py

import regex_syntax
import regex

def compile(pattern, syntax):
    syntax = regex.set_syntax(syntax)
    try:
        pattern = regex.compile(pattern)
    finally:
        # restore original syntax
        regex.set_syntax(syntax)
    return pattern

def compile_awk(pattern):
    return compile(pattern, regex_syntax.RE_SYNTAX_AWK)

def compile_grep(pattern):
    return compile(pattern, regex_syntax.RE_SYNTAX_GREP)

def compile_emacs(pattern):
    return compile(pattern, regex_syntax.RE_SYNTAX_EMACS)
```

The find Module

(Only 1.5.2, Obsolete) The find module provides a single function, with the same name as the module: find(pattern, directory) $\Rightarrow$ list scans a given directory and all its subdirectories for files matching a given pattern, as Example 14-36 shows.

For more information on the pattern syntax, see the fnmatch module.

Example 14-36. Using the find Module

```
File: find-example-1.py

import find

# find all JPEG files in or beneath the current directory
for file in find.find("*.jpg", "."):
    print file
```

.\samples\sample.jpg

Index

We'd like to hear your suggestions for improving our indexes. Send email to *index@oreilly.com*.

G

gauss function, 81
gdbm module, 217
    anydbm module and, 213
GET request handler, 199
get value method, 69
getcwd function, 21
getgrall function, using grp module, 228
getgrgid function, using grp module, 228
getgrnam function, using grp module, 228
getitem function, 96
_ _getitem_ _ method, 35
getmembers function, 6
getopt module, 76
getpall function, using pwd module, 228
getpass module, 78
getrefcount function, 49
gettime function, 167
ghostscript viewer, using mailcap module, 157
gif file formats, 206
glob module, 78
global interpreter lock, 95
GNU dbm database handler, using gdbm module, 217
gopherlidb module, 188
grep module, 260
groupinfo function, 229
grp module, 228
GZIP formats
    gzip module and, 148
    support for, 127
gzip module, 148

H

handle_accept method, 171
handle_close method, 171
handle_connect method, 171
handle_error(type, value, traceback) method, 171
handle_expt method, 171
handle_read method, 171
handle_write method, 171
Hangul syllable properties, in Python 2.0, 204
HEAD request handler, 199
<header> tag, 125
help methods, 252
helper class for MimeWriter module, 154

hexadecimal strings, converting to/from binary data, 124
HLS color value, using functions for converting to, 212
host platforms, checking, 49
HSV color values, using functions for converting to, 212
HTML (Hypertext Markup Language), 125
htmllib module, 137, 176
htmllib parser, 126
HTTP (Hypertext Transfer Protocol), 164
HTTP servers
    BaseHTTPServer module and, 198
    CGIHTTPServer module and, 200
    posting data to, 189
httplib module, 188-190

I

ihooks module, 243
IMAP (Internet Message Access Protocol), 191
imaplib module, 191
imghdr module, 206
imNumberType function, using operator module, 45
imp module, 240
import behaviors, implementing with imp module, 240
_ _import_ _ function, 4, 214
import statement, 48
ImportError(StandardError), 17
indent methods, adding structure, 15
IndentationError(SyntaxError), 18
index function, 33
IndexError(LookupError), 18
infolist method, 146
inMappingType function, using operator module, 45
inplace keyword, 66
input function, 66
input/output, working with, 51
int function, 38
InteracticeConsole class, 93
internationalization, 203-205
Internet Message Access Protocol (IMAP), 191
Internet Time Protocol, 162
I/O streams, working with, 51

Z

About the Author

Fredrik Lundh is a principal of Secret Labs, Inc., the creators of PythonWorks, an integrated development environment (IDE) for Python. He is an expert on the use of Python with images and graphics and is also the creator of the Python Imaging Library (PIL). He is an active member of the Python community and a frequent contributor to the Python newsgroups.

Colophon

Our look is the result of reader comments, our own experimentation, and feedback from distribution channels. Distinctive covers complement our distinctive approach to technical topics, breathing personality and life into potentially dry subjects.

The animals on the cover of *Python Standard Library* are harvest mice. Many species of harvest mice populate North American grasslands and marshes, while only one species—*Micromys minutus*, the Old World harvest mouse—resides in the grasslands and farmlands of Europe and Asia.

Smaller than the common house mouse, the harvest mouse sports prominent ears and a very long hairy tail, and its hind feet have an opposable fifth toe for grasping and climbing stems. Behaviorally, harvest mice set themselves apart from other mice species by building breeding nests suspended in high grasses. These nests are baseball-sized globes of woven grass with small entrance holes and are lined with soft plant material, such as dandelion fluff, to keep the young warm. The young are born in litters of three to six, completely dependent on the mother (the father is not allowed in the nest). By the time they are five weeks old, however, they are independent and sexually mature. Overall, harvest mice typically live for six to eighteen months in the wild—enough time for a female to produce one to six litters in her lifetime. These numbers are much higher for mice in captivity.

The harvest mouse is a "cover dependent" species, as it relies on brush and vegetation to hide its small, brown body from predators as it forages for seeds and insect larvae. It moves slowly and adopts a still "camouflage posture" as further defense; overall, it is much more calm than the common house mouse.

The Western, Eastern, and Fulvous harvest mice (*Reithrodontomys megalotis*, *Reithrodontomys humulis*, and *Reithrodontomys fulvescens*, respectively) currently populate various regions of the United States and Canada with relative success, challenged somewhat by habitat loss due to crop farming, cattle grazing, and urbanization. However, their cousin the Saltmarsh harvest mouse (*Reithrodontomys raviventris*) suffers severe threat due to the filling in of its dwindling marshland home in the San Francisco Bay Area. The only endangered harvest mouse species, its members number in only the hundreds to the few thousands.

Catherine Morris was the production editor and proofreader, and Linley Dolby was the copyeditor for *Python Standard Library*. Emily Quill, Matt Hutchinson, and Claire Cloutier provided quality control. Joe Wizda wrote the index. Interior composition was done by Gabe Weiss, Matt Hutchinson, and Catherine Morris.

Hanna Dyer designed the cover of this book, based on a series design by Edie Freedman. The cover image is a 19th-century engraving from the Dover Pictorial Archive. Emma Colby produced the cover layout with QuarkXPress 4.1 using Adobe's ITC Garamond font. Emma Colby also designed the CD label.

David Futato designed the interior layout based on a series design by Nancy Priest. The print version of this book was created by translating the DocBook SGML markup of its source files into a set of gtroff macros using a filter developed at O'Reilly & Associates by Norman Walsh. Steve Talbott designed and wrote the underlying macro set on the basis of the GNU *troff –gs* macros; Lenny Muellner adapted them to SGML and implemented the book design. The GNU groff text formatter Version 1.11.1 was used to generate PostScript output. The text and heading fonts are ITC Garamond Light and Garamond Book; the code font is Constant Willison. This colophon was written by Sarah Jane Shangraw.

Whenever possible, our books use a durable and flexible lay-flat binding. If the page count exceeds this binding's limit, perfect binding is used.

More Titles from O'Reilly

Scripting Languages

Exploring Expect

By Don Libes
1st Edition December 1994
602 pages, ISBN 1-56592-090-2

Written by the author of Expect, this is the first book to explain how this part of the UNIX toolbox can be used to automate Telnet, FTP, passwd, rlogin, and hundreds of other interactive applications. Based on Tcl (Tool Command Language), Expect lets you automate interactive applications that have previously been extremely difficult to handle with any scripting language.

Python Programming on Win32

By Mark Hammond & Andy Robinson
1st Edition January 2000
674 pages, ISBN 1-56592-621-8

Despite Python's increasing popularity on Windows, *Python Programming on Win32* is the first book to demonstrate how to use it as a serious Windows development and administration tool. This book addresses all the basic technologies for common integration tasks on Windows, explaining both the Windows issues and the Python code you need to glue things together.

Programming Python, 2nd Edition

By Mark Lutz
2nd Edition March 2001
1256 pages, Includes CD-ROM
ISBN 0-596-00085-5

Programming Python, 2nd Edition, focuses on advanced applications of Python, an increasingly popular object-oriented scripting language. Endorsed by Python creator Guido van Rossum, it demonstrates advanced Python programming techniques, and addresses software design issues such as reusability and object-oriented programming. The enclosed platform-neutral CD-ROM has book examples and various Python-related packages, including the full Python Version 2.0 source code distribution.

Learning Python

By Mark Lutz & David Ascher
1st Edition April 1999
384 pages, ISBN 1-56592-464-9

Learning Python is an introduction to the increasingly popular Python programming language – an interpreted, interactive, object-oriented, and portable scripting language. This book thoroughly introduces the elements of Python: types, operators, statements, classes, functions, modules, and exceptions. It also demonstrates how to perform common programming tasks and write real applications.

Tcl/Tk Tools

By Mark Harrison
1st Edition September 1997
678 pages, Includes CD-ROM
ISBN 1-56592-218-2

One of the greatest strengths of Tcl/Tk is the range of extensions written for it. This book clearly documents the most popular and robust extensions – by the people who created them – and contains information on configuration, debugging, and other important tasks. The CD-ROM includes Tcl/Tk, the extensions, and other tools documented in the text both in source form and as binaries for Solaris and Linux.

Tcl/Tk in a Nutshell

By Paul Raines & Jeff Tranter
1st Edition March 1999
456 pages, ISBN 1-56592-433-9

The Tcl language and Tk graphical toolkit are powerful building blocks for custom applications. This quick reference briefly describes every command and option in the core Tcl/Tk distribution, as well as the most popular extensions. Keep it on your desk as you write scripts, and you'll be able to quickly find the particular option you need.

O'REILLY®

TO ORDER: **800-998-9938** • **order@oreilly.com** • **http://www.oreilly.com/**
OUR PRODUCTS ARE AVAILABLE AT A BOOKSTORE OR SOFTWARE STORE NEAR YOU.
FOR INFORMATION: **800-998-9938** • **707-829-0515** • **info@oreilly.com**

Scripting Languages

VBScript in a Nutshell

By Paul Lomax, Matt Childs, & Ron Petrusha
1st Edition May 2000
512 pages, ISBN 1-56592-720-6

Whether you're using VBScript to create client-side scripts, ASP applications, WSH scripts, or programmable Outlook forms, *VBScript in a Nutshell* is the only book you'll need by your side – a complete and easy-to-use language reference.

VBScript Pocket Reference

By Paul Lomax, Matt Childs & Ron Petrusha
1st Edition January 2001
126 pages, ISBN 0-596-00126-6

Based on the bestselling *VBScript in a Nutshell*, this small book details every VBScript language element – every statement, function, and object – both in VBScript itself and in the Microsoft Scripting Runtime Library. Entries are arranged alphabetically by topic. In addition, appendixes list VBScript operators and VBScript intrinsic constants. The *VBScript Pocket Reference* is the consummate quick reference for writing scripts with VBScript.

Python Pocket Reference

By Mark Lutz
1st Edition November 1998
80 pages, ISBN 1-56592-500-9

The *Python Pocket Reference* is a companion volume to two O'Reilly Animal Guides, *Programming Python* and *Learning Python*. This small book summarizes Python statements and types, built-in functions, commonly used library modules, and other prominent Python language features.

Tcl/Tk Pocket Reference

By Paul Raines
1st Edition October 1998
94 pages, ISBN 1-56592-498-3

A companion volume to *Tcl/Tk in a Nutshell*, the *Tcl/Tk Pocket Reference* is a handy reference guide to the basic Tcl language elements, Tcl and Tk commands, and Tk widgets. It provides easy access to just what you need and includes easy-to-understand summaries of Tcl/Tk language elements. Covers Tcl Version 8 and Tk Version 8.

How to stay in touch with O'Reilly

1. Visit Our Award-Winning Web Site

http://www.oreilly.com/

★ "Top 100 Sites on the Web" —*PC Magazine*
★ "Top 5% Web sites" —*Point Communications*
★ "3-Star site" —*The McKinley Group*

Our web site contains a library of comprehensive product information (including book excerpts and tables of contents), downloadable software, background articles, interviews with technology leaders, links to relevant sites, book cover art, and more. File us in your Bookmarks or Hotlist!

2. Join Our Email Mailing Lists

New Product Releases
To receive automatic email with brief descriptions of all new O'Reilly products as they are released, send email to:
ora-news-subscribe@lists.oreilly.com
Put the following information in the first line of your message (*not* in the Subject field):
subscribe ora-news

O'Reilly Events
If you'd also like us to send information about trade show events, special promotions, and other O'Reilly events, send email to:
ora-news-subscribe@lists.oreilly.com
Put the following information in the first line of your message (*not* in the Subject field):
subscribe ora-events

3. Get Examples from Our Books via FTP

There are two ways to access an archive of example files from our books:

Regular FTP
- ftp to:
  ftp.oreilly.com
  (login: anonymous
  password: your email address)
- Point your web browser to:
  ftp://ftp.oreilly.com/

FTPMAIL
- Send an email message to:
  ftpmail@online.oreilly.com
  (Write "help" in the message body)

4. Contact Us via Email

order@oreilly.com
To place a book or software order online. Good for North American and international customers.

subscriptions@oreilly.com
To place an order for any of our newsletters or periodicals.

books@oreilly.com
General questions about any of our books.

software@oreilly.com
For general questions and product information about our software. Check out O'Reilly Software Online at **http://software.oreilly.com/** for software and technical support information. Registered O'Reilly software users send your questions to: **website-support@oreilly.com**

cs@oreilly.com
For answers to problems regarding your order or our products.

booktech@oreilly.com
For book content technical questions or corrections.

proposals@oreilly.com
To submit new book or software proposals to our editors and product managers.

international@oreilly.com
For information about our international distributors or translation queries. For a list of our distributors outside of North America check out:
http://www.oreilly.com/distributors.html

5. Work with Us

Check out our website for current employment opportunites:
http://jobs.oreilly.com/

O'Reilly & Associates, Inc.
101 Morris Street, Sebastopol, CA 95472 USA
TEL   707-829-0515 or 800-998-9938
       (6am to 5pm PST)
FAX   707-829-0104

O'REILLY®

International Distributors

UK, EUROPE, MIDDLE EAST AND AFRICA (EXCEPT FRANCE, GERMANY, AUSTRIA, SWITZERLAND, LUXEMBOURG, AND LIECHTENSTEIN)

INQUIRIES
O'Reilly UK Limited
4 Castle Street
Farnham
Surrey, GU9 7HS
United Kingdom
Telephone: 44-1252-711776
Fax: 44-1252-734211
Email: information@oreilly.co.uk

ORDERS
Wiley Distribution Services Ltd.
1 Oldlands Way
Bognor Regis
West Sussex PO22 9SA
United Kingdom
Telephone: 44-1243-843294
UK Freephone: 0800-243207
Fax: 44-1243-843302 (Europe/EU orders)
or 44-1243-843274 (Middle East/Africa)
Email: cs-books@wiley.co.uk

FRANCE

INQUIRIES & ORDERS
Éditions O'Reilly
18 rue Séguier
75006 Paris, France
Tel: 1-40-51-71-89
Fax: 1-40-51-72-26
Email: france@oreilly.fr

GERMANY, SWITZERLAND, AUSTRIA, LUXEMBOURG, AND LIECHTENSTEIN

INQUIRIES & ORDERS
O'Reilly Verlag
Balthasarstr. 81
D-50670 Köln, Germany
Telephone: 49-221-973160-91
Fax: 49-221-973160-8
Email: anfragen@oreilly.de (inquiries)
Email: order@oreilly.de (orders)

CANADA (FRENCH LANGUAGE BOOKS)

Les Éditions Flammarion ltée
375, Avenue Laurier Ouest
Montréal (Québec) H2V 2K3
Tel: 00-1-514-277-8807
Fax: 00-1-514-278-2085
Email: info@flammarion.qc.ca

HONG KONG

City Discount Subscription Service, Ltd.
Unit A, 6th Floor, Yan's Tower
27 Wong Chuk Hang Road
Aberdeen, Hong Kong
Tel: 852-2580-3539
Fax: 852-2580-6463
Email: citydis@ppn.com.hk

KOREA

Hanbit Media, Inc.
Chungmu Bldg. 210
Yonnam-dong 568-33
Mapo-gu
Seoul, Korea
Tel: 822-325-0397
Fax: 822-325-9697
Email: hant93@chollian.dacom.co.kr

PHILIPPINES

Global Publishing
G/F Benavides Garden
1186 Benavides Street
Manila, Philippines
Tel: 632-254-8949/632-252-2582
Fax: 632-734-5060/632-252-2733
Email: globalp@pacific.net.ph

TAIWAN

O'Reilly Taiwan
1st Floor, No. 21, Lane 295
Section 1, Fu-Shing South Road
Taipei, 106 Taiwan
Tel: 886-2-27099669
Fax: 886-2-27038802
Email: mori@oreilly.com

INDIA

Shroff Publishers & Distributors Pvt. Ltd.
12, "Roseland", 2nd Floor
180, Waterfield Road, Bandra (West)
Mumbai 400 050
Tel: 91-22-641-1800/643-9910
Fax: 91-22-643-2422
Email: spd@vsnl.com

CHINA

O'Reilly Beijing
SIGMA Building, Suite B809
No. 49 Zhichun Road
Haidian District
Beijing, China PR 100080
Tel: 86-10-8809-7475
Fax: 86-10-8809-7463
Email: beijing@oreilly.com

JAPAN

O'Reilly Japan, Inc.
Yotsuya Y's Building
7 Banch 6, Honshio-cho
Shinjuku-ku
Tokyo 160-0003 Japan
Tel: 81-3-3356-5227
Fax: 81-3-3356-5261
Email: japan@oreilly.com

SINGAPORE, INDONESIA, MALAYSIA AND THAILAND

TransQuest Publishers Pte Ltd
30 Old Toh Tuck Road #05-02
Sembawang Kimtrans Logistics Centre
Singapore 597654
Tel: 65-4623112
Fax: 65-4625761
Email: wendiw@transquest.com.sg

ALL OTHER ASIAN COUNTRIES

O'Reilly & Associates, Inc.
101 Morris Street
Sebastopol, CA 95472 USA
Tel: 707-829-0515
Fax: 707-829-0104
Email: order@oreilly.com

AUSTRALIA

Woodslane Pty., Ltd.
7/5 Vuko Place
Warriewood NSW 2102
Australia
Tel: 61-2-9970-5111
Fax: 61-2-9970-5002
Email: info@woodslane.com.au

NEW ZEALAND

Woodslane New Zealand, Ltd.
21 Cooks Street (P.O. Box 575)
Waganui, New Zealand
Tel: 64-6-347-6543
Fax: 64-6-345-4840
Email: info@woodslane.com.au

ARGENTINA

Distribuidora Cuspide
Suipacha 764
1008 Buenos Aires
Argentina
Phone: 5411-4322-8868
Fax: 5411-4322-3456
Email: libros@cuspide.com

O'REILLY®